C000104423

POCKET WORLD IN FIGURES

The
Economist

=== POCKET ===

WORLD IN
FIGURES

THE ECONOMIST IN ASSOCIATION WITH
PROFILE BOOKS LTD

Published by Profile Books Ltd,
62 Queen Anne Street, London W1M 9LA

First published by The Economist Books Ltd 1991

Copyright © The Economist Newspaper Ltd, 1991, 1992,
1993, 1994, 1995, 1996

Material researched and compiled by Andrew Bevan, Chris
Coulman, Robert Eves, Carol Howard, Stella Jones,
Liz Mann, David McKelvey, Justene McNeice,
Nick Wiseman, Simon Wright

Design and makeup Jonathan Harley, Liz Conway

Printed in Great Britain by
The Bath Press

A CIP catalogue record for this book is available
from the British Library

ISBN 1 86197 002 1

Contents

CONTENTS

Notes

This edition of the annual *Economist Pocket World in Figures* has been expanded to include a larger number of countries. The country profiles cover some 63 major countries, including Russia and Ukraine, and a selection of statistics for the other ex-Soviet republics. The world rankings consider 170: all those with a population of at least 1m or a GDP of at least $1bn; they are listed on page 217. The extent and quality of the statistics available varies from country to country. Every care has been taken to specify the broad definitions on which the data are based and to indicate cases where data quality or technical difficulties are such that interpretation of the figures is likely to be seriously affected. Nevertheless, figures from individual countries will often differ from standard international statistical definitions.

Statistics do not yet fully reflect the changes that have taken place in the Czech Republic and Slovakia, ex-Yugoslavia and the former Soviet Union. In ex-Yugoslavia, Serbia and Montenegro now constitute the Federal Republic of Yugoslavia, and Macedonia is officially known as the Former Yugoslav Republic of Macedonia. Data for Cyprus normally refer to Greek Cyprus only. For other countries such as Morocco they exclude disputed areas. Data for the EU refer to its 12 members prior to the enlargement of the Union on January 1 1995.

Statistical basis

The all-important factor in a book of this kind is to be able to make reliable comparisons between countries. Although this is never quite possible for the reasons stated above, the best route, which this book takes, is to compare data for the same year or period and to use actual, not estimated, figures wherever possible. The research for this edition of *The Economist Pocket World in Figures* was carried out in 1996 using the latest available sources that present data on an internationally comparable basis. Data, therefore, unless otherwise indicated, refers to the year ending December 31 1994.

In the country profiles, population density, population under 15 and over 65, and number of men per 100 women refer to forecasts for 1995; life expectancy, crude birth, death and fertility rates are based on 1995–2000 averages; human development indices are for 1992 and GDP per head in purchasing power parity to 1992; energy data refer to 1993;

structure of manufacturing data to 1993; household data and marriage and divorce data refer to the latest year with available figures, 1985–92. In a number of cases, data are shown for the latest year within a range.

Other definitions

Data shown on country profiles may not always be consistent with those shown on the world rankings because the definitions or years covered can differ. Data may also differ between two different rankings.

Most countries' national accounts are now compiled on a GDP basis so, for simplicity, the term GDP has been used interchangeably with GNP. GDP figures in this book come from the World Bank. It bases its rouble conversions on purchasing power parities.

Statistics for principal exports and principal imports are normally based on customs statistics. These are generally compiled on different definitions to the visible exports and imports figures shown in the balance of payments section.

Definitions of the statistics shown are given on the relevant page or in the glossary at the end of the book. Figures may not add exactly to totals, or percentages to 100, because of rounding or, in the case of GDP, statistical adjustment. Sums of money have generally been converted to US dollars at the official exchange rate ruling at the time to which the figures refer.

Energy consumption data are not always reliable, particularly for the major oil producing countries. Consumption per head data may therefore be higher than in reality. Energy exports can exceed production and imports can exceed consumption if transit operations distort trade data or oil is imported for refining and re-exported.

Abbreviations

bn	billion (one thousand million)	GNP	Gross national product
CAR	Central African Republic	GRT	Gross tonnage
CIS	Commonwealth of Independent	m	million
	States	NDP	Net domestic product
EU	European Union	NMP	Net material product
kg	kilogram	PPP	Purchasing power parity
km	kilometre	UAE	United Arab Emirates
GDP	Gross domestic product	...	not available

═══ Part I ═══
WORLD
RANKINGS

Countries: *natural facts*

Countries: *the largest[a]*
'000 sq km

1	Russia	17,075	31	Nigeria	924
2	Canada	9,970	32	Venezuela	912
3	China	9,561	33	Namibia	824
4	United States	9,373	34	Pakistan	804
5	Brazil	8,512	35	Mozambique	799
6	Australia	7,682	36	Turkey	779
7	India	3,287	37	Chile	757
8	Argentina	2,767	38	Zambia	753
9	Kazakhstan	2,717	39	Myanmar	677
10	Sudan	2,506	40	Afghanistan	652
11	Algeria	2,382	41	Somalia	638
12	Zaire	2,345	42	CAR	622
13	Saudi Arabia	2,200	43	Ukraine	604
14	Mexico	1,973	44	Madagascar	587
15	Indonesia	1,919	45	Kenya	583
16	Libya	1,760	46	Botswana	581
17	Iran	1,648	47	France	544
18	Mongolia	1,565	48	Yemen	528
19	Peru	1,285	49	Thailand	513
20	Chad	1,284	50	Spain	505
21	Niger	1,267	51	Turkmenistan	488
22	Angola	1,247	52	Cameroon	475
23	Mali	1,240	53	Papua New Guinea	463
24	South Africa	1,226	54	Sweden	450
25	Colombia	1,142	55	Morocco	447
26	Ethiopia	1,134	56	Uzbekistan	447
27	Bolivia	1,099	57	Iraq	438
28	Mauritania	1,031	58	Paraguay	407
29	Egypt	1,000	59	Zimbabwe	390
30	Tanzania	945	60	Japan	378

Mountains: *the highest[b]*

	Name	Location	Height (m)
1	Everest	Nepal-China	8,848
2	K2 (Godwin Austen)	Pakistan	8,611
3	Kangchenjunga	Nepal-Sikkim	8,586
4	Lhotse	Nepal-China	8,516
5	Makalu	Nepal-China	8,463
6	Cho Oyu	Nepal-China	8,201
7	Dhaulagiri	Nepal	8,167
8	Manaslu	Nepal	8,163
9	Nanga Parbat	Pakistan	8,125
10	Annapurna I	Nepal	8,091
11	Gasherbrum I	Pakistan-China	8,068
12	Broad Peak	Pakistan-China	8,047
13	Xixabangma (Gosainthan)	China	8,046
14	Gasherbrum II	Pakistan-China	8,035

a Includes freshwater.
b Includes separate peaks which are part of the same massif.

Rivers: *the longest*

	Name	Location	Length (km)
1	Nile	Africa	6,695
2	Amazon	South America	6,516
3	Yangtze	Asia	6,380
4	Mississippi-Missouri	North America	6,019
5	Ob'-Irtysh	Asia	5,570
6	Yenisey-Angara	Asia	5,550
7	Hwang He (Yellow)	Asia	5,464
8	Congo	Africa	4,667
9	Parana	South America	4,500
10	Mekong	Asia	4,425
11	Amur	Asia	4,416
12	Lena	Asia	4,400
13	Mackenzie	North America	4,250
14	Niger	Africa	4,030
15	Missouri	North America	3,969
16	Mississippi	North America	3,779
17	Murray-Darling	Australia	3,750
18	Volga	Europe	3,688
19	Kolyma	Asia	3,513
20	Madeira	South America	3,200
21	Yukon	North America	3,185
22	Indus	Asia	3,180
23	Syrdar'ya	Asia	3,078
24	Salween	Asia	3,060
25	Sao Francisco	South America	2,900
26	Rio Grande	North America	2,870
27	Danube	Europe	2,850
28	Brahmaputra	Asia	2,840
29	Euphrates	Asia	2,815
30	Para-Tocantis	South America	2,750

Waterfalls: *the highest*

	Name	Location	Height (m)
1	Angel	Venezuela	979
2	Tugela	South Africa	948
3	Utigard	Norway	800
4	Mongefossen	Norway	774
5	Yosemite	California, USA	739
6	Mardalsfossen	Norway	656
7	Tyssestrengane	Norway	646
8	Cuquenan	Venezuela	609
9	Ribbon	California, USA	491
10	Della	Canada	440

Notes: Estimates of the lengths of different rivers vary widely according to the rules adopted concerning the selection of tributaries to be followed, the path to take through a delta, where different hydrological systems begin and end etc. The Nile is normally taken as the world's longest river but some estimates put the Amazon as longer if a southerly path through its delta leading to the River Para is followed. Likewise, difficulties in waterfall measurements exist depending on which breaks in the fall are counted. The more famous waterfalls, Niagara and Victoria, are surprisingly small, 50m and 108m respectively; their notoriety evolving from their width and accessibility.

Population: *explosions revealed*

Largest populations, 1994
Millions

1	China	1,190.92	31	Argentina	34.18
2	India	913.60	32	Canada	29.12
3	United States	260.53	33	Tanzania	28.85
4	Indonesia	189.91	34	Sudan	27.36
5	Brazil	159.14	35	Algeria	27.33
6	Russia	148.37	36	Morocco	26.49
7	Pakistan	126.28	37	Kenya	26.02
8	Japan	124.78	38	North Korea	23.47
9	Bangladesh	117.79	39	Peru	23.33
10	Nigeria	107.90	40	Romania	22.74
11	Mexico	91.86	41	Uzbekistan	22.35
12	Germany	81.14	42	Venezuela	21.38
13	Vietnam	72.50	43	Nepal	21.36
14	Philippines	66.19	44	Taiwan	21.13
15	Iran	65.76	45	Iraq	19.95
16	Turkey	60.77	46	Malaysia	19.50
17	Thailand	58.72	47	Afghanistan	18.88
18	United Kingdom	58.09	48	Uganda	18.59
19	France	57.73	49	Sri Lanka	18.13
20	Egypt	57.56	50	Australia	17.84
21	Italy	57.15	51	Saudi Arabia	17.50
22	Ethiopia	53.44	52	Kazakhstan	17.03
23	Ukraine	51.47	53	Ghana	16.94
24	Myanmar	45.56	54	Mozambique	16.61
25	South Korea	44.56	55	Netherlands	15.39
26	Zaire	42.55	56	Syria	14.17
27	South Africa	41.59	57	Chile	14.04
28	Spain	39.55	58	Yemen	13.87
29	Poland	38.34	59	Côte d'Ivoire	13.78
30	Colombia	36.33	60	Madagascar	13.10

Largest populations, 2010
Millions

1	China	1,388.47	13	Iran	95.22
2	India	1,189.08	14	Philippines	88.16
3	United States	297.49	15	Ethiopia	85.08
4	Indonesia	239.60	16	Egypt	81.49
5	Pakistan	210.10	17	Germany	80.47
6	Brazil	199.33	18	Turkey	77.88
7	Nigeria	168.37	19	Zaire	68.88
8	Bangladesh	162.50	20	Thailand	67.13
9	Russia	143.13	21	Myanmar	61.60
10	Japan	127.15	22	France	60.13
11	Mexico	117.65	23	United Kingdom	59.92
12	Vietnam	98.45	24	South Africa	56.40

Fastest growing populations, 1985–94
Average annual growth, %

1	Jordan	5.2	11	Syria	3.5
2	Malawi	4.5	12	Swaziland	3.4
	Qatar	4.5	13	Botswana	3.3
4	Oman	4.4		Iran	3.3
5	Gambia, The	4.1		UAE	3.3
	Yemen	4.1		Zaire	3.3
7	Macao	3.7		Zambia	3.3
8	Côte d'Ivoire	3.6	18	Angola	3.2
	Libya	3.6		Liberia	3.2
	Saudi Arabia	3.6		Niger	3.2

Slowest growing populations, 1985–94
Average annual growth, %

1	Kuwait	-0.5		Belgium	0.2
2	Hungary	-0.4		Romania	0.2
3	Bulgaria	-0.2	15	Barbados	0.3
4	Latvia	-0.1		Poland	0.3
	Portugal	-0.1		Spain	0.3
6	Czech Republic	0.0		United Kingdom	0.3
	Estonia	0.0	19	Finland	0.4
	Ireland	0.0		Georgia	0.4
9	Denmark	0.1		Japan	0.4
	Italy	0.1		Lithuania	0.4
	Ukraine	0.1		Norway	0.4
12	Belarus	0.2		Slovakia	0.4

Fastest growing populations, 1995–2010
Average annual growth, %

1	Oman	3.8		Saudi Arabia	3.2
2	Afghanistan	3.6		Syria	3.2
3	Côte d'Ivoire	3.3	10	Jordan	3.1
4	Algeria	3.2		Liberia	3.1
	Angola	3.2		Madagascar	3.1
	Libya	3.2		Yemen	3.1
	Niger	3.2			

Slowest growing populations, 1995–2010
Average annual growth, %

1	Bulgaria	-0.4		Ukraine	-0.2
	Latvia	-0.4	9	Belarus	-0.1
3	Estonia	-0.3		Germany	-0.1
	Hungary	-0.3		Italy	-0.1
5	Croatia	-0.2		Serbia	-0.1
	Romania	-0.2		Slovenia	-0.1
	Russia	-0.2			

Population density

Highest population density
Population per sq km, 1995

1	Macao[a]	20,482		21	El Salvador	274
2	Hong Kong	5,612		22	Israel	267
3	Singapore	4,608		23	Réunion	260
4	Bermuda	1,189		24	Haiti	259
5	Malta	1,159		25	Trinidad & Tobago	255
6	Bangladesh	836		26	Guadeloupe	251
7	Bahrain	831		27	Netherlands Antilles	248
8	Barbados	609		28	United Kingdom	239
9	Taiwan[b]	587		29	Burundi	230
10	Mauritius	547		30	Germany	229
11	South Korea	454		31	Philippines	225
12	Puerto Rico	413			Vietnam	225
13	Netherlands	380		33	Jamaica	223
14	Martinique	344		34	North Korea	198
15	Belgium	331		35	Italy	190
	Japan	331		36	Pakistan	176
17	Rwanda	302		37	Switzerland	174
18	Lebanon	289		38	Dominican Republic	161
19	India	285		39	Luxembourg	157
20	Sri Lanka	280		40	Nepal	156

Lowest population density
Population per sq km, 1995

1	Australia	2			Papua New Guinea	9
	Mauritania	2			Russia	9
	Mongolia	2		23	Oman	10
	Namibia	2		24	Sudan	11
5	Botswana	3		25	Algeria	12
	Canada	3			Paraguay	12
	Iceland	3		27	Argentina	13
	Libya	3			New Zealand	13
	Suriname	3			Norway	13
10	CAR	5			Zambia	13
	Chad	5		31	Finland	15
	Gabon	5			Somalia	15
13	Kazakhstan	6		33	Uruguay	18
14	Bolivia	7		34	Brazil	19
	Niger	7			Chile	19
16	Congo	8			Peru	19
	Saudi Arabia	8			Zaire	19
	Turkmenistan	8		38	Bahamas	20
19	Angola	9			Mozambique	20
	Mali	9			Sweden	20

a 1993.
b 1994.
Note: Estimates of population density refer to the total land area of a country. In countries such as Japan and Canada, where much of the land area is virtually uninhabitable, the effective population densities of the habitable areas are much greater than the figures suggest.

Biggest cities
Population millions, latest year

1	Seoul	10.61
2	Mumbai (Bombay)	9.93
3	Sao Paulo	9.48
4	Mexico City	8.83
5	Moscow	8.75
6	Tokyo	8.28
7	Shanghai	8.21
8	Jakarta	7.89
9	Beijing	7.36
10	Istanbul	7.33
11	New York	7.31
12	Delhi	7.21
13	Cairo	6.80
	London	6.80
15	Lima[a]	6.41
16	Tehran	6.04
17	Bangkok	5.88
18	Tianjin	5.80
19	Rio de Janeiro	5.34
20	Karachi[a]	5.18
21	Qingdo	5.12
22	Shenyang	4.66
23	St. Petersburg	4.44
24	Calcutta	4.40
25	Santiago	4.39
26	Bogota[a]	4.18
27	Guangzhou	3.92
28	Baghdad	3.84
	Madras	3.84
30	Wuhan	3.83

Quality of life index[b]
New York=100, November 1994

1	Geneva	106.00
2	Vancouver	105.29
3	Vienna	105.24
4	Toronto	105.20
5	Luxembourg	105.19
6	Zurich	105.09
7	Montreal	104.97
8	Dusseldorf	104.78
9	Singapore	104.76
10	Auckland	104.51
11	Oslo	104.50
12	Calgary	104.48
	Munich	104.48
14	Brussels	104.27
15	Amsterdam	104.01
16	Sydney	103.97
17	Frankfurt	103.84
18	Copenhagen	103.73
19	Melbourne	103.70
20	Wellington	103.67
21	London	103.52
22	Stockholm	103.41
23	Perth	103.34
24	Paris	103.14
25	Brisbane	102.92
26	Helsinki	102.88
27	Hamburg	102.70
28	Tokyo	102.31
29	Berlin	102.18
30	Boston	102.09

Highest urban pop.
% pop. living in urban areas, latest year

1	Bermuda	100
	Singapore	100
3	Macao	99
4	Belgium	97
	Kuwait	97
6	Hong Kong	93
7	Iceland	91
	Qatar	91
8	Israel	90
	Uruguay	90

Lowest urban pop.
% pop. living in urban areas, latest year

1	Burundi	5
	Rwanda	5
3	Bhutan	6
4	Uganda	11
5	Cambodia	13
	Oman	13
7	Bangladesh	14
	Nepal	14

a Urban agglomeration.
b Based on 42 factors as diverse as personal security and political stability.
Note: Estimates of cities' populations vary according to where geographical boundaries are defined. As far as possible the data refer to the city proper; urban agglomeration includes adjacent suburbs, eg, the population of the extended agglomeration of Paris (which includes 309 communes) is 9.32m; the population of Paris excluding these communes is 2.15m.

Population: *age and sex*

Youngest populations
% aged under 15, 1995

1	Côte d'Ivoire	49.1	21	Nicaragua	45.9
2	Uganda	48.8	22	Tanzania	45.8
3	Niger	48.4		Togo	45.8
4	Zaire	48.0	24	Congo	45.6
5	Kenya	47.7	25	Nigeria	45.5
6	Oman	47.5	26	Ghana	45.3
	Somalia	47.5		Libya	45.3
	Zambia	47.5	28	Burkina Faso	44.9
9	Benin	47.4		Cambodia	44.9
	Mali	47.4	30	Laos	44.8
11	Syria	47.3	31	Mozambique	44.7
12	Angola	47.1	32	Senegal	44.5
	Guinea	47.1	33	Guatemala	44.3
14	Malawi	46.8		Pakistan	44.3
15	Yemen	46.7	35	Sierra Leone	44.2
16	Ethiopia	46.4	36	Zimbabwe	44.1
17	Burundi	46.3	37	Cameroon	44.0
18	Madagascar	46.1	38	Honduras	43.8
19	Liberia	46.0		Sudan	43.8
	Rwanda	46.0	40	Iraq	43.6

Oldest populations
% aged over 65, 1995

1	Sweden	17.3	21	Netherlands	13.2
2	Italy	16.0	22	Croatia	12.8
3	Greece	15.9		Estonia	12.8
	Norway	15.9	24	Belarus	12.6
5	Belgium	15.8		United States	12.6
6	United Kingdom	15.5	26	Czech Republic	12.5
7	Denmark	15.2	27	Slovenia	12.4
	Germany	15.2	28	Uruguay	12.3
9	Austria	14.9	29	Lithuania	12.2
	France	14.9	30	Russia	12.1
	Spain	14.9	31	Barbados	11.8
12	Bulgaria	14.5		Canada	11.8
13	Switzerland	14.2		Romania	11.8
14	Finland	14.1	34	Australia	11.6
	Japan	14.1	35	Georgia	11.4
	Portugal	14.1		Serbia, Montenegro	11.4
17	Hungary	14.0	37	New Zealand	11.3
	Ukraine	14.0	38	Ireland	11.2
19	Luxembourg	13.9	39	Iceland	11.1
20	Latvia	13.3	40	Malta	11.0

Most male populations
Number of men per 100 women[a], 1995

1	Qatar	197.1			Iraq	103.7
2	UAE	176.6	22	Dominican Republic	103.4
3	Bahrain	134.4			Iran	103.4
4	Saudi Arabia	125.8	24	Fiji	103.2
5	Oman	110.4	25	Côte d'Ivoire	102.8
6	Brunei	109.6			Paraguay	102.8
7	Libya	108.7	27	Singapore	102.5
8	Pakistan	107.2	28	Algeria	102.4
9	India	106.9	29	Costa Rica	102.3
10	Papua New Guinea	106.6			Panama	102.3
11	Bangladesh	106.5	31	Tunisia	102.2
12	Taiwan[b]	106.2	32	Liberia	102.1
13	China	106.0	33	Guatemala	102.0
14	Afghanistan	105.3	34	Malaysia	101.8
15	Albania	105.0	35	Mongolia	101.7
	Jordan	105.0			Syria	101.7
17	Turkey	104.7	37	Honduras	101.6
18	Hong Kong	104.6	38	Venezuela	101.5
19	Nepal	104.0	39	Ethiopia	101.4
20	Egypt	103.7	40	Macedonia, FYR	101.3

Most female populations
Number of men per 100 women, 1995

1	Latvia	85.7	21	Finland	94.8
2	Ukraine	86.8		Kazakhstan	94.8
3	Russia	88.3	23	Poland	94.9
4	Belarus	88.6	24	Uruguay	95.0
5	Estonia	88.9	25	France	95.1
6	Lithuania	89.9		Lebanon	95.1
7	Georgia	91.2		Slovakia	95.1
8	Moldova	91.4	28	Czech Republic	95.2
9	Hungary	91.9		Netherlands Antilles	95.2
10	Swaziland	92.0	30	Germany	95.3
11	Cambodia	93.0	31	United States	95.4
12	Barbados	93.1	32	Austria	95.5
13	Portugal	93.4		Nicaragua	95.5
14	Croatia	93.7	34	Congo	95.7
	Puerto Rico	93.7		United Kingdom	95.7
16	Slovenia	93.8	36	El Salvador	95.8
17	CAR	93.9		Guadeloupe	95.8
18	Martinique	94.0	38	Botswana	95.9
19	Macao[c]	94.2		Burundi	95.9
20	Italy	94.6		Réunion	95.9

a Large numbers of immigrant workers, mostly men, result in the high male ratios of several Middle East countries.
b 1994.
c 1993.

Population: *matters of breeding*

Highest crude birth rates
No. of live births per 1,000 population, 1995–2000

1	Afghanistan	50.5	26	Chad	41.6
2	Niger	50.2	27	Madagascar	41.2
3	Angola	48.4	28	Senegal	41.1
	Uganda	48.4		Tanzania	41.1
5	Côte d'Ivoire	47.6	30	Gambia, The	40.9
	Guinea	47.6	31	Guinea-Bissau	40.6
7	Malawi	47.4		Laos	40.6
	Mali	47.4	33	Libya	40.0
9	Somalia	47.3	34	Cameroon	39.4
10	Sierra Leone	46.3		Ghana	39.4
11	Yemen	46.0	36	CAR	39.3
12	Benin	45.8	37	Syria	38.9
13	Ethiopia	45.4	38	Gabon	38.5
14	Zaire	44.8	39	Sudan	38.4
15	Liberia	44.5	40	Mauritania	38.3
16	Burkina Faso	44.2	41	Jordan	37.5
17	Kenya	42.8	42	Cambodia	37.3
18	Mozambique	42.6		Pakistan	37.3
19	Congo	42.5	44	Bhutan	37.0
	Rwanda	42.5	45	Nicaragua	36.6
21	Nigeria	42.3	46	Nepal	36.4
22	Burundi	42.1		Swaziland	36.4
23	Zambia	41.9	48	Guatemala	36.3
24	Oman	41.8	49	Zimbabwe	36.0
	Togo	41.8	50	Iraq	35.8

Highest fertility rates
Average no. of children per woman, 1995–2000

1	Yemen	7.14	21	Rwanda	6.00
2	Niger	7.10	22	Nigeria	5.97
3	Côte d'Ivoire	6.88	23	Saudi Arabia	5.94
4	Uganda	6.72	24	Libya	5.92
5	Angola	6.69	25	Congo	5.87
	Malawi	6.69	26	Kenya	5.76
7	Oman	6.67	27	Gabon	5.70
8	Benin	6.60	28	Madagascar	5.65
	Mali	6.60	29	Senegal	5.62
10	Ethiopia	6.51	30	Pakistan	5.59
	Guinea	6.51	31	Ghana	5.53
	Somalia	6.51	32	Chad	5.51
13	Afghanistan	6.37	33	Zambia	5.49
14	Liberia	6.33	34	Tanzania	5.48
15	Burundi	6.28	35	Guinea-Bissau	5.42
16	Zaire	6.24	36	Sudan	5.37
17	Togo	6.08	37	Syria	5.36
18	Mozambique	6.06	38	Cameroon	5.30
	Sierra Leone	6.06	39	CAR	5.29
20	Laos	6.03	40	Iraq	5.25

Lowest crude birth rates
Number of live births per 1,000 population, 1995–2000

1	Germany	9.2		Netherlands	12.3
2	Italy	9.6		Switzerland	12.3
3	Greece	9.8	**23**	France	12.4
	Hong Kong	9.8		Hungary	12.4
	Spain	9.8	**25**	Finland	12.5
6	Japan	10.5		Luxembourg	12.5
7	Bulgaria	10.6	**27**	United Kingdom	12.9
	Slovenia	10.6	**28**	Lithuania	13.0
9	Russia	10.8	**29**	Poland	13.5
10	Croatia	11.1	**30**	Sweden	13.6
	Estonia	11.1	**31**	Czech Republic	13.8
12	Latvia	11.3	**32**	Malta	13.9
13	Austria	11.4		Singapore	13.9
14	Ukraine	11.5	**34**	Canada	14.1
15	Romania	11.6	**35**	Australia	14.2
16	Belarus	11.8		Norway	14.2
	Belgium	11.8		Serbia	14.2
	Portugal	11.8		Serbia, Montenegro	14.2
19	Denmark	12.0	**39**	United States	14.7
20	Bosnia & Hercegovina	12.3	**40**	Slovakia	14.8

Lowest fertility rates
Average number of children per woman, 1995–2000

1	Hong Kong	1.21	**21**	Denmark	1.70
2	Spain	1.23	**22**	Belgium	1.71
3	Italy	1.27		Hungary	1.71
4	Germany	1.30	**24**	Luxembourg	1.72
5	Greece	1.40	**25**	Singapore	1.73
6	Slovenia	1.45	**26**	France	1.74
7	Bulgaria	1.50	**27**	South Korea	1.80
	Japan	1.50		Taiwan	1.80
	Romania	1.50	**29**	United Kingdom	1.81
10	Russia	1.53	**30**	Cuba	1.82
11	Portugal	1.55	**31**	Barbados	1.83
12	Austria	1.60		Czech Republic	1.83
	Bosnia & Hercegovina	1.60		Lithuania	1.83
14	Estonia	1.61	**34**	Australia	1.87
	Netherlands	1.61	**35**	Poland	1.88
16	Latvia	1.64	**36**	Finland	1.92
	Ukraine	1.64		Slovakia	1.92
18	Belarus	1.65	**38**	Canada	1.93
	Croatia	1.65	**39**	China	1.95
20	Switzerland	1.67		Martinique	1.95

Notes: The crude birth rate is the number of live births in one year per 1,000 population. In addition to the fertility rate (see below) it depends on the population's age structure and will tend to be higher if there is a large proportion of women of childbearing age.
  The fertility rate is the average number of children born to a woman who completes her childbearing years.

The world economy

Biggest economies
GDP, $bn

1	United States	6,737		49	Egypt	41
2	Japan	4,321		50	UAE	40
3	Germany	2,075		51	Hungary	39
4	France	1,355		52	Czech Republic	33
5	Italy	1,101		53	Kuwait	31
6	United Kingdom	1,069		54	Morocco	30
7	China	630			Nigeria	30
8	Canada	570		56	Romania	28
9	Brazil	536		57	Bangladesh	27
10	Spain	525			Puerto Rico	27
11	Russia	392		59	Syria	24
12	Mexico	369		60	Belarus	22
13	South Korea	366			Libya	22
14	Netherlands	338		62	North Korea	21
15	Australia	321			Uzbekistan	21
16	India	279		64	Kazakhstan	19
17	Argentina	276		65	Iraq	18
18	Switzerland	265		66	Luxembourg	16
19	Taiwan	241			Tunisia	16
20	Belgium	231		68	Ecuador	15
21	Sweden	206			Uruguay	15
22	Austria	197			Zaire	15
23	Indonesia	168		71	Slovenia	14
24	Turkey	149			Vietnam	14
25	Denmark	145		73	Croatia	12
26	Thailand	130			Guatemala	12
27	Saudi Arabia	127			Slovakia	12
28	Hong Kong	126			Sri Lanka	12
29	South Africa	125		77	Oman	11
30	Norway	114		78	Bulgaria	10
31	Finland	96			Cuba	10
32	Poland	95			Dominican Republic	10
33	Portugal	92			Lebanon	10
34	Ukraine	81		82	Cameroon	9
35	Greece	80			Liberia[a]	9
36	Israel	78			Myanmar	9
37	Malaysia	69		85	Costa Rica	8
38	Singapore	66			El Salvador	8
39	Philippines	63			Paraguay	8
40	Colombia	59			Qatar	8
	Iran	59		89	Côte d'Ivoire	7
	Venezuela	59			Cyprus	7
43	Pakistan	56			Ethiopia	7
44	Chile	50			Ghana	7
45	Ireland	48			Iceland	7
46	New Zealand	47			Kenya	7
47	Algeria	46			Panama	7
48	Peru	44				

a Estimate.

Regional GDP

$bn, 1994		*growth 1985–94*	
World	25,664	World	3.1
Industrial countries	20,068	Industrial countries	2.5
G7	17,230	G7	2.6
EU12	7,078	EU12	2.4
EU15	7,577		
Asia[a]	1,910	Asia[a]	7.5
Latin America	1,055	Latin America	2.8
Eastern Europe	774	Eastern Europe	-4.4
Middle East and Europe[b]	642	Middle East and Europe[b]	3.0
Africa	379	Africa	2.1

Regional GDP per head

$bn, 1994		*growth 1985–94*	
World	4,613		
Industrial countries	22,926	Industrial countries	1.8
G7	25,772	G7	1.8
EU12	20,305	EU12	2.0
EU15	20,463		
Asia[a]	661	Asia[a]	5.8
Latin America	3,042	Latin America	0.7
Eastern Europe	2,094	Eastern Europe	-4.8
Middle East and Europe[b]	2,327	Middle East and Europe[b]	0.2
Africa	601	Africa	-0.6

Regional trade: value

Exports, $bn, 1994		*Imports, $bn 1994*	
World	4,095		
Industrial countries	2,801	Industrial countries	2,717
G7	2,125	G7	2,089
EU12	1,497	EU12	1,449
EU15	1,633	EU15	1,580
Asia[a]	726	Asia[a]	737
Latin America	159	Latin America	178
Middle East and Europe[b]	163	Middle East and Europe[b]	157
Africa	77	Africa	78

Regional trade: volume growth, %

Exports, $bn, 1985–94		*Imports, 1985–94*	
World	6.1		
Industrial countries	5.5	Industrial countries	5.9
G7	5.5	G7	6.0
EU12	4.6	EU12	5.5
Asia[a]	13.5	Asia[a]	12.9
Latin America	5.0	Latin America	8.6
Middle East and Europe[b]	5.9	Middle East and Europe[b]	2.2
Africa	1.9	Africa	-0.3

a Excludes Japan.
b Includes Turkey.

Living standards

Highest GDP per head
$

1	Luxembourg	39,833
2	Switzerland	37,179
3	Japan	34,629
4	Bermuda	29,857
5	Denmark	28,104
6	Norway	26,477
7	United States	25,860
8	Germany	25,578
9	Austria	24,949
10	Iceland	24,605
11	Sweden	23,631
12	France	23,474
13	Singapore	23,357
14	Belgium	22,735
15	Netherlands	21,970
16	Hong Kong	21,650
17	UAE	21,515
18	Canada	19,572
19	Italy	19,268
20	Kuwait	19,039
21	Finland	18,850
22	United Kingdom	18,411
23	Australia	17,976
24	Qatar	14,544
25	Israel	14,412
26	Brunei	14,247
27	Ireland	13,625
28	Spain	13,282
29	New Zealand	13,191
30	Bahamas	11,790
31	Taiwan	11,412
32	Malta	10,140
33	Reunion[a]	9,976
34	Cyprus	9,803
35	Portugal	9,370
36	Macao[a]	8,750
37	South Korea	8,224
38	Argentina	8,065
39	Greece	7,705
40	Bahrain	7,507
41	Puerto Rico	7,284
42	Saudi Arabia	7,235
43	Slovenia	7,141
44	Martinique[b]	6,965
45	Netherlands Antilles[a]	6,807
46	Barbados	6,529
47	Oman	5,200
48	Guadeloupe[b]	4,931
49	Uruguay	4,650
50	Libya	4,238
51	Mexico	4,014
52	Hungary	3,839
53	Trinidad & Tobago	3,745
54	Chile	3,564
55	Gabon	3,545
56	Malaysia	3,522
57	Brazil	3,370
58	Czech Republic	3,210
59	Mauritius	3,183
60	Liberia	3,060
61	South Africa	3,011
62	Estonia	2,823
63	Botswana	2,798
64	Venezuela	2,761
65	Panama	2,671
66	Russia	2,645
67	Lebanon	2,611
68	Croatia	2,530
69	Poland	2,468
70	Turkey	2,452

Lowest GDP per head
$

1	Sudan	63
2	Somalia	74
3	Mozambique	80
4	Tanzania	85
5	Afghanistan[a]	111
6	Ethiopia	130
7	Malawi	144
8	Burundi	146
9	Sierra Leone	152
10	Chad	186
11	Vietnam	190
12	Cambodia	191
13	Rwanda	193
14	Nepal	195
15	Myanmar	197
16	Uganda	200
17	Haiti[a]	219
18	Bangladesh	226
19	Niger	231
20	Madagascar	233

a 1992.
b Estimate.

Highest purchasing power[a]
GDP per head in PPP (USA = 100), 1992

1	United States	100.0	36	Trinidad & Tobago	41.1
2	Switzerland	95.0	37	Barbados[b]	40.7
3	Qatar	94.2	38	South Korea	38.9
4	UAE	91.9	39	Argentina	37.3
5	Luxembourg	90.6	40	Venezuela	35.9
6	Germany	88.9	41	Chile	35.4
7	Brunei	86.7	42	Greece	35.0
8	Canada	86.4		Kuwait	35.0
	Japan	86.4	44	Malta	34.9
10	Hong Kong	85.6	45	Malaysia	32.8
11	France	82.1	46	Czech Republic	32.4
12	Denmark	80.3	47	Mexico	30.7
13	Austria	78.7	48	Estonia	28.2
14	Belgium	78.4		Slovakia	28.2
15	Norway	78.2	50	Hungary	27.7
16	Singapore	77.1	51	Belarus	27.1
	Sweden	77.1	52	Russia	25.8
18	Australia	76.7	53	Latvia	25.5
19	Italy	76.1		Uruguay	25.5
20	Netherlands	74.8	55	Thailand	25.0
21	Iceland	74.3	56	Belize	23.6
22	Bahamas	73.1		Panama	23.6
23	United Kingdom	72.2	58	Colombia	23.1
24	Finland	68.5		Costa Rica	23.1
25	Cyprus	63.3	60	Fiji	22.8
26	New Zealand	63.1		Iran	22.8
27	Israel	61.9	62	Brazil	22.1
28	Bahrain	61.4	63	Turkey	22.0
29	Spain	56.4	64	Tunisia	21.7
30	Ireland	54.0	65	Botswana	21.5
31	Oman	49.3	66	Ukraine	21.1
32	Mauritius	49.2	67	Syria	20.9
33	Saudi Arabia	41.6	68	Algeria	20.5
34	Portugal	41.5	69	Poland	20.3
35	Libya	41.2	70	Ecuador	18.3

Lowest purchasing power[a]
GDP per head in PPP (USA = 100), 1992

1	Ethiopia	1.4		Bhutan	3.2
2	Mozambique	1.6		Chad	3.2
3	Zaire	2.2		Myanmar[b]	3.2
4	Mali	2.3	14	Afganistan[b]	3.4
5	Guinea	2.5		Burkina Faso	3.4
6	Tanzania	2.6	16	Guinea-Bissau	3.5
7	Burundi	3.0		Malawi	3.5
	Madagascar	3.0		Niger	3.5
	Rwanda	3.0	19	Uganda	3.6
10	Angola[b]	3.2	20	Sierra Leone	3.7

a See glossary for explanation of purchasing power parity.
b Estimate.

The quality of life

Human development index

1	Canada	95.0	41	Belarus	86
2	Japan	93.7	42	Bahrain	86
	United States	93.7		Estonia	86
4	Netherlands	93.6	44	UAE	86
5	Finland	93.4	45	Fiji	86
6	Iceland	93.3	46	Venezuela	85
7	Norway	93.2	47	Latvia	85
8	France	93.0	48	Hungary	85
	Spain	93.0		Panama	85
10	Sweden	92.9	50	Poland	85
11	Australia	92.7	51	Russia	84
12	Belgium	92.6	52	Mexico	84
13	Austria	92.5		Ukraine	84
	Switzerland	92.5	54	Qatar	83
15	Germany	92.1	55	Colombia	83
16	Denmark	92.0	56	Thailand	82
17	New Zealand	91.9	57	Malaysia	82
18	United Kingdom	91.6	58	Kuwait	82
19	Ireland	91.5		Mauritius	82
20	Italy	91.2	60	Brazil	80
21	Greece	90.7	61	Kazakhstan	79
	Israel	90.7	62	Bulgaria	79
23	Cyprus	90.6	63	Turkey	79
24	Hong Kong	90.5	64	Ecuador	78
25	Barbados	90.0	65	Iran	77
26	Bahamas	89.4	66	Cuba	76
27	Luxembourg	89.3		Lithuania	76
28	Belize	88.3	68	Libya	76
	Costa Rica	88.3	69	Botswana	76
30	Argentina	88.2		Tunisia	76
	South Korea	88.2	71	Saudi Arabia	76
32	Uruguay	88.1		Suriname	76
33	Chile	88.0	73	Syria	76
	Malta	88.0	74	Jordan	75
35	Singapore	87.8	75	Moldova	75
36	Portugal	87.4	76	Albania	73
37	Czech Republic	87.2	77	North Korea	73
	Slovakia	87.2	78	Algeria	73
	Trinidad & Tobago	87.2	79	Turkmenistan	72
40	Brunei	86.8	80	Paraguay	72

Notes: GDP or GDP per head is often taken as a measure of how developed a country is but its usefuless is limited as it refers only to economic welfare. In 1990 the UN Development Programme published its first estimate of a Human Development Index, which combined statistics on two other indicators – adult literacy and life expectancy – with income levels to give a better, though still far from perfect, indicator of human development. In 1991 average years of schooling was combined with adult literacy to give a knowledge variable. The index is shown here scaled from 0 to 100; countries scoring over 80 are considered to have high human development, those scoring from 50 to 79 have medium human development and those under 50 have low human development.

Economic freedom index

1	Hong Kong	1.25		Italy	2.70
2	Singapore	1.30		Jamaica	2.70
3	Bahrain	1.70		Morocco	2.70
4	New Zealand	1.75		Spain	2.70
5	Switzerland	1.80	46	Bolivia	2.75
6	Netherlands	1.85	47	Botswana	2.80
7	United States	1.90		Costa Rica	2.80
8	Denmark	1.95		Greece	2.80
	Luxembourg	1.95		Jordan	2.80
	Taiwan	1.95		Uruguay	2.80
	United Kingdom	1.95	52	Uganda	2.83
12	Bahamas	2.00	53	Guatemala	2.85
	Canada	2.00		Indonesia	2.85
	Czech Republic	2.00		Oman	2.85
15	Austria	2.05	56	Hungary	2.90
	Japan	2.05		Israel	2.90
17	Australia	2.10		Philippines	2.90
	Belgium	2.10		Saudi Arabia	2.90
	Germany	2.10		Swaziland	2.90
	UAE	2.10	61	Benin	2.95
21	Ireland	2.20		Lebanon	2.95
22	Finland	2.30		Slovakia	2.95
	France	2.30		Zambia	2.95
	South Korea	2.30	65	Barbados	3.00
	Thailand	2.30		Colombia	3.00
26	Estonia	2.35		Peru	3.00
27	Kuwait	2.40		South Africa	3.00
	Malaysia	2.40		Turkey	3.00
	Panama	2.40	70	Kenya	3.05
30	Chile	2.45		Latvia	3.05
	El Salvador	2.45		Malta	3.05
	Norway	2.45		Pakistan	3.05
33	Trinidad & Tobago	2.50		Poland	3.05
34	Sweden	2.55	75	Gabon	3.06
35	Cyprus	2.60	76	Fiji	3.10
	Portugal	2.60		Mali	3.10
37	Argentina	2.65		Papua New Guinea	3.10
	Paraguay	2.65	79	Ecuador	3.15
	Sri Lanka	2.65		Honduras	3.15
	Tunisia	2.65	81	Ghana	3.20
41	Belize	2.70	82	Algeria	3.25

Notes: The index of economic freedom, published by the Heritage Foundation, ranks countries on the basis of ten indicators of how government intervention can restrict the economic relations between individuals. The economic indicators are trade policy, taxation, monetary policy, the banking system, foreign-investment rules, property rights, the amount of economic output consumed by the government, regulation policy, the size of the black market and the extent of wage and price controls. A country can score between 1 and 5 in each category, 1 being the most free and 5 being the least free.

Economic growth

Fastest economic growth, 1985–94
Average annual % increase in real GDP

1	China	9.4		21	Cambodia[c]	5.4
	Thailand	9.4		22	Pakistan	5.2
3	South Korea	8.7		23	India	5.0
4	Singapore	8.2		24	Nepal	4.9
5	Malaysia	7.5			Papua New Guinea	4.9
6	Swaziland[a]	7.2		26	Laos	4.8
7	Botswana	7.0		27	Ghana	4.7
8	Lesotho	6.9			Israel	4.7
9	Chile	6.8		29	Costa Rica	4.6
10	Hong Kong	6.7			Oman	4.6
	Mauritius	6.7		31	Bangladesh	4.5
12	Taiwan	6.6		32	Colombia	4.4
13	Indonesia	6.5		33	Sri Lanka	4.3
	Mozambique	6.5		34	Ireland	4.2
15	Bhutan	6.3			Nigeria	4.2
16	Macao[b]	6.2			Tanzania	4.2
17	Vietnam	6.1		37	Turkey	4.1
18	Uganda	5.8			Uruguay	4.1
19	Cyprus	5.7		39	Guinea	3.9
20	Malta	5.6			Sudan	3.9

Slowest economic growth, 1985–94
Average annual % increase in real GDP

1	Georgia[d]	-25.6			Slovakia[b]	-5.5
2	Russia[e]	-14.8		22	Zaire	-5.0
3	Azerbaijan[d]	-14.5		23	Czech Republic[b]	-4.9
4	Lithuania[d]	-14.1		24	Lebanon[f]	-4.4
5	Armenia[d]	-14.0		25	Cameroon	-3.5
6	Tajikistan[d]	-12.8		26	Afghanistan	-3.4
7	Kirgizstan[d]	-11.9			Haiti	-3.4
8	Ukraine[d]	-11.8		28	Angola[g]	-3.2
9	Moldova[d]	-11.6		29	Romania	-3.0
10	Macedonia[b]	-11.5		30	Albania	-2.2
11	Kazakhstan[d]	-11.0			Slovenia	-2.2
12	Cuba[d]	-10.3		32	Bulgaria	-2.1
13	Iraq	-9.2		33	Uzbekistan[d]	-2.0
14	Latvia[d]	-9.0		34	North Korea[g]	-1.7
15	Rwanda	-8.2		35	Nicaragua	-1.5
16	Turkmenistan[d]	-7.7		36	Somalia[g]	-1.1
17	Belarus[d]	-6.9		37	Hungary	-1.0
18	Croatia[d]	-6.1		38	Congo	-0.6
	Estonia[d]	-6.1			Trinidad & Tobago	-0.6
20	Libya	-5.5		40	Côte d'Ivoire	-0.4

a 1987–93
b 1990–94
c 1988–94
d 1989–94

e 1991–94.
f 1987–94.
g Estimate.

Fastest economic growth, 1975–84
Average annual % increase in real GDP

1	Botswana	12.4		Malta		7.2
2	Oman	10.3	12	Egypt		7.1
3	Jordan	9.0	13	Malaysia		7.0
4	Hong Kong	8.9		Thailand		7.0
5	Taiwan	8.6	15	Cameroon		6.8
6	Singapore	8.0	16	Paraguay		6.6
	South Korea	8.0	17	Mongolia		6.5
8	Congo	7.6	18	Bahrain		6.2
9	Niger	7.4	19	Vietnam		6.1
10	China	7.2	20	Bhutan		6.0

Slowest economic growth, 1975–84
Average annual % increase in real GDP

1	Kuwait	-1.7	11	Madagascar	-0.2
2	Ghana	-1.5	12	El Salvador	-0.1
3	Nicaragua	-1.4		Zambia	-0.1
	Nigeria	-1.4	14	Switzerland	0.0
5	Chad	-1.3	15	Argentina	0.1
6	Gabon	-0.9		Mozambique	0.1
7	Zaire	-0.8	17	Uganda	0.2
8	Afghanistan	-0.6	18	Papua New Guinea	0.6
9	Lesotho	-0.5	19	Jamaica	0.7
10	Liberia	-0.4	20	Sierra Leone	0.8

Highest industrial growth, 1980–93
Average annual % increase in real terms

1	South Korea	12.1	6	Botswana	9.2
2	Bhutan[a]	11.8		Oman	9.2
3	China	11.5	8	Mauritius	8.8
4	Thailand	11.0	9	Malaysia	8.2
5	Lesotho	9.3	10	Pakistan	7.2

Highest services growth, 1980–93
Average annual % increase in real terms

1	Botswana	11.6	6	Singapore	7.4
2	China	11.1	7	Egypt	6.9
3	South Korea	8.3		Indonesia	6.9
4	Bhutan[a]	7.7		Turkmenistan[b]	6.9
	Thailand	7.7	10	Ghana	6.8

Highest agricultural growth, 1980–93
Average annual % increase in real terms

1	UAE	9.7	6	China	5.3
2	Jordan[c]	8.1	7	Benin	4.9
3	Oman	6.9		Tanzania	4.9
4	Guinea-Bissau	6.1		Togo	4.9
5	Chile	5.5	10	Tunisia	4.8

a 1980–92.
b Estimate.
c 1980–91.

Trading places

Biggest traders
% of total world exports (visible & invisible)

1	United States	13.95	21	Australia	1.09
2	Japan	9.98		Malaysia	1.09
3	Germany	9.43	23	Hong Kong	1.02
4	France	7.06	24	Thailand	0.97
5	United Kingdom	6.43	25	Brazil	0.85
6	Italy	4.63		Norway	0.85
7	Belgium/Luxembourg	4.09	27	Saudi Arabia	0.82
8	Netherlands	3.89	28	Indonesia	0.77
9	Canada	3.18	29	Ireland	0.67
10	Switzerland	2.20	30	Finland	0.61
11	China	2.08	31	Turkey	0.52
12	Spain	1.95	32	India	0.50
13	South Korea	1.92	33	South Africa	0.49
14	Taiwan	1.88	34	Portugal	0.45
15	Singapore	1.49	35	Israel	0.40
16	Sweden	1.40	36	Poland	0.37
17	Austria	1.37	37	Philippines	0.35
18	Russia	1.33	38	Argentina	0.33
19	Denmark	1.29		Czech Republic	0.33
20	Mexico	1.23	40	UAE	0.32

Most trade dependent
Trade as % of GDP[a]

1	Singapore	93.0
2	Panama	90.3
3	Bahrain	87.4
4	Malaysia	81.7
5	Swaziland	77.5
6	Macedonia, FYR	69.8
7	Suriname	67.0
8	Ireland	59.7
9	Netherlands Antilles	59.6
10	Macao	57.0
11	Slovakia	56.1
12	Malta	51.1
13	Belgium/Luxembourg	49.6
14	UAE	49.5
15	Sudan[b]	49.4
16	Slovenia	48.6
17	Gambia, The	47.4
18	Yemen	47.2
19	Congo	47.0
20	Brunei	45.3

Least trade dependent
Trade as % of GDP[a]

1	Zaire	2.7
2	Myanmar	3.1
3	Iraq[b]	3.5
4	Liberia	3.8
5	North Korea	5.1
6	Haiti	6.4
7	Ethiopia	6.5
8	Argentina	6.7
9	Brazil	7.2
	Japan	7.2
11	United States	8.7
12	India	9.3
13	Burkina Faso	9.9
14	Somalia[b]	11.2
15	CAR	11.6
	Niger	11.6
	Peru	11.6
18	Armenia	13.0
	Belarus	13.0
20	Cuba	13.3

Notes: The figures are drawn from balance of payment statistics and, therefore, have differing technical definitions from trade statistics taken from customs or similar sources. The invisible trade figures do not show some countries, notably ex-Soviet republics, due to unavailable data. For Hong Kong and Singapore, domestic exports and retained imports only are used.

Biggest visible traders
% of world visible exports

1	United States	12.56	21	Austria	1.11
2	Germany	10.71		Thailand	1.11
3	Japan	9.56	23	Brazil	1.10
4	France	5.56	24	Denmark	1.04
5	United Kingdom	5.13		Saudi Arabia	1.04
6	Italy	4.72	26	Indonesia	1.00
7	Canada	4.07	27	Norway	0.87
8	Netherlands	3.43	28	Ireland	0.84
9	Belgium/Luxembourg	2.93	29	Finland	0.73
10	China	2.55	30	Hong Kong	0.72
11	South Korea	2.33	31	India[c]	0.62
12	Taiwan	2.30		South Africa	0.62
13	Switzerland	2.06	33	Turkey	0.48
14	Spain	1.85	34	UAE	0.47
15	Russia	1.69	35	Portugal	0.46
16	Mexico	1.52	36	Poland	0.43
17	Sweden	1.50	37	Israel	0.41
18	Singapore	1.45	38	Venezuela	0.40
19	Malaysia	1.42	39	Argentina[b]	0.39
20	Australia	1.17	40	Iran[b]	0.37

Biggest invisible traders
% of world invisible exports

1	United States	16.76	22	Thailand	0.71
2	Japan	10.82	23	Mexico	0.66
3	France	10.09	24	Russia	0.62
4	United Kingdom	9.04	25	Turkey	0.59
5	Germany	6.84	26	Greece	0.52
6	Belgium/Luxembourg	6.41	27	Egypt	0.47
7	Netherlands	4.82	28	Malaysia	0.45
8	Italy	4.42	29	Portugal	0.44
9	Switzerland	2.49	30	Israel	0.38
10	Spain	2.15		Philippines[b]	0.38
11	Austria	1.89		Saudi Arabia	0.38
12	Denmark	1.79	33	Brazil	0.36
13	Hong Kong	1.63		Finland	0.36
14	Singapore	1.57	35	Ireland	0.34
15	Canada	1.39	36	Indonesia	0.30
16	Sweden	1.19		Kuwait	0.30
17	China	1.12	38	Czech Republic	0.29
18	South Korea	1.08	39	India[c]	0.27
19	Taiwan	1.04	40	Poland	0.25
20	Australia	0.93	41	South Africa	0.23
21	Norway	0.80	42	Argentina[b]	0.21

a Average of imports and exports of goods as % of GDP.
b 1993.
c 1992.

Current account

Largest surpluses
$bn

1	Japan	129.24	21	Colombiaᶜ	0.91
2	Switzerland	18.50	22	Sweden	0.83
3	Italy	14.59	23	Slovakia	0.72
4	Belgium/Luxembourg	12.75	24	Croatia	0.63
5	Singapore	11.95	25	Papua New Guinea	0.57
6	Netherlands	11.55	26	Turkmenistan	0.50
7	Russia	11.37	27	Slovenia	0.46
8	France	8.13	28	Gabon	0.32
9	China	6.53	29	Bangladesh	0.24
10	Taiwan	5.97	30	Senegal	0.22
11	Norway	3.65		Trinidad & Tobago	0.22
12	Ireland	3.20	32	Botswana	0.20
13	Kuwait	3.03		Latvia	0.20
14	Hong Kong	2.70	34	Namibia	0.19
15	Denmark	2.66	35	Bulgaria	0.14
16	Turkey	2.63	36	Iceland	0.13
17	Venezuela	2.45	37	Kenyaᵈ	0.12
18	Algeriaᵃ	2.37		Tajikistan	0.12
19	Libyaᵇ	2.20	39	Lesotho	0.11
20	Finland	1.07	40	Kazakhstanᵈ	0.10

Largest deficits
$bn

1	United States	-150.93	26	Ukraine	-1.40
2	Mexico	-28.78	27	Panama	-1.21
3	Germany	-21.68	28	Brazil	-1.15
4	Canada	-17.39	29	Omanᵈ	-1.07
5	Australia	-15.22	30	Portugal	-1.04
6	Saudi Arabia	-9.07	31	Congo	-0.87
7	Thailand	-8.42	32	Ecuador	-0.81
8	Argentinaᵈ	-7.45	33	Angolaᵈ	-0.77
9	Spain	-6.42	34	Chile	-0.76
10	Iranᵈ	-4.22	35	Paraguay	-0.75
11	Malaysia	-4.15	36	Morocco	-0.72
12	Indiaᶜ	-4.11	37	Nicaragua	-0.69
13	Hungary	-4.05	38	Syria	-0.64
14	Israel	-4.01		Zaireᵇ	-0.64
15	South Korea	-3.86	40	Guatemala	-0.63
16	Philippinesᵈ	-3.29	41	South Africa	-0.57
17	Pakistanᵈ	-2.94	42	Sri Lanka	-0.55
18	Indonesia	-2.79	43	Cameroonᵈ	-0.51
19	Poland	-2.55		Sudanᶜ	-0.51
20	Austria	-2.45	45	Georgia	-0.50
21	United Kingdom	-2.39	46	Costa Rica	-0.46
22	Peru	-2.25	47	Uzbekistan	-0.43
23	Nigeria	-2.13	48	Tanzaniaᵈ	-0.41
24	New Zealand	-2.01	49	Jordan	-0.40
25	Belarus	-1.84	50	Uruguay	-0.39

a 1991. c 1992.
b 1990. d 1993.

Largest surpluses as % of GDP
%

1	Singapore	18.15		21	Netherlands	3.41
2	Suriname	16.21		22	Latvia	3.40
3	Papua New Guinea	11.72		23	Mongolia[d]	3.29
4	Libya[b]	9.95		24	Slovenia	3.21
5	Kuwait	9.62		25	Norway	3.19
6	Gabon	8.72		26	Japan	2.99
7	Lesotho	7.73		27	Russia	2.90
8	Switzerland	6.98		28	Taiwan	2.47
9	Ireland	6.63		29	Swaziland	2.29
10	Namibia	6.24		30	Hong Kong	2.14
11	Slovakia	6.03		31	Gambia, The	2.08
12	Tajikistan	5.59		32	Colombia[c]	2.05
13	Belgium/Luxembourg	5.52		33	Iceland	1.91
14	Croatia	5.17			Benin	1.84
15	Botswana	4.93		35	Kenya[d]	1.84
16	Algeria[a]	4.53		36	Denmark	1.83
17	Trinidad & Tobago	4.51		37	Turkey	1.77
18	Senegal	4.48		38	Bulgaria	1.36
19	Venezuela	4.15			Jamaica	1.35
20	Barbados[d]	3.95		40	Italy	1.33

Largest deficits as % of GDP
%

1	Congo	-54.01		26	Netherlands Antilles	-7.20
2	Nicaragua	-49.75		27	Iran[d]	-7.16
3	Mozambique[c]	-36.85			Saudi Arabia	-7.16
4	Guinea-Bissau[d]	-26.61		29	Nigeria	-7.09
5	Malawi	-17.56		30	Jordan	-6.81
6	Panama	-17.51		31	Mali	-6.77
7	Angola[d]	-17.48		32	Mauritius	-6.55
8	Georgia	-16.28		33	Thailand	-6.48
9	Tanzania[d]	-16.18		34	Madagascar	-6.44
10	Mauritania[d]	-12.79		35	Laos	-6.22
11	Albania	-12.77		36	Malaysia	-6.04
12	Oman[d]	-11.10		37	Philippines[d]	-6.02
13	Hungary	-10.39		38	Costa Rica	-5.89
14	Macedonia FYR	-10.28		39	Pakistan[d]	-5.51
15	Paraguay	-9.85		40	Ecuador	-5.49
16	Chad[d]	-9.38		41	Togo	-5.45
17	Zambia[a]	-9.02		42	Cameroon[d]	-5.30
18	Guinea	-8.64		43	Israel	-5.13
19	Cambodia	-8.53		44	Guatemala	-5.11
20	Nepal	-8.43		45	Peru	-5.10
21	Honduras[d]	-8.42		46	Azerbaijan	-4.80
22	Belarus	-8.40		47	Australia	-4.75
23	Sierra Leone[d]	-7.99		48	Rwanda[c]	-4.69
24	Zaire[b]	-7.92			Sri Lanka	-4.69
25	Mexico	-7.81		50	Moldova	-4.67

Inflation

Highest inflation, 1994–95
% consumer price inflation

1	Zaire[a]	23,760.0		31	Romania	40.0
2	Turkmenistan	1,800.0		32	Madagascar[a]	39.1
3	Angola[a]	950.0		33	Benin[a]	38.6
4	Belarus	700.0		34	Suriname	37.1
5	Azerbaijan	425.0		35	Gabon[a]	36.1
6	Ukraine	350.0		36	Nigera	36.0
7	Uzbekistan	325.0		37	Iran[a]	35.2
8	Georgia	250.0		38	Lithuania	35.0
9	Armenia	210.0			Mexico	35.0
10	Russia	197.7			Moldova	35.0
11	Kazakhstan[a]	180.0		41	Malawi[a]	34.6
12	Tajikistan	120.0		42	Malia	33.8
13	Sudan[a]	102.0		43	Senegal[a]	32.3
14	Turkey	93.6		44	Kirgizstan	31.9
15	Mongolia[a]	87.6		45	Jamaica[a]	30.0
16	Yemen[a]	71.8			Libya[a]	30.0
17	Bulgaria	68.0		47	Kenya[a]	29.0
18	Brazil	66.0			Tanzania[a]	29.0
19	Nigeria	65.0		49	Hungary	28.2
20	Rwanda[a]	64.0		50	Poland	28.1
21	Mozambique[a]	63.1		51	Cambodia[a]	26.0
22	Iraq[a]	60.0			Côte d'Ivoire[a]	26.0
23	Venezuela	59.6		53	Estonia	25.0
24	Congo[a]	56.9			Latvia	25.0
25	Zambia[a]	53.0		55	Ghana[a]	24.9
26	Macedonia	50.0		56	Burkina Faso[a]	24.7
27	Uruguay[a]	44.7		57	CAR[a]	24.5
28	Haiti[a]	42.6		58	Somalia[b]	24.3
29	Togo[a]	41.4		59	Algeria[a]	22.5
30	Chad[a]	41.3			Honduras[a]	22.5

Highest inflation, 1989–95
% average annual consumer price inflation

1	Serbia[c]	110,611.3		16	Mongolia[f]	263.1
2	Zaire[d]	1,500.0		17	Moldova[e]	236.6
3	Brazil	1,025.0		18	Russia	222.1
4	Kazakhstan[c]	773.4		19	Uzbekistan	216.9
5	Nicaragua[d]	678.2		20	Argentina	215.5
6	Georgia[e]	635.4		21	Slovenia[d]	213.5
7	Turkmenistan	469.8		22	Croatia[d]	202.2
8	Armenia	441.6		23	Kirgizstan[e]	195.0
9	Azerbaijan[e]	412.5		24	Lithuania	141.3
10	Ukraine	378.6		25	Zambia[d]	121.6
11	Angola[f]	373.7		26	Estonia	107.6
12	Belorussia	369.1		27	Poland	101.6
13	Peru	364.7		28	Romania	94.3
14	Tajikistan[e]	328.3		29	Latvia	92.2
15	Macedonia, FYR[e]	301.7		30	Sudan[d]	90.6

Lowest inflation, 1994–95

% consumer price inflation

1	Oman[a]	-0.7	26	United States	2.8
2	Serbia[a]	-0.2	27	Papua New Guinea[a]	2.9
3	Japan	-0.1	28	Brunei[a]	3.0
4	Bahrain[a]	0.9		Croatia	3.0
5	Finland	1.0		Qatar[a]	3.0
6	Barbados[b]	1.1	31	Bahamas[a]	3.2
7	Panama[a]	1.3		Bangladesh[a]	3.2
8	Belgium	1.5	33	Argentina	3.4
	Ethiopia[a]	1.5		Malaysia	3.4
	Fiji[a]	1.5		United Kingdom	3.4
11	France	1.7	36	Jordan[a]	3.5
	Iceland	1.7	37	Taiwan	3.7
13	Germany	1.8	38	New Zealand	3.8
	Singapore	1.8		Puerto Rico[a]	3.8
	Switzerland	1.8	40	Gambia, The[a]	4.0
16	Luxembourg	1.9	41	Guinea[a]	4.1
	Netherlands	1.9		Mauritania[a]	4.1
18	Netherlands Antilles	2.0		Portugal	4.1
19	Denmark	2.1	44	South Korea	4.5
20	Austria	2.2	45	Australia	4.6
	Canada	2.2		UAE[a]	4.6
22	Bermuda[b]	2.5	47	Cyprus[a]	4.7
	Ireland	2.5		Kuwait[a]	4.7
	Norway	2.5		Spain	4.7
	Sweden	2.5	50	Saudi Arabia	5.0

Lowest inflation, 1989–95

% average annual consumer price inflation

1	Panama[d]	1.0	16	Malta[d]	2.9
2	Bahrain[d]	1.1		Norway	2.9
3	Japan	1.8	18	Canada	3.0
4	Saudi Arabia	1.9		Luxembourg	3.0
5	Brunei[c]	2.1	20	Austria	3.1
	Cameroon[d]	2.1		Germany	3.1
7	Oman	2.4	22	New Zealand	3.2
8	Denmark	2.5	23	Finland	3.3
9	France	2.6		Qatar[d]	3.3
	Netherlands	2.6	25	Puerto Rico[d]	3.5
11	Belgium	2.7		Switzerland	3.5
	CAR[d]	2.7	27	Malaysia	3.6
	Netherlands Antilles	2.7	28	Burkina Faso[d]	3.7
	Singapore	2.7		United States	3.7
15	Ireland	2.8	30	Chad[d]	3.9

a	1993–94.	d	1989–94.
b	1992–93.	e	1990–95.
c	1990–94.	f	1991–94.

Notes: Inflation is measured as the % increase in the consumer price index between two dates. The figures shown are based on the average level of the index during the relevant years.

Debt

Highest foreign debt[a]

$m

1	Brazil	151,104	21	Chile	22,93?
2	Mexico	128,302	22	Iran	22,71?
3	China	100,536	23	Peru	22,62?
4	India	98,990	24	Morocco	22,51?
5	Indonesia	96,500	25	Syria	20,55?
6	Russia	94,232	26	Colombia	19,41?
7	Argentina	77,388	27	Côte d'Ivoire	18,45?
8	Turkey	66,332	28	Sudan	17,71?
9	Thailand	60,991	29	Bangladesh	16,56?
10	South Korea	54,542	30	Ecuador	14,95?
11	Poland	42,160	31	Ex-Yugoslavia	13,55?
12	Philippines	39,302	32	Zaire	12,33?
13	Venezuela	36,850	33	Nicaragua	11,01?
14	Egypt	33,358	34	Czech Republic	10,69?
15	Algeria	29,898	35	Angola	10,60?
16	Pakistan	29,579	36	Bulgaria	10,46?
17	Nigeria	28,479	37	Tunisia	9,25?
18	Hungary	28,016	38	Sri Lanka	7,81?
19	Vietnam	25,115	39	Tanzania	7,44?
20	Malaysia	24,767	40	Cameroon	7,27?

Highest debt service[b]

$m

1	Mexico	19,049	21	Chile	2,90?
2	Brazil	16,114	22	Czech Republic	2,46?
3	Indonesia	14,792	23	Egypt	2,27?
4	China	11,135	24	Nigeria	1,91?
5	India	10,516	25	Tunisia	1,42?
6	Turkey	10,213	26	Côte d'Ivoire	1,27?
7	Thailand	9,237	27	Peru	1,05?
8	South Korea	7,923	28	Ecuador	98?
9	Argentina	6,692	29	Kenya	88?
10	Hungary	5,692	30	Papua New Guinea	87?
11	Algeria	5,105	31	Slovakia	83?
12	Malaysia	5,042	32	Bulgaria	76?
13	Philippines	4,534	33	Trinidad & Tobago	67?
14	Iran	4,314	34	Bangladesh	65?
15	Venezuela	3,691	35	Zimbabwe	60?
16	Colombia	3,686	36	Jamaica	59?
17	Russia	3,661	37	Romania	58?
18	Pakistan	3,423	38	Congo	55?
19	Poland	3,093	39	Oman	55?
20	Morocco	2,920	40	Uruguay	50?

a Foreign debt is debt owed to non-residents and repayable in foreign currency; the figures shown include liabilities of government, public and private sectors. Developed countries have been excluded.

b Debt service is the sum of interest and principal repayments (amortization) due on outstanding foreign debt. The debt service ratio is debt service expressed as a percentage of the country's exports of goods and services.

Highest foreign debt burden
Foreign debt as % of GDP

1	Nicaragua	800.6	21	Laos	135.6
2	Congo	454.1	22	Burundi	125.3
3	Mozambique	450.3	23	Gabon	122.5
4	Guinea-Bissau	340.7	24	Jordan	121.8
5	Côte d'Ivoire	338.9	25	Syria[a]	116.9
6	Tanzania[c]	316.8	26	Gambia, The	112.4
7	Somalia[d]	293.9		Kenya	112.4
8	Sudan[e]	272.8	28	Zaire[h]	111.9
9	Mauritania	239.1	29	Jamaica	110.1
10	Madagascar	225.3	30	Benin	109.4
11	Zambia	203.8	31	Ethiopia	108.2
12	Sierra Leone	187.8	32	Cameroon	107.0
13	Rwanda	164.8	33	Panama	106.3
14	Yemen	161.8	34	Bulgaria	105.7
15	Vietnam	161.3	35	Niger	104.2
16	Liberia[f]	160.4	36	Nigeria	102.5
17	Malawi	160.3	37	CAR	101.8
18	Togo	156.6	38	Ghana	101.5
19	Mali	151.8	39	Senegal	99.1
20	Honduras	151.6	40	Guinea	94.7

Highest debt service ratios[b]
%

1	Sierra Leone	100.0	21	Bolivia	28.6
2	Algeria	55.3	22	Mali	27.2
3	Hungary	52.2	23	Zimbabwe	26.9
4	Congo	51.5	24	India	26.3
5	Uganda	44.0	25	Niger	26.1
6	Côte d'Ivoire	40.1	26	Burundi	25.2
7	Nicaragua	38.2	27	Ghana	24.6
8	Honduras	34.9	28	Mauritania	23.2
9	Pakistan	34.8	29	Mozambique	23.0
10	Mexico	33.9	30	Jamaica	22.2
	Trinidad & Tobago	33.9	31	Ecuador	21.8
12	Kenya	33.3		Iran	21.8
13	Morocco	32.1	33	Tanzania	20.4
14	Argentina	31.8	34	Peru	20.2
	Brazil	31.8	35	Venezuela	19.9
16	Zambia	31.3	36	Dominican Republic	19.6
17	Turkey	31.2		Nigeria	19.6
18	Indonesia	30.0	38	Chile	19.2
19	Colombia	29.8	39	Gambia, The	19.0
20	Papua New Guinea	29.0	40	Philippines	18.5

c	1993.		f	1987.
d	1990.		g	1991.
e	1992.		h	1989.

Aid

Largest bilateral and multilateral donors

$m

1	Japan	13,239	13	Australia	1,08
2	United States	9,927	14	Switzerland	98
3	France[a]	8,466	15	Belgium	72
4	Germany	6,818	16	Austria	65
5	United Kingdom	3,197	17	Kuwait	55
6	Italy	2,705	18	Saudi Arabia	31
7	Netherlands	2,517	19	Portugal	30
8	Canada	2,250	20	Finland	29
9	Sweden	1,819	21	South Korea	14
10	Denmark	1,446	22	New Zealand	11
11	Spain	1,305	23	Ireland	10
12	Norway	1,137	24	UAE	10

Largest recipients of bilateral and multilateral aid

$m

1	China	3,232	36	Burkina Faso	43
2	Egypt	2,695	37	Mexico	43
3	India	2,324	38	Algeria	42
4	Bangladesh	1,757	39	Peru	41
5	Ex-Yugoslavia	1,716	40	Sudan	41
6	Indonesia	1,642	41	Niger	37
7	Pakistan	1,606	42	Jordan	37
8	Côte d'Ivoire	1,594	43	Congo	36
9	Israel	1,237	44	Guinea	36
10	Mozambique	1,231	45	Cambodia	33
11	Ethiopia	1,070	46	Brazil	33
12	Philippines	1,057	47	Papua New Guinea	32
13	Tanzania	968	48	El Salvador	31
14	Vietnam	897	49	Burundi	31
15	Uganda	753	50	Honduras	29
16	Syria	745	51	South Africa	29
17	Cameroon	731	52	Madagascar	28
18	Zambia	719	53	Sierra Leone	27
19	Rwanda	713	54	Mauritania	26
20	Kenya	676	55	Iraq	25
21	Senegal	644	56	Benin	25
22	Morocco	631	57	Zaire	24
23	Haiti	601	58	Lebanon	23
24	Nicaragua	600	59	Afghanistan	22
25	Sri Lanka	595	60	Argentina	22
26	Bolivia	578	61	Guatemala	22
	Thailand	578	62	Laos	21
28	Zimbabwe	561	63	Ecuador	21
29	Ghana	546	64	Chad	21
30	Somalia	538	65	Nigeria	19
31	West Bank and Gaza	478	66	Mongolia	18
32	Malawi	470	67	Gabon	18
33	Angola	451	68	Guinea-Bissau	17
34	Nepal	448	69	Yemen	17
35	Mali	442	70	CAR	16

argest bilateral and multilateral donors
% of GDP

1 Kuwait	2.29		13 Austria	0.33
2 Norway	1.05		14 Belgium	0.32
3 Denmark	1.03		15 Finland	0.31
4 Sweden	0.96		United Kingdom	0.31
5 Netherlands	0.76		17 Japan	0.29
6 France[a]	0.64		18 Spain	0.28
7 Canada	0.43		UAE	0.28
8 Luxembourg	0.40		20 Italy	0.27
9 Switzerland	0.36		21 Ireland	0.25
0 Australia	0.35		Saudi Arabia	0.25
Portugal	0.35		23 New Zealand	0.24
2 Germany	0.34		24 United States	0.15

argest recipients of bilateral and multilateral aid
$ per head

1 West Bank and Gaza	232		35 Honduras	54
2 Israel	228		36 Syria	53
3 Netherlands Antilles	193		37 Fiji	52
4 Gabon	176		38 CAR	51
5 Guinea-Bissau	169		Zimbabwe	51
6 Congo	144		40 Burundi	50
Suriname	144		41 Benin	49
8 Nicaragua	140		42 Albania	48
9 Mauritania	121		43 Egypt	47
0 Côte d'Ivoire	116		44 Bhutan	46
1 Malta	115		Jamaica	46
2 Namibia	92		Laos	46
Rwanda	92		Mali	46
4 Jordan	88		Oman	46
5 Haiti	85		49 Burkina Faso	43
6 Bahrain	80		Malawi	43
Bolivia	80		Niger	43
8 Senegal	79		52 Angola	42
9 Mongolia	78		53 Uganda	41
Papua New Guinea	78		54 Armenia	38
Zambia	78		55 Chad	35
2 Mozambique	74		56 Cambodia	34
3 Ex-Yugoslavia	72		Tanzania	34
4 Gambia, The	65		58 Kirgizstan	33
5 Botswana	62		Sri Lanka	33
Swaziland	62		60 Ghana	32
7 Cyprus	60		61 Togo	31
Lebanon	60		62 Uruguay	27
Sierra Leone	60		63 Kenya	26
0 Lesotho	59		64 Morocco	24
Somalia	59		65 Costa Rica	23
2 Cameroon	57		66 Guatemala	22
3 El Salvador	56		Madagascar	22
4 Guinea	55			

a Including overseas territories.

Industry

Largest industrial output
$bn, 1993

1	Japan	1,728	21	Turkey	4
2	United States	1,440	22	South Africa	4
3	Germany	726	23	Norway	3
4	France	363	24	Poland	3
5	Italy	317	25	Denmark	3
6	United Kingdom	270	26	Iran	3
7	China	204	27	Venezuela	2
8	Russia	168	28	Finland	2
9	Brazil	164	29	Greece	2
10	South Korea	142		Singapore	2
11	Mexico	96		UAE	2
12	Netherlands	87	32	Colombia	1
13	Australia	84		Hong Kong	1
14	Argentina	79	34	Peru	1
15	Austria	64		Philippines	1
16	India	61	36	Algeria	1
17	Indonesia	56	37	Belarus	1
18	Sweden	52		Puerto Rico	1
19	Ukraine	51	39	Czech Republic	1
20	Thailand	49		Nigeria	1

Highest growth in industrial output
Average annual real % growth, 1980–93

1	South Korea	12.1	12	Indonesia	6.
2	Bhutan[a]	11.8	13	India	6.
3	China	11.5		Singapore	6.
4	Thailand	11.0	15	Turkey	5.
5	Lesotho	9.3	16	Gambia, The	5.
6	Botswana	9.2	17	Norway	5.
	Oman	9.2	18	Bangladesh	5.
8	Mauritius	8.8	19	Papua New Guinea	5.
9	Malaysia	8.2	20	Chad	5.
10	Syria[a]	7.6		Japan	5.
11	Pakistan	7.2		Sri Lanka	5.

Lowest growth in industrial output
Average annual real % growth, 1980–93

1	Mozambique	-4.4	12	Moldova	-1.
2	Romania	-4.4	13	Estonia	-0.
3	Trinidad & Tobago	-4.1	14	Namibia	-0.
4	Albania	-4.0	15	Cambodia	-0.
5	Poland	-3.2	16	South Africa	-0.
6	Nicaragua	-2.9	17	Philippines	-0.
7	Georgia	-1.8	18	Guinea-Bissau	0.
8	Latvia	-1.7		Togo	0.
9	Hungary	-1.6	20	Russia	0.
10	Sierra Leone	-1.5		Uruguay	0.
	UAE	-1.5			

a 1980-92.

Largest chemicals output
$bn, 1992

1	United States	131.87	11	Spain	10.07
2	Japan	102.30	12	Netherlands	9.36
3	Germany	67.87	13	South Korea	8.55
4	United Kingdom	26.24	14	Belgium	7.52
5	France	24.40	15	Puerto Rico	6.70
6	Canada	19.46	16	Argentina	6.00
7	China	17.68	17	India	5.82
8	Italy	15.02	18	Sweden	4.36
9	Brazil	12.61	19	Austria	3.74
10	Mexico	11.42	20	Australia	3.49

Largest machinery and transport output
$bn, 1992

1	Japan	388.76	11	Brazil	19.81
2	United States	340.67	12	Mexico	16.79
3	Germany	231.90	13	Sweden	14.39
4	Italy	82.61	14	Netherlands	14.03
5	France	81.34	15	Austria	13.09
6	United Kingdom	60.56	16	Thailand	12.47
7	Canada	50.59	17	Belgium	11.82
8	China	39.77	18	India	10.39
9	Spain	26.17	19	Australia	8.74
10	South Korea	25.64	20	Singapore	7.33

Largest textiles and clothing output
$bn, 1992

1	United States	54.95	11	Spain	8.05
2	Japan	51.15	12	India	6.23
3	Italy	35.05	13	Argentina	5.00
4	Germany	22.62	14	Thailand	4.99
5	China	19.15	15	Indonesia	4.46
6	France	16.27	16	Belgium	4.30
7	South Korea	10.25	17	Hong Kong	4.21
8	United Kingdom	10.09	18	Turkey	3.85
9	Brazil	9.91	19	Mexico	3.36
10	Canada	9.73	20	Austria	2.80

Largest processed food output
$bn, 1992

1	United States	142.86	11	Brazil	13.51
2	Japan	102.30	12	Netherlands	12.28
3	Germany	56.56	13	Argentina	10.50
4	France	37.96	14	Belgium	9.13
5	Canada	33.08	15	South Korea	8.55
6	United Kingdom	30.28	16	Australia	7.86
7	Italy	25.03	17	Austria	7.01
8	China	19.15	18	Indonesia	6.41
9	Spain	18.12	19	Denmark	5.40
10	Mexico	16.12	20	Thailand	4.99

Agriculture

Most economically dependent on agriculture
% of GDP from agriculture

1	Georgia	68.0	21	Moldova	41.7
2	Somalia	65.5	22	Rwanda	40.5
3	Tanzania	57.1	23	Madagascar	39.1
4	Laos	56.3	24	Niger	38.5
5	Myanmar	54.8	25	Côte d'Ivoire	37.4
6	Ethiopia	54.3	26	Benin	36.8
7	Afghanistan	52.6	27	Haiti	36.7
8	Cambodia	52.2	28	Sudan	33.8
9	Burundi	51.9	29	West Bank and Gaza	32.9
10	Albania	51.8	30	Kirgizstan	32.8
11	CAR	49.9	31	Zambia	32.0
12	Uganda	49.6	32	Burkina Faso	31.8
13	Togo	49.2		India	31.8
14	Chad	48.8	34	Malawi	31.3
15	Armenia	48.6	35	Azerbaijan	31.1
16	Ghana	47.6	36	Nigeria	30.7
17	Guinea-Bissau	44.4	37	Bangladesh	30.4
18	Nepal	43.3	38	Liberia	30.3
19	Sierra Leone	42.9	39	Ukraine	30.2
20	Mali	42.4		Zaire	30.2

Least economically dependent on agriculture
% of GDP from agriculture

1	Hong Kong	0.2	22	Sweden	3.1
	Singapore	0.2		Switzerland	3.1
3	Puerto Rico	0.5	24	Italy	3.3
4	Netherlands Antilles	0.9		Oman	3.3
5	Germany	1.0	26	Denmark	3.6
	Qatar	1.0		Netherlands	3.6
7	Bahrain	1.1		Taiwan	3.6
8	Luxembourg	1.2	29	Spain	3.7
9	United States	1.7	30	Bahamas	4.5
10	Belgium	1.8		Libya	4.5
11	United Kingdom	2.0	32	South Africa	4.7
12	Japan	2.1	33	Slovenia	4.9
13	Brunei	2.2	34	Iraq	5.1
14	Austria	2.3	35	Botswana	5.2
15	Iceland	2.4		Tajikistan	5.2
	Israel	2.4	37	Slovakia	5.3
	Trinidad & Tobago	2.4	38	Cyprus	5.5
18	UAE	2.5	39	Czech Republic	5.8
19	France	2.6	40	Finland	6.0
20	Norway	2.7		Portugal	6.0
21	Canada	2.8			

Fastest growth
% average annual growth per head, 1980–93

1	Saudi Arabia	13.9	8	Belgium	2.4
2	Malaysia	4.0	9	Cambodia	2.3
3	Lebanon	3.4		Nigeria	2.3
4	Burkino Faso	3.0	11	Algeria	2.1
5	Indonesia	2.7		Denmark	2.1
6	China	2.5	13	Ireland	2.0
	Portugal	2.5		Morocco	2.0

Slowest growth
% average annual growth per head, 1980–93

1	Netherlands Antilles	-12.4	8	Haiti	-3.2
2	Somalia	-6.2	9	Romania	-3.1
3	Liberia	-6.1	10	Botswana	-2.9
4	Singapore	-5.0		Mongolia	-2.9
5	Nicaragua	-4.6	12	Angola	-2.7
6	Macao	-4.5		Suriname	-2.7
7	Afghanistan	-4.0	14	Iceland	-2.6

Biggest producers
'000 tonnes

Cereals

1	China	397,212	6	Indonesia	52,862
2	United States	357,377	7	Canada	47,054
3	India	212,482	8	Brazil	45,930
4	Russia	78,709	9	Germany	36,353
5	France	53,641	10	Ukraine	32,862

Meat

1	China	44,814	6	Germany	5,789
2	United States	32,965	7	India	4,117
3	Brazil	8,080	8	Italy	4,030
4	Russia	7,475	9	Spain	3,765
5	France	6,140	10	Argentina	3,574

Fruit

1	China	37,298	6	Spain	11,648
2	India	33,235	7	France	10,649
3	Brazil	32,515	8	Turkey	9,700
4	United States	28,854	9	Mexico	9,547
5	Italy	17,972	10	Uganda	9,239

Vegetables

1	China	128,811	6	Italy	13,629
2	India	65,137	7	Spain	10,680
3	United States	36,443	8	South Korea	10,503
4	Turkey	19,354	9	Russia	10,190
5	Japan	13,870	10	Iran	10,050

Commodities

Wheat

Top 10 producers
'000 tonnes

1	China	102,000
2	EU 15	85,300
3	United States	63,200
4	Ex-Soviet Union	61,600
5	India	58,000
6	Canada	23,200
7	Pakistan	15,100
8	Turkey	15,000
9	Iran	11,500
10	Argentina	11,100

Top 10 consumers
'000 tonnes

1	China	115,000
2	Ex-Soviet Union	78,000
3	EU 15	73,900
4	India	57,200
5	United States	35,000
6	Pakistan	18,200
7	Turkey	15,400
8	Iran	14,000
9	Egypt	9,900
10	Poland	8,900

Rice

Top 10 producers[a]
'000 tonnes

1	China	175,930
2	India	121,898
3	Indonesia	46,638
4	Bangladesh	25,252
5	Vietnam	24,091
6	Thailand	21,361
7	Myanmar	16,034
8	Japan	14,973
9	Brazil	10,885
10	Philippines	10,475

Top 10 consumers[b]
'000 tonnes

1	China	129,000
2	India	77,307
3	Indonesia	32,740
4	Bangladesh	17,842
5	Vietnam	13,900
6	Japan	9,350
7	Myanmar	8,521
8	Thailand	8,400
9	Brazil	8,100
10	Philippines	7,180

Sugar[c]

Top 10 producers
'000 tonnes

1	EU 15	16,702
2	Brazil	12,270
3	India	11,900
4	United States	6,921
5	China	6,325
6	Ex-Soviet Union	5,732
7	Australia	5,217
8	Thailand	4,168
9	Mexico	4,025
10	Cuba	4,017

Top 10 consumers
'000 tonnes

1	EU 15	14,523
2	India	13,700
3	Ex-Soviet Union	10,075
4	United States	8,454
5	China	7,900
6	Brazil	7,874
7	Mexico	4,350
8	Indonesia	2,900
	Pakistan	2,900
10	Japan	2,657

Coarse grains[d]

Top 5 producers
'000 tonnes

1	United States	284,800
2	China	114,600
3	EU 15	88,600
4	Ex-Soviet Union	85,000
5	Brazil	35,800

Top 5 consumers
'000 tonnes

1	United States	208,000
2	China	115,000
3	Ex-Soviet Union	88,000
4	EU 15	85,000
5	Brazil	38,000

Tea

Top 10 producers		*Top 10 consumers*	
'000 tonnes		*'000 tonnes*	
1 India	744	1 India	580
2 China	588	2 China	409
3 Sri Lanka	244	3 United Kingdom	148
4 Kenya	209	4 Turkey	129
5 Turkey	134	5 Japan	127
6 Indonesia	130	6 Pakistan	107
7 Japan	86	7 United States	96
8 Bangladesh	52	8 Russia	83
9 Iran	45	9 Iran	75
10 Argentina	42	10 Egypt	55

Coffee

Top 10 producers		*Top 10 consumers*	
'000 tonnes		*'000 tonnes*	
1 Brazil	1,266	1 United States	1,053
2 Colombia	778	2 Germany	604
3 Indonesia	385	3 Brazil	540
4 India	253	4 Japan	365
5 Mexico	249	5 France	307
6 Guatemala	220	6 Italy	286
7 Vietnam	211	7 Spain	167
8 Côte d'Ivoire	179	8 United Kingdom	160
9 Uganda	158	9 Indonesia	139
10 Ethiopia	152	10 Netherlands	127

Cocoa

Top 10 producers		*Top 10 consumers*	
'000 tonnes		*'000 tonnes*	
1 United States	546	1 Côte d'Ivoire	884
2 Germany	244	2 Brazil	270
3 United Kingdom	182	3 Indonesia	260
4 France	157	4 Ghana	255
5 Russia	148	5 Malaysia	205
6 Japan	116	6 Nigeria	135
7 Brazil	88	7 Cameroon	98
8 Italy	81	8 Ecuador	80
9 Spain	65	9 Dominican Republic	60
10 Belgium	60	10 Colombia	52

a Paddy (unmilled rice, in the husk).
b Milled rice.
c Raw.
d Includes: maize (corn), barley, sorghum, rye, oats and millet.

Commodities

Copper

Top 10 producers[a]
'000 tonnes

1	Chile	2,220
2	United States	1,796
3	Canada	617
4	Russia	448
5	Australia	416
6	China	396
7	Zambia	384
8	Poland	377
9	Peru	360
10	Indonesia	334

Top 10 consumers[b]
'000 tonnes

1	United States	2,678
2	Japan	1,375
3	Germany	1,000
4	China	798
5	Taiwan	547
6	France	513
7	Italy	480
8	South Korea	476
9	Belgium	407
10	United Kingdom	377

Lead

Top 10 producers[a]
'000 tonnes

1	Australia	465
2	China	462
3	United States	372
4	Peru	217
5	Mexico	175
6	Canada	173
7	Sweden	113
8	South Africa	96
9	Morocco	70
10	Kazakhstan	69

Top 10 consumers[b]
'000 tonnes

1	United States	1,495
2	Germany	355
3	Japan	348
4	China	295
5	United Kingdom	268
6	France	237
7	Italy	230
8	South Korea	172
9	Mexico	162
10	Spain	120

Zinc

Top 10 producers[a]
'000 tonnes

1	Canada	1,009
2	China	990
3	Australia	971
4	Peru	674
5	United States	592
6	Mexico	369
7	Ireland	195
8	Spain	170
9	Sweden	160
10	Poland	151

Top 10 consumers[c]
'000 tonnes

1	United States	1,118
2	Japan	721
3	China	612
4	Germany	520
5	Italy	320
6	South Korea	318
7	France	241
8	Belgium	225
9	Australia	215
10	United Kingdom	197

Tin

Top 5 producers[a]
'000 tonnes

1	China	54.1
2	Indonesia	38.5
3	Peru	20.0
4	Brazil	19.7
5	Bolivia	16.1

Top 5 consumers[b]
'000 tonnes

1	United States	33.0
2	China	32.1
3	Japan	28.7
4	Germany	18.2
5	United Kingdom	10.4

Nickel

Top 10 producers[a]		*Top 10 consumers*[b]	
'000 tonnes		*'000 tonnes*	
1 Russia	212.0	1 Japan	181.1
2 Canada	150.1	2 United States	131.0
3 New Caledonia	96.0	3 Germany	87.8
4 Indonesia	81.2	4 Russia	66.7
5 Australia	79.0	5 France	44.4
6 China	36.9	6 Italy	44.0
7 Cuba	31.0	7 China	42.0
8 Dominican Republic	30.9	8 United Kingdom	38.0
9 South Africa	30.1	9 Finland	30.4
10 Colombia	20.8	10 Spain	25.7

Aluminium

Top 10 producers[d]		*Top 10 consumers*[b]	
'000 tonnes		*'000 tonnes*	
1 United States	3,299	1 United States	5,407
2 Russia	2,671	2 Japan	2,346
3 Canada	2,255	3 China	1,484
4 China	1,498	4 Germany	1,460
5 Australia	1,311	5 France	735
6 Brazil	1,185	6 Italy	660
7 Norway	857	7 South Korea	604
8 Venezuela	585	8 Canada	533
9 Germany	505	9 United Kingdom	500
10 India	472	10 Russia	476

Precious metals

Gold[a]		*Silver*[a]	
Top 10 producers		*Top 10 producers*	
tonnes		*tonnes*	
1 South Africa	583.9	1 Mexico	2,325
2 United States	331.0	2 Peru	1,667
3 Australia	256.2	3 United States	1,380
4 Russia	164.7	4 Australia	1,045
5 Canada	146.1	5 Chile	959
6 China	130.0	6 Poland	800
7 Brazil	75.4	7 Canada	775
8 Uzbekistan	64.4	8 Kazakhstan	408
9 Papua New Guinea	60.6	9 Bolivia	352
10 Indonesia	55.3	10 Morocco	333

a Mine production.
b Refined consumption.
c Slab consumption.
d Primary refined production.

Commodities

Rubber (natural and synthetic)

| *Top 10 producers* | | *Top 10 consumers* | |
'000 tonnes		'000 tonnes	
1 United States	2,390	1 United States	3,119
2 Thailand	1,722	2 Japan	1,666
3 Indonesia	1,361	3 China	1,425
4 Japan	1,349	4 Germany	713
5 Malaysia	1,101	5 South Korea	610
6 China	835	6 India	589
7 Germany	642	7 France	505
8 Russia	590	8 Brazil	448
9 India	523	9 Italy	390
10 France	520	10 United Kingdom	365

Raw wool

| *Top 10 producers* [a] | | *Top 10 consumers* [b] | |
'000 tonnes		'000 tonnes	
1 Australia	726	1 China	439
2 Ex-Soviet Union	340	2 Italy	175
3 New Zealand	289	3 Japan	90
4 China	260	4 United Kingdom	74
5 Argentina	90	5 United States	65
Uruguay	90	6 South Korea	61
7 Turkey	74	7 Ex-Soviet Union	60
8 Pakistan	70	8 Germany	56
9 South Africa	66	Turkey	56
United Kingdom	66	10 India	53

Cotton

| *Top 10 producers* | | *Top 10 consumers* | |
'000 tonnes		'000 tonnes	
1 China	4,341	1 China	4,341
2 United States	4,281	2 United States	2,438
3 India	2,361	3 India	2,275
4 Pakistan	1,478	4 Pakistan	1,524
5 Uzbekistan	1,254	5 Turkey	850
6 Turkey	628	6 Brazil	844
7 Brazil	564	7 Indonesia	460
8 Argentina	350	8 Japan	387
9 Australia	335	9 South Korea	360
Greece	335	10 Russia	350

Major oil seeds [c]

| *Top 5 producers* | | *Top 5 consumers* | |
'000 tonnes		'000 tonnes	
1 United States	79,546	1 United States	43,469
2 China	37,716	2 EU 15	27,385
3 Brazil	26,802	3 China	25,494
4 India	20,080	4 Brazil	20,354
5 Argentina	18,567	5 India	16,605

Oil[d]

Top 15 producers '000 barrels per day, 1994		Top 15 consumers '000 barrels per day, 1994	
1 Saudi Arabia[e]	8,965	**1** United States	16,915
2 United States	8,355	**2** Japan	5,770
3 Russia	6,385	**3** Russia	3,265
4 Iran[e]	3,600	**4** China	3,030
5 Mexico	3,265	**5** Germany	2,880
6 China	2,905	**6** France	1,930
7 Norway	2,755	**7** Italy	1,915
8 United Kingdom	2,675	**8** South Korea	1,805
Venezuela[e]	2,675	**9** United Kingdom	1,775
10 UAE[e]	2,490	**10** Canada	1,735
11 Canada	2,280	**11** Mexico	1,660
12 Kuwait[e]	2,085	**12** Brazil	1,440
13 Nigeria[e]	1,880	**13** India	1,400
14 Indonesia[e]	1,585	**14** Spain	1,120
15 Libya[e]	1,410	**15** Indonesia	830

Natural gas

Top 10 producers '000 terajoules, 1993		Top 10 consumers '000 terajoules, 1993	
1 Russia	20,497	**1** United States	22,362
2 United States	20,008	**2** Russia	14,745
3 Canada	5,263	**3** Ukraine	3,367
4 Netherlands	2,930	**4** Canada	2,884
5 United Kingdom	2,537	**5** Germany	2,763
6 Turkmenistan	2,219	**6** United Kingdom	2,692
7 Algeria	2,102	**7** Japan	2,223
8 Indonesia	2,062	**8** Italy	1,952
9 Uzbekistan	1,529	**9** Netherlands	1,589
10 Saudi Arabia	1,401	**10** Uzbekistan	1,481

Coal

Top 10 producers Million tonnes, 1993		Top 10 consumers Million tonnes, 1993	
1 China	1,150	**1** China	1,129
2 United States	858	**2** United States	799
3 Russia	304	**3** Russia	315
4 Germany	286	**4** Germany	304
5 India	263	**5** India	268
6 Australia	224	**6** Poland	178
7 Poland	199	**7** South Africa	140
8 South Africa	183	**8** Ukraine	121
9 Ukraine	116	**9** Japan	119
10 Kazakhstan	112	**10** Australia	100

a   Greasy basis.
b   Clean basis.
c   Soybeans, sunflower seed, cottonseed, groundnuts and rapeseed.
d   Includes crude oil, shale oil, oil sands and natural gas liquids.
e   Opec members.

Energy

Largest producers
Million tonnes coal equivalent, 1993

1	United States	2,236.5	16	France	161.9
2	Russia	1,486.0	17	Algeria	156.4
3	China	1,070.0	18	Ukraine	153.6
4	Saudi Arabia	654.1	19	Kuwait	147.7
5	Canada	450.2	20	South Africa	141.4
6	United Kingdom	329.7	21	Nigeria	141.3
7	Iran	288.3	22	Kazakhstan	137.3
8	India	276.0	23	Poland	132.3
9	Mexico	275.3	24	Japan	118.3
10	Indonesia	243.8	25	Netherlands	106.2
11	Venezuela	238.5	26	Libya	104.2
12	Australia	227.2	27	North Korea	91.1
13	Norway	217.2	28	Brazil	85.0
14	Germany	210.8	29	Egypt	83.1
15	UAE	179.9	30	Turkmenistan	82.9

Largest consumers
Million tonnes coal equivalent, 1993

1	United States	2,789.4	16	Brazil	129.7
2	Russia	1,025.0	17	South Africa	122.1
3	China	1,012.7	18	Kazakhstan	115.4
4	Japan	597.3	19	Spain	114.6
5	Germany	468.3	20	Netherlands	112.8
6	United Kingdom	324.8	21	Iran	111.4
7	India	318.6	22	Saudi Arabia	100.1
8	Canada	313.8	23	North Korea	99.8
9	France	312.3	24	Indonesia	90.7
10	Ukraine	274.9	25	Venezuela	71.1
11	Italy	230.3	26	Argentina	68.9
12	Mexico	168.6	27	Turkey	67.5
13	South Korea	153.7	28	Belgium	67.4
14	Poland	138.4	29	Uzbekistan	64.9
15	Australia	133.6	30	Romania	60.1

Energy efficiency

Most efficient			*Least efficient*		
GDP per kg of energy, 1993, $			*GDP per kg of energy, 1993, $*		
1	Myanmar[a]	22.2	1	Mongolia	0.2
2	Benin	20.4	2	Azerbaijan	0.3
3	Burkina Faso	17.7		Kazakhstan	0.3
4	Macao	15.2	4	Lithuania	0.5
5	Mali	14.4		Russia	0.5
6	CAR	13.4		Suriname	0.5
7	Chad	12.1		Turkmenistan	0.5
8	Bhutan	10.9		Ukraine	0.5
9	Cameroon	10.2		Uzbekistan	0.5
10	Bermuda	9.8	10	Bulgaria	0.6
				China	0.6

a 1992.

Largest exporters
Million tonnes coal equivalent, 1993

1	Saudi Arabia	512.6	14	United States	113.6
2	Russia	471.5	15	Algeria	112.3
3	Canada	193.9	16	Mexico	110.3
4	Iran	191.1	17	Libya	87.6
5	Norway	187.7	18	Turkmenistan	62.6
6	Venezuela	161.3	19	Kazakhstan	55.6
7	UAE	143.1	20	Malaysia	54.7
8	Indonesia	131.6	21	Singapore	53.4
9	Australia	130.4	22	Oman	53.3
10	Kuwait	128.2	23	China	52.9
11	United Kingdom	121.6	24	South Africa	43.0
12	Nigeria	118.5	25	Egypt	37.4
13	Netherlands	117.2			

Largest importers
Million tonnes coal equivalent, 1993

1	United States	701.1	14	India	66.9
2	Japan	532.4	15	Russia	57.6
3	Germany	294.4	16	Canada	57.4
4	Italy	201.7	17	Turkey	48.1
5	France	194.7	18	Belarus	40.6
6	South Korea	169.9		Sweden	40.6
7	Ukraine	133.8	20	Kazakhstan	37.2
8	Netherlands	132.1	21	Thailand	36.1
9	United Kingdom	124.2	22	China	35.6
10	Singapore	104.8	23	Greece	29.8
11	Spain	103.9	24	Poland	28.9
12	Belgium	87.5	25	Australia	27.1
13	Brazil	67.3			

Largest consumption per head
Kg coal equivalent, 1993

1	Qatar	36,015	16	Finland	6,838
2	UAE	19,524	17	Kazakhstan	6,805
3	Bahrain	17,606	18	Belgium	6,711
4	Brunei	16,047	19	Sweden	6,516
5	Luxembourg	13,848	20	Saudi Arabia	5,846
6	Canada	10,891	21	Germany	5,791
7	United States	10,815	22	United Kingdom	5,586
8	Singapore	9,102	23	New Zealand	5,530
9	Kuwait	9,054	24	Czech Republic	5,499
10	Australia	7,586	25	Netherlands Antilles	5,497
11	Netherlands	7,381	26	France	5,428
12	Norway	7,172	27	Ukraine	5,333
13	Trinidad & Tobago	7,133	28	Denmark	5,032
14	Iceland	7,053	29	Turkmenistan	4,828
15	Russia	6,937	30	Japan	4,796

Note: Consumption data for small countries, especially oil producers, can be unreliable, often leading to unrealistically high consumption per head rates.

Workers of the world

Highest % of population in labour force
1993–94 or latest

1	Singapore	57.0		Suriname	48.2
2	Denmark	55.8	27	Portugal	47.9
3	Switzerland	55.4	28	New Zealand	47.8
4	Latvia	55.1	29	Australia	47.7
5	Iceland	54.7	30	Burkina Faso	47.6
6	Japan	53.1	31	Moldova	47.5
7	Burundi	52.9		Panama	47.5
8	Czech Republic	52.6	33	Slovenia	47.0
	Thailand	52.6	34	Slovakia	46.9
10	Belarus	52.5	35	Austria	46.7
11	Germany	52.3	36	Bulgaria	46.3
12	United States	51.3		Netherlands Antilles	46.3
13	Lithuania	50.8		Rwanda	46.3
	Ukraine	50.8	39	Romania	45.9
15	Bahamas	50.7	40	Colombia	45.4
16	Estonia	50.5	41	Poland	45.2
17	Hong Kong	50.3	42	Bangladesh	45.0
18	Canada	50.1	43	France	44.8
19	Sweden	49.6	44	Uruguay	44.7
20	Norway	49.4	45	Bahrain	44.6
	United Kingdom	49.4		Paraguay	44.6
22	Finland	49.2	47	Jamaica	44.5
	Russia	49.2	48	South Korea	44.4
24	CAR	48.2	49	Macao	44.3
	Cyprus	48.2	50	Mauritius	44.1

Most male workforce
% male workers, 1993–94 or latest

1	Iran	90.4	21	Ireland	68.4
2	Pakistan	86.3	22	Honduras	68.3
3	Bahrain	82.0	23	Côte d'Ivoire	67.7
	Syria	82.0	24	Chile	67.3
5	Tunisia	79.1	25	Nigeria	66.7
6	Egypt	75.9	26	Sri Lanka	66.1
7	Kuwait	75.7	27	Mauritius	65.9
8	Saudi Arabia	74.4		Nicaragua	65.9
9	Guatemala	74.2	29	Malaysia	65.7
10	Morocco	73.9	30	Luxembourg	63.5
11	Ecuador	73.6	31	Spain	63.2
12	Malta	73.2	32	Italy	63.1
13	Argentina	72.1	33	Greece	63.0
14	India	71.4		Trinidad & Tobago	63.0
15	Panama	70.8	35	Philippines	62.8
16	Costa Rica	69.9	36	Hong Kong	62.6
17	Turkey	69.2	37	Netherlands	62.4
18	Mexico	69.1	38	Suriname	62.2
19	Brazil	69.0	39	Cyprus	62.1
20	Venezuela	68.8	40	Indonesia	61.8

Lowest % of population in labour force
1993–94 or latest

1	Iran	26.0	**26**	Kuwait	38.9
2	Syria	27.8	**27**	Mexico	38.9
3	Pakistan	27.9	**28**	Bolivia	39.4
4	Egypt	29.2		Côte d'Ivoire	39.4
5	Tunisia	29.8	**30**	Spain	39.8
6	Nigeria	31.1	**31**	Italy	40.1
7	Puerto Rico	32.4	**32**	Hungary	40.4
8	Morocco	32.5	**33**	Trinidad & Tobago	40.5
9	Botswana	33.3	**34**	Barbados	40.6
10	Guatemala	33.5		El Salvador	40.6
11	Senegal	34.0	**36**	Greece	40.7
12	Zimbabwe	34.6	**37**	Brazil	40.8
13	Nicaragua	34.7		Philippines	40.8
14	Ecuador	34.8	**39**	Sri Lanka	41.0
	Honduras	34.8	**40**	Argentina	41.5
16	Malaysia	35.1	**41**	Indonesia	41.9
17	Fiji	35.2		Netherlands	41.9
18	Malta	36.1	**43**	Belgium	42.1
19	Venezuela	36.3	**44**	Taiwan	42.6
20	Israel	36.9	**45**	Cambodia	43.1
21	India	37.5		Macedonia, FYR	43.1
	South Africa	37.5	**47**	Malawi	43.3
23	Ireland	37.8		Peru	43.3
24	Chile	38.6	**49**	Ethiopia	43.4
25	Costa Rica	38.7	**50**	Luxembourg	43.5

Most female workforce
% female workers, 1993–94 or latest

1	Cambodia	55.7		Slovenia	46.7
2	Lithuania	53.8	**22**	Jamaica	46.5
3	Rwanda	53.5	**23**	Slovakia	46.1
4	Burundi	52.6	**24**	Poland	46.0
5	Malawi	51.0		United States	46.0
6	Latvia	50.0	**26**	Norway	45.4
7	Estonia	49.9	**27**	El Salvador	45.3
8	Ukraine	49.2	**28**	Canada	45.2
9	Belarus	49.0	**29**	Netherlands Antilles	45.1
10	Burkina Faso	48.7	**30**	Portugal	44.7
11	Russia	48.5		Romania	44.7
12	Barbados	48.4	**32**	Hungary	44.5
	Bulgaria	48.4		Thailand	44.5
14	Sweden	48.1	**34**	France	44.1
15	Zimbabwe	47.8	**35**	United Kingdom	43.8
16	Czech Republic	47.6	**36**	New Zealand	43.6
17	Bahamas	47.5	**37**	Colombia	43.4
18	Finland	47.0	**38**	Switzerland	43.3
19	CAR	46.8	**39**	Germany	43.2
20	Denmark	46.7	**40**	Paraguay	42.4

Banking and business

Largest banks
By capital, $m

1	Sanwa Bank	Japan	22,648
2	Dai-Ichi Kangyo Bank	Japan	22,370
3	Fuji Bank	Japan	22,210
4	Sumitomo Bank	Japan	22,002
5	Sakura Bank	Japan	21,395
6	Mitsubishi Bank	Japan	19,832
7	HSBC Holdings	United Kingdom	17,972
8	Crédit Agricole	France	17,288
9	Citicorp	United States	17,216
10	Union Bank of Switzerland	Switzerland	16,244
11	Industrial Bank of Japan	Japan	15,794
12	BankAmerica Corp	United States	13,865
13	Deutsche Bank	Germany	13,089
14	Bank of Tokyo	Japan	12,495
15	Long-Term Credit Bank of Japan	Japan	12,394
16	Tokai Bank	Japan	12,376
17	C.S. Holding	Switzerland	12,055
18	Asahi Bank	Japan	11,938
19	Swiss Bank Corp	Switzerland	11,607
20	Compagnie Financière de Paribas	France	10,827
21	Groupe Caisse d'Epargne	France	10,544
22	Banque Nationale de Paris	France	10,425
23	Industrial & Commercial Bank of China	China	10,380
24	National Westminster Bank	United Kingdom	10,293
25	ABN-AMRO Bank	Netherlands	10,262
26	Barclays Bank	United Kingdom	10,172
27	Chemical Banking Corp	United States	10,002
28	Mitsubishi Trust & Banking Corporation	Japan	9,878
29	NationsBank	United States	9,761
30	Sumitomo Trust & Banking	Japan	9,559
31	Rabobank Nederland	Netherlands	9,476
32	Bank of China	China	8,981
33	Société Générale	France	8,921
34	J.P. Morgan & Co.	United States	8,863
35	Dresdner Bank	Germany	8,856
36	Crédit Lyonnais	France	8,708
37	Chase Manhattan Corp	United States	8,162
38	Westdeutsche Landesbank Girozentrale	Germany	7,887
39	Mitsui Trust & Banking	Japan	7,683
40	Banc One Corp	United States	7,152

Notes: Capital is essentially equity and reserves.
Figures for Japanese banks refer to the year ended March 31, 1995. Figures for all other countries refer to the year ended December 31, 1994.

Largest businesses
By sales, $bn

1	Mitsubishi[a]	Japan	175.8
2	Mitsui[a]	Japan	171.5
3	Itochu[a]	Japan	167.8
4	Sumitomo[a]	Japan	162.5
5	General Motors	United States	155.0
6	Marubeni[a]	Japan	150.2
7	Ford Motor	United States	128.4
8	Exxon	United States	101.5
9	Nissho Iwai[a]	Japan	100.9
10	Royal Dutch/Shell Group	United Kingdom/Netherlands	94.9
11	Toyota Motor[b]	Japan	88.2
12	Wal-Mart Stores[c]	United States	83.4
13	Hitachi[a]	Japan	76.4
14	Nippon Life Insurance[a]	Japan	75.4
15	AT&T[d]	United States	75.1
16	Nippon Telegraph & Telephone[a]	Japan	70.8
17	Matsushita Electric Industrial[a]	Japan	69.9
	Tomen[a]	Japan	69.9
19	General Electric	United States	64.7
20	Daimler-Benz	Germany	64.2
21	Intl. Business Machines	United States	64.1
22	Mobil	United States	59.6
23	Nissan Motor[a]	Japan	58.7
24	Nichimen[a]	Japan	56.2
25	Kanematsu[a]	Japan	55.9
26	Dai-Ichi Mutual Life Insurance[a]	Japan	54.9
27	Sears Roebuck	United States	54.8
28	Philip Morris	United States	53.8
29	Chrysler	United States	52.2
30	Siemens[f]	Germany	51.1
31	British Petroleum	United Kingdom	50.7
32	Tokyo Electric Power[a]	Japan	50.4
33	U.S. Postal Service[ef]	United States	49.4
	Volkswagen	Germany	49.4
35	Sumitomo Life Insurance[a]	Japan	49.0
36	Toshiba[a]	Japan	48.2
37	Unilever	United Kingdom/Netherlands	45.5
38	IRI[e]	Italy	45.4
39	Nestlé	Switzerland	41.6
40	Deutsche Telekom	Germany	41.1

a   Year ended March 31, 1995.
b   Year ended June 30, 1994.
c   Year ended January 31, 1995.
d   Acquired McCaw Cellular.
e   Government owned.
f   Year ended September 30, 1994.

Notes: All companies shown have derived at least half of their sales from
manufacturing and/or mining. Figures refer to the year ended December 31, 1994,
except where specified. They include sales of consolidated subsidiaries but exclude
excise taxes collected by manufacturers, thus differing, in some instances, from
figures published by the companies themselves.

Stockmarkets

Largest market capitalisation
$m, end 1994

1	United States	5,081,810		26	Denmark	54,339
2	Japan	3,719,914		27	Indonesia	47,241
3	United Kingdom	1,210,245		28	China	43,521
4	Germany	470,519		29	Saudi Arabia	38,693
5	France	451,263		30	Finland	38,278
6	Canada	315,009		31	Argentina	36,864
7	Switzerland	284,092		32	Norway	36,469
8	Netherlands	283,251		33	Israel	32,730
9	Hong Kong	269,508		34	Austria	30,272
10	Taiwan	247,325		35	Russia	30,000
11	South Africa	225,718		36	Luxembourg	28,511
12	Australia	219,188		37	New Zealand	27,217
13	Malaysia	199,276		38	Turkey	21,605
14	South Korea	191,778		39	Portugal	16,249
15	Brazil	189,281		40	Greece	14,921
16	Italy	180,135		41	Colombia	14,028
17	Spain	154,858		42	Czech Republic	12,589
18	Singapore	134,516		43	Pakistan	12,263
19	Thailand	131,479		44	Kuwait	10,517
20	Sweden	130,939		45	Namibia	9,574
21	Mexico	130,246		46	Ireland	8,408
22	India	127,515		47	Peru	8,178
23	Belgium	84,103		48	Jordan	4,594
24	Chile	68,195		49	Morocco	4,376
25	Philippines	55,519		50	Egypt	4,263

Highest growth in market capitalisation, $ terms
% increase, 1985–94

1	Indonesia	40,277		21	Spain	715
2	Portugal	8,363		22	Sri Lanka	690
3	Philippines	8,199		23	Hong Kong	681
4	Thailand	6,984		24	Jamaica	559
5	Mexico	3,314		25	Austria	558
6	Chile	3,289		26	Finland	554
7	Colombia	3,272		27	Kenya[b]	550
8	South Korea	2,498		28	France	471
9	Taiwan	2,271		29	Zimbabwe	408
10	Turkey[a]	2,211		30	Netherlands	377
11	Greece	1,850		31	Brazil	343
12	Argentina	1,710		32	Israel	329
13	Morocco	1,616		33	Tunisia	327
14	Malaysia	1,128		34	South Africa	307
15	Singapore	1,115		35	Belgium	303
16	Uruguay	1,033		36	Japan	280
17	Peru	976		37	United Kingdom	269
18	Bangladesh	828		38	Australia	264
19	Pakistan	795			Venezuela	264
20	India	788		40	Norway	262

Highest growth in value traded, $ terms
% increase, 1985–94

1	Indonesia	393,267	24	Denmark	2,052
2	Turkey[a]	166,762	25	Zimbabwe	1,856
3	Portugal	105,400	26	Spain	1,717
4	Greece	30,165	27	Argentina	1,702
5	Sri Lanka	23,233	28	Hong Kong	1,412
6	Taiwan	14,420	29	United Kingdom	1,257
7	Thailand	14,018	30	Pakistan	1,255
8	Philippines	12,467	31	Côte d'Ivoire	1,100
9	Bangladesh	10,600	32	Netherlands	912
10	Chile	9,133	33	Costa Rica[c]	900
11	Peru	8,005	34	Sweden	786
12	Colombia	7,203	35	Italy	755
13	South Korea	6,773	36	New Zealand	666
14	Morocco	5,962	37	Luxembourg	647
15	Singapore	5,761	38	Belgium	583
16	Malaysia	5,316	39	Germany	544
17	France	4,094	40	Australia	502
18	Mexico	3,415	41	Jamaica	500
19	Israel	3,257		Uruguay[a]	500
20	Venezuela	2,919	43	South Africa	463
21	Tunisia	2,860	44	India	450
22	Finland	2,528	45	Brazil	410
23	Austria	2,288	46	Kuwait	403

Highest growth in number of listed companies[d]
% increase, 1985–94

1	Indonesia	800	20	South Africa	39
2	Portugal	713	21	Peru	37
3	Turkey[a]	340	22	Philippines	37
4	Thailand	289	23	Netherlands	37
5	Taiwan	146	24	Jamaica	32
6	Israel	139	25	Mexico	31
7	Costa Rica	127	26	Finland	30
8	Egypt	121	27	Canada	30
9	Malaysia	115	28	Sri Lanka	26
10	South Korea	104	29	Chile	22
11	Hong Kong	103	30	Japan	21
12	Pakistan	100	31	Côte d'Ivoire	20
13	Singapore	97	32	Zimbabwe	16
14	Greece	89	33	Australia	14
15	Nigeria	84	34	Spain	13
16	Switzerland	81	35	Colombia	11
17	Austria	73	36	Kenya	4
18	India	61	37	Denmark	4
19	Italy	52	38	Brazil	1

a 1986–94.
b 1988–94.
c 1987–94.
d Only 38 stockmarkets experienced an increase in number of listed companies.

Transport: *roads and cars*

Longest road networks
Km, 1994 or latest

1	United States	6,284,039	16	Indonesia	244,164
2	India	1,923,248	17	Argentina	215,578
3	Brazil	1,824,364	18	Pakistan	204,346
4	Japan	1,137,453	19	Austria	200,000
5	Canada	901,903	20	Philippines	182,537
6	France	812,550	21	South Africa	182,329
7	Australia	810,264	22	Ukraine	172,315
8	Germany	639,805	23	Hungary	158,633
9	Romania	461,880	24	Kazakhstan	158,581
10	Turkey	381,028	25	Saudi Arabia	156,084
11	Poland	370,510	26	Zaire	145,000
12	United Kingdom	366,477	27	Belgium	140,978
13	Spain	341,230	28	Sweden	135,920
14	Italy	305,388	29	Greece	116,150
15	Mexico	245,433	30	Colombia	107,377

Densest road networks
Km of road per km² land area, 1994 or latest

1	Belgium	4.60	16	France	1.47
2	Bahrain	4.50	17	Ireland	1.31
3	Singapore	4.42	18	Poland	1.18
4	Japan	3.01	19	Cyprus	1.10
5	Netherlands	2.80	20	Italy	1.04
6	Ukraine	2.70	21	Latvia	1.00
7	Luxembourg	1.99	22	Mauritius	0.98
8	Germany	1.80	23	Lithuania	0.94
9	Hungary	1.71	24	Greece	0.88
10	Switzerland	1.70	25	South Korea	0.74
11	Denmark	1.65	26	Slovenia	0.73
12	United Kingdom	1.58	27	Czech Republic	0.71
13	Hong Kong	1.54	28	Spain	0.68
14	Austria	1.50	29	Romania	0.64
	Sri Lanka	1.50		United States	0.64

Highest car ownership
Number of cars per 100 people, 1994 or latest

1	Luxembourg	57		France	43
2	United States	56	12	Belgium	41
3	Italy	50	13	Sweden	41
4	Canada	49	14	Netherlands	38
5	Germany	48		Norway	38
6	Australia	46	16	Finland	37
	New Zealand	46	17	United Kingdom	36
8	Switzerland	45	18	Japan	34
9	Iceland	44		Spain	34
10	Austria	43	20	Cyprus	33

Most crowded road networks
Number of vehicles per km of road network, 1994 or latest

1	Hong Kong	289		Czech Republic	57
2	Taiwan	227		Japan	57
3	Singapore	157	18	Bulgaria	49
4	Kuwait	140		Malaysia	49
5	South Korea	100		Spain	49
6	Brunei	96	21	Switzerland	48
7	Israel	93	22	Slovenia	47
8	Thailand	92	23	Mexico	46
9	Italy	91	24	Luxembourg	45
10	Ukraine	73	25	Saudi Arabia	43
11	Germany	65	26	France	37
	Netherlands	65		Jordan	37
	Slovakia	65		Mauritius	37
14	United Kingdom	63	29	Macedonia, FYR	35
15	Bahrain	57	30	Romania	33

Most used road networks
'000 vehicle-km per year per km of road network, 1994 or latest

1	Hong Kong	6,225.8	16	Saudi Arabia	603.1
2	Kuwait	3,474.6	17	Japan	601.1
3	Israel	1,909.1	18	France	568.0
4	Thailand	1,593.0	19	Denmark	559.9
5	Bahrain	1,432.9	20	United States	559.3
6	Madagascar	1,194.6	21	Finland	537.5
7	Italy	1,187.5	22	Macedonia,FYR	489.1
8	United Kingdom	1,108.1	23	Colombia	474.4
9	Netherlands	948.0	24	Slovenia	469.8
10	Germany	834.9	25	Oman	425.7
11	Luxembourg	763.1	26	Spain	425.0
12	Sweden	745.3	27	Belgium	424.8
13	Iraq	745.0	28	Poland	305.0
14	Switzerland	693.1	29	Ireland	276.5
15	South Korea	613.7	30	Ecuador	274.9

Most accidents
Number of people injured per 100m vehicle-km, 1994 or latest

1	Malawi	2,730	11	Sri Lanka	209
2	Rwanda	1,764	12	Canada	207
3	South Korea	725		Morocco	207
4	Jordan	658	14	Hong Kong	194
5	Costa Rica	406	15	Belgium	143
6	Kenya	363	16	Israel	132
7	Turkey	329	17	Japan	129
8	Honduras	317		South Africa	129
9	Portugal	234	19	Latvia	125
10	Egypt	222	20	United States	96

Transport: *planes and trains*

Most air passenger-km
Million passenger-km[a] per year, 1991

1	United States	823,717	21	Saudi Arabia	18,250
2	United Kingdom	139,088	22	India	17,581
3	Japan	117,996	23	New Zealand	16,946
4	France	67,217	24	Philippines	13,977
5	Russia	65,144	25	South Africa	12,352
6	Australia	61,124	26	Argentina	11,093
7	Germany	56,903	27	Pakistan	10,409
8	China	51,395	28	Israel	9,662
9	Singapore	44,947	29	Sweden	9,417
10	Canada	43,490	30	Turkey	8,548
11	Netherlands	42,435	31	Greece	8,429
12	South Korea	39,579	32	UAE	8,267
13	Brazil	31,864	33	Norway	7,663
14	Italy	31,738	34	Portugal	7,638
15	Spain	26,654	35	Belgium	7,496
16	Thailand	25,242	36	Venezuela	7,372
17	Mexico	23,521	37	Finland	6,720
18	Indonesia	21,166	38	Egypt	6,324
19	Malaysia	20,335	39	Austria	5,806
20	Switzerland	18,858	40	Chile	5,398

Busiest airports
Number of passengers '000, 1993

1	Chicago	O'Hare	65,091
2	Dallas	Dallas/Ft. Worth	49,655
3	Los Angeles	Los Angeles Intl.	47,845
4	London	Heathrow	47,601
5	Tokyo[b]	Haneda	41,981
6	Atlanta[b]	Hartsfield	37,915
7	San Francisco	San Francisco Intl.	32,042
8	Frankfurt	Frankfurt/Main	31,767
9	Miami	Miami Intl.	28,660
10	Denver[b]	Stapleton	28,285

Busiest international airports
Number of international passengers '000, 1993

1	London	Heathrow	40,848
2	Frankfurt	Frankfurt/Main	25,119
3	Hong Kong	Hong Kong Intl.	24,421
4	Paris	Charles de Gaulle	23,336
5	Amsterdam	Schipol	20,658
6	Tokyo	New Tokyo Intl. (Narita)	18,947
7	Singapore	Changi	18,796
8	London	Gatwick	18,656
9	New York	Kennedy	14,821
10	Zurich	Zurich	13,129

a Air passenger–km data refer to the distance travelled by each aircraft of national origin.
b 1991.

Longest railway networks
'000 km

1	United States	239.0	21	Czech Republic	9.4
2	Russia	87.5	22	Pakistan[d]	8.8
3	India	62.5	23	Turkey	8.5
4	China	54.0	24	Hungary	7.8
5	Germany	40.4	25	Chile[c]	6.3
6	Australia[a]	35.8	26	Finland	5.9
7	Argentina[b]	34.2	27	Austria	5.6
8	France	32.3	28	Belarus	5.5
9	South Africa	28.7	29	Iran	5.1
10	Mexico[a]	26.5	30	Philippines[a]	4.9
11	Poland	24.3	31	Cuba[c]	4.8
12	Ukraine	22.6		Sudan[a]	4.8
13	Brazil[c]	22.1	33	Egypt	4.7
14	Japan	20.3	34	North Korea[a]	4.5
15	United Kingdom	16.5	35	Bulgaria	4.3
16	Italy	16.0		New Zealand[d]	4.3
17	Canada	13.5		Serbia, Montenegro	4.3
18	Spain	12.6	38	Algeria	4.2
19	Romania	11.4		Indonesia[e]	4.2
20	Sweden	9.7	40	Zaire	4.1

Most rail passengers
Km per year per person

1	Japan	1,956	11	Slovakia	850
2	Switzerland	1,785	12	Czech Republic	821
3	Belarus	1,552	13	Romania	806
4	Russia	1,531	14	Egypt	794
5	Ukraine	1,358	15	Germany	751
6	Austria	1,147	16	Luxembourg	723
7	France	1,015	17	Latvia	704
8	Netherlands	939	18	Sweden	670
9	Denmark	938	19	Belgium	655
10	Italy	855	20	South Korea	649

Most rail freight
Million tonnes-km per year

1	United States	1,752,849	11	Australia[a]	50,670
2	China	1,242,602	12	France	48,750
3	Russia	1,195,473	13	Mexico[f]	32,988
4	India	252,411	14	Belarus	27,963
5	Ukraine	200,423	15	Japan	24,100
6	South Africa	169,202	16	Czech Republic	22,793
7	Canada[c]	101,806	17	Romania	21,554
8	Brazil[b]	92,838	18	Italy	20,575
9	Germany	70,554	19	Sweden	18,591
10	Poland	64,719	20	South Korea	14,070

a	1989.	d	1992.
b	1987.	e	1990.
c	1988.	f	1991.

Transport: *sail away*

Largest merchant fleets
Number of vessels over 100 GRT[a], mid-1995

1	Japan	9,438	21	Germany	1,146
2	Panama	5,777	22	Ukraine	1,142
3	United States	5,292	23	Turkey	1,075
4	Russia	5,261	24	Netherlands	1,059
5	China	2,948	25	India	916
6	South Korea	2,246	26	Canada	886
7	Norway	2,215	27	France	824
8	Indonesia	2,196	28	Malaysia	685
9	Greece	1,863	29	Taiwan	683
10	Spain	1,762	30	Peru	671
11	Cyprus	1,674	31	Mexico	630
12	Liberia	1,666	32	Australia	627
13	United Kingdom	1,612	33	Sweden	621
14	Philippines	1,524	34	Brazil	551
15	Honduras	1,409	35	Poland	516
16	Italy	1,397	36	Thailand	501
17	Singapore	1,344	37	Morocco	475
18	Bahamas	1,176	38	Argentina	471
19	Denmark	1,166	39	Vietnam	447
20	Malta	1,164	40	Chile	446

Largest ports[b]
Total cargo traffic, '000 tonnes[c]

1	Rotterdam	293,794	21	Port Hedland	53,337
2	Singapore	290,000	22	Virginia	53,199
3	Chiba	173,688	23	London	51,593
4	Kobe	170,970	24	New York	47,299
5	Melbourne	147,657	25	Tampa	44,591
6	Hong Kong	147,184	26	Forth	44,359
7	Nagoya	137,261	27	Tees and Hartlepool	42,994
8	Houston	128,820	28	Genoa	42,406
9	Yokohama	128,275	29	Grimsby-Immingham	40,921
10	Antwerp	109,494	30	Warri	40,654
11	Marseilles	91,062	31	Sydney	40,000
12	Long Beach	87,065	32	Sullom Voe	38,592
13	Bergen	75,525	33	Arzew	38,308
14	Corpus Christi	70,439	34	Trieste	37,840
15	Richard's Bay	68,735	35	Dunkirk	37,168
16	Hamburg	68,439	36	Duluth	35,076
17	Vancouver	67,633	37	Gladsone	35,027
18	Yokkaichi	58,534	38	Wilheimshaven	34,902
19	Le Havre	54,376	39	Kelang	33,858
20	Newcastle	53,491	40	Zeebrugge	32,134

a Gross Tonnage (GRT) = total volume within the hull and above deck. 1 GRT=100 cu ft.
b Recent figures for some Asian and American ports are not available.
c Total cargo loaded and discharged.

Tourism

Most tourist arrivals
Number of arrivals, '000

#	Country	Value	#	Country	Value
1	France	60,640	21	Thailand	6,166
2	United States	45,504	22	Turkey	6,034
3	Spain	43,232	23	Russia	4,643
4	Italy	27,480	24	Macao	4,489
5	Hungary	21,425	25	Ireland	4,309
6	China	21,070	26	Bulgaria	4,055
7	United Kingdom	20,855	27	Indonesia	4,006
8	Poland	18,800	28	South Africa	3,897
9	Austria	17,894	29	Argentina	3,866
10	Mexico	17,113	30	Tunisia	3,856
11	Czech Republic	17,000	31	South Korea	3,580
12	Canada	15,971	32	Morocco	3,465
13	Germany	14,494	33	Australia	3,362
14	Switzerland	12,200	34	Belgium	3,304
15	Greece	10,072	35	Puerto Rico	3,042
16	Hong Kong	9,331	36	Norway	2,830
17	Portugal	9,132	37	Romania	2,796
18	Malaysia	7,197	38	Egypt	2,356
19	Singapore	6,268	39	Croatia	2,293
20	Netherlands	6,178	40	Uruguay	2,175

Biggest tourist spending
$m

#	Country	Value	#	Country	Value
1	United States	43,562	11	Belgium	7,735
2	Germany	41,753	12	Switzerland	6,325
3	Japan	30,715	13	Mexico	5,363
4	United Kingdom	18,303	14	Sweden	4,878
5	France	13,875	15	Australia	4,339
6	Italy	12,181	16	Spain	4,106
7	Canada	11,676	17	South Korea	4,088
8	Netherlands	10,983	18	Norway	3,930
9	Austria	9,330	19	Singapore	3,665
10	Taiwan	7,885	20	Denmark	3,583

Largest tourist receipts
$m

#	Country	Value	#	Country	Value
1	United States	60,406	11	Singapore	7,067
2	France	25,629	12	Mexico	6,318
3	Italy	23,927	13	Canada	6,309
4	Spain	21,853	14	Poland	6,150
5	United Kingdom	15,176	15	Australia	5,955
6	Austria	13,160	16	Thailand	5,762
7	Germany	11,091	17	Netherlands	5,612
8	Hong Kong	8,317	18	Belgium	5,182
9	Switzerland	7,570	19	Indonesia	4,785
10	China	7,323	20	Turkey	4,321

Education

Highest primary enrolment

Number enrolled as % of relevant age group, 1992

1	Gabon[a]	134		Philippines	109
2	Namibia	124		Syria[c]	109
3	China	121	20	Hong Kong	108
4	Portugal	120		Uruguay	108
5	Peru	119		Vietnam	108
	Zimbabwe	119	23	Argentina	107
7	Ecuador[b]	118		Australia	107
	UAE	118		Canada	107
9	Colombia	117		Germany	107
	Tunisia	117		Singapore	107
11	Botswana	116		Sri Lanka	107
12	Indonesia	115	29	Brazil	106
13	Mexico	113		France	106
14	Turkey	112		Jamaica	106
15	Togo	111		Lesotho	106
16	Paraguay	110		Mauritius	106
17	Iran	109		Panama	106

Lowest primary enrolment

Number enrolled as % of relevant age group, 1992

1	Ethiopia	22	14	Mozambique	60
2	Afghanistan[b]	24	15	Kuwait	61
3	Mali	25	16	Chad	65
4	Bhutan[d]	26	17	Benin	66
5	Niger	29		Malawi	66
6	Burkina Faso	31	19	CAR[c]	68
7	Liberia[a]	35		Tanzania	68
8	Guinea	42	21	Burundi	69
9	Pakistan	46		Côte d'Ivoire	69
10	Sierra Leone	48		Gambia, The	69
11	Sudan[d]	49		Morocco	69
12	Mauritania	55	25	Rwanda	71
13	Senegal	58		Uganda	71

Highest tertiary enrolment[e]

Number enrolled as % of relevant age group, 1992

1	Canada	99		Spain	40
2	United States	76	11	Netherlands	39
3	Finland	57		Peru	39
4	New Zealand	50	13	Belgium	38
5	Norway	49		Denmark	38
6	France	46		Ireland	38
7	Argentina	43	16	Austria	37
8	South Korea	42	17	Germany	36
9	Australia	40	18	Israel	34

Notes: The gross enrolment ratios shown are the actual number enrolled as a percentage of the number of children in the official primary age group. They may exceed 100 when children outside the primary age group are receiving primary education either because they have not moved on to secondary education or because they have started primary education early.

Least literate
% adult literacy rate

1	Burkina Faso	19.9		Oman		35.0
2	Sierra Leone	23.7	15	Mali		35.9
3	Benin	25.0	16	Pakistan		36.4
4	Guinea	26.9	17	Bangladesh		36.6
5	Nepal	27.0	18	Cambodia		37.8
	Somalia	27.0	19	Guinea-Bissau		39.0
7	Sudan	28.2	20	Namibia		40.0
8	Gambia, The	30.0		Senegal		40.0
9	Niger	31.2	22	CAR		40.2
10	Afghanistan	31.6	23	Bhutan		40.9
11	Chad	32.5	24	Yemen		41.1
12	Mozambique	33.5	25	Angola		42.5
13	Mauritania	35.0		Liberia		42.5

Highest mean years of schooling
1992

1	United States	12.4	15	Japan	10.8
2	Canada	12.2	16	New Zealand	10.7
3	Norway	12.1	17	Luxembourg	10.5
4	Australia	12.0	18	Israel	10.2
	France	12.0	19	Hungary	9.8
6	United Kingdom	11.7	20	Barbados	9.4
7	Germany	11.6	21	South Korea	9.3
	Switzerland	11.6	22	Argentina	9.2
9	Austria	11.4		Ex-Czechoslovakia	9.2
	Sweden	11.4		Iceland	9.2
11	Belgium	11.2	25	Estonia	9.0
12	Netherlands	11.1		Latvia	9.0
13	Denmark	11.0		Lithuania	9.0
14	Finland	10.9		Russia	9.0

Lowest mean years of schooling
1992

1	Burkina Faso	0.2		Guinea	0.9
	Niger	0.2		Oman	0.9
3	Bhutan	0.3		Senegal	0.9
	Chad	0.3		Sierra Leone	0.9
	Somalia	0.3		Yemen	0.9
6	Burundi	0.4	19	Papua New Guinea	1.0
	Guinea-Bissau	0.4	20	CAR	1.1
	Mali	0.4		Ethiopia	1.1
	Mauritania	0.4		Rwanda	1.1
10	Gambia, The	0.6		Uganda	1.1
11	Benin	0.7	24	Nigeria	1.2
12	Sudan	0.8	25	Angola	1.5
13	Afghanistan	0.9			

a 1988.   b 1989.   c 1991.   d 1990.
e Tertiary education includes all levels of post-secondary education including courses leading to awards not equivalent to a university degree, courses leading to a first university degree and postgraduate courses.

Life: *the chances*

Highest life expectancy
Years, 1995–2000

1	Japan	79.9		Puerto Rico	76.0
2	Hong Kong	79.1		Singapore	76.0
3	Sweden	79.0	33	Denmark	75.8
4	Iceland	78.8	34	Guadeloupe	75.5
5	Switzerland	78.6		Portugal	75.5
6	Australia	78.3	36	Brunei	75.1
	Italy	78.3	37	Réunion	74.8
8	Spain	78.2		UAE	74.8
9	Canada	78.1	39	Chile	74.4
	Greece	78.1		Jamaica	74.4
11	Netherlands	78.0	41	Bahamas	74.3
12	Cyprus	77.8	42	Netherlands Antilles	74.0
13	France	77.6	43	Panama	73.9
14	Belgium	77.4	44	Georgia	73.6
	Israel	77.4	45	Armenia	73.4
16	Norway	77.3		Slovenia	73.4
17	Austria	77.1	47	Argentina	73.2
18	Martinique	77.0		Bosnia & Hercegovina	73.2
	United Kingdom	77.0	49	Sri Lanka	73.1
20	Malta	76.9	50	Bahrain	72.9
21	Costa Rica	76.8		Uruguay	72.8
	Germany	76.8	52	Albania	72.8
	United States	76.8		Trinidad & Tobago	72.8
24	Finland	76.5		Venezuela	72.8
	Luxembourg	76.5		Serbia, Montenegro	72.8
26	Barbados	76.4	56	Macedonia, FYR	72.7
	New Zealand	76.4	57	Fiji	72.6
28	Ireland	76.1	58	South Korea	72.4
29	Cuba	76.0	59	Croatia	72.2
	Kuwait	76.0		North Korea	72.2

Highest male life expectancy
Years, 1995–2000

1	Japan	76.8	6	Greece	75.5
2	Iceland	76.3	7	Australia	75.4
3	Hong Kong	76.2		Israel	75.4
4	Sweden	76.1		Switzerland	75.4
5	Cyprus	75.6	10	Spain	75.3

Highest female life expectancy
Years, 1995–2000

1	Japan	82.9	6	France	81.3
2	Hong Kong	82.3		Iceland	81.3
3	Sweden	81.9	8	Australia	81.2
4	Switzerland	81.7		Canada	81.2
5	Italy	81.4	10	Spain	81.0

Lowest life expectancy
Years, 1995–2000

1	Sierra Leone	41.0		Mauritania	53.5
2	Uganda	43.3	**32**	Cambodia	54.1
3	Malawi	44.8	**33**	Kenya	54.2
4	Afghanistan	45.5	**34**	Sudan	55.0
	Guinea-Bissau	45.5	**35**	Gabon	55.5
6	Zambia	46.1	**36**	Nepal	56.5
7	Guinea	46.5	**37**	Togo	57.0
8	Rwanda	46.6	**38**	Liberia	57.5
9	Burkina Faso	46.7	**39**	Papua New Guinea	57.9
10	Mozambique	46.8	**40**	Ghana	58.0
11	Gambia, The	47.0	**41**	Bangladesh	58.1
12	Mali	48.0	**42**	Haiti	58.4
13	Niger	48.5	**43**	Cameroon	58.5
14	Benin	48.9	**44**	Madagascar	59.0
15	Angola	49.0	**45**	Swaziland	60.0
	Somalia	49.0	**46**	Myanmar	60.1
17	Chad	49.5	**47**	Namibia	61.3
	Côte d'Ivoire	49.5	**48**	Bolivia	61.5
19	Congo	49.9	**49**	India	62.8
	Ethiopia	49.9	**50**	Lesotho	63.0
21	CAR	50.1	**51**	Pakistan	63.9
22	Zimbabwe	50.8	**52**	Indonesia	65.1
23	Burundi	51.2	**53**	South Africa	65.2
24	Senegal	51.3	**54**	Libya	65.2
25	Tanzania	51.5	**55**	Morocco	65.7
26	Zaire	51.9	**56**	Mongolia	65.8
27	Yemen	52.2	**57**	Egypt	66.0
28	Nigeria	52.4	**58**	Turkmenistan	66.7
29	Bhutan	53.2	**59**	Guatemala	67.2
30	Laos	53.5	**60**	Botswana	67.3

Lowest male life expectancy
Years, 1995–2000

1	Sierra Leone	39.4	**6**	Burkina Faso	45.1
2	Uganda	42.2	**7**	Rwanda	45.2
3	Guinea-Bissau	43.9	**8**	Gambia, The	45.4
4	Malawi	44.3		Mozambique	45.4
5	Afghanistan	45.0		Zambia	45.4

Lowest female life expectancy
Years, 1995–2000

1	Sierra Leone	42.6	**6**	Guinea	47.0
2	Uganda	44.3	**7**	Guinea-Bissau	47.1
3	Malawi	45.4	**8**	Rwanda	48.0
4	Afghanistan	46.0	**9**	Burkina Faso	48.1
5	Zambia	46.8	**10**	Mozambique	48.3

Death: *the chances*

Highest death rates[a]
Number of deaths per 1,000 population

1	Sierra Leone	22.9		Togo	11.4
2	Albania	21.6	52	Germany	10.9
3	Afghanistan	20.3		Sweden	10.9
4	Malawi	19.6		United Kingdom	10.9
5	Guinea-Bissau	19.5	55	Haiti	10.8
6	Uganda	19.4		Moldova	10.8
7	Guinea	18.3		Norway	10.8
8	Burkina Faso	18.0	58	Cameroon	10.7
9	Mozambique	17.6		Poland	10.7
10	Gambia, The	17.3		Slovenia	10.7
11	Mali	17.1	61	Slovakia	10.6
	Niger	17.1	62	Belgium	10.5
13	Angola	16.9		Ghana	10.5
14	Rwanda	16.7		Portugal	10.5
15	Somalia	16.6	65	Uruguay	10.4
16	Benin	16.4	66	Bangladesh	10.2
17	Chad	16.3		Finland	10.2
18	Zambia	16.2	68	Austria	10.1
19	Ethiopia	15.9		Greece	10.1
20	CAR	15.7		Madagascar	10.1
21	Côte d'Ivoire	15.3	71	Italy	9.9
22	Congo	15.2		Luxembourg	9.9
23	Hungary	14.5		Papua New Guinea	9.9
	Senegal	14.5	74	Myanmar	9.8
25	Burundi	14.4	75	France	9.6
26	Gabon	14.3		Serbia, Montenegro	9.6
27	Nigeria	13.9	77	Spain	9.3
	Zaire	13.9	78	Namibia	9.2
29	Yemen	13.7		Swaziland	9.2
30	Ukraine	13.6	80	Bolivia	9.1
31	Bhutan	13.5	81	Georgia	9.0
	Tanzania	13.5		Switzerland	9.0
33	Latvia	13.4	83	India	8.9
34	Bulgaria	13.3	84	Barbados	8.8
35	Estonia	13.2		Ireland	8.8
	Laos	13.2		Netherlands	8.8
	Zimbabwe	13.2	87	United States	8.7
38	Mauritania	13.1	88	Lesotho	8.6
39	Russia	13.0	89	Japan	8.3
40	Czech Republic	12.9	90	New Zealand	8.2
41	Liberia	12.6	91	Argentina	8.0
42	Cambodia	12.1		Malta	8.0
43	Belarus	12.0	93	South Africa	7.9
44	Sudan	11.9	94	Pakistan	7.8
45	Denmark	11.8	95	Canada	7.7
	Kenya	11.8	96	Indonesia	7.6
47	Croatia	11.7	97	Puerto Rico	7.5
48	Lithuania	11.6	98	Australia	7.4
49	Romania	11.5		Macedonia, FYR	7.4
50	Nepal	11.4	100	Bosnia & Hercegovina	7.3

Highest infant mortality[a]
Number of deaths per 1,000 live births

1	Afghanistan	154	26	Mauritania	92
	Sierra Leone	154	27	Côte d'Ivoire	88
3	Mali	149	28	Laos	86
4	Malawi	136		Nepal	86
	Mozambique	136		Zaire	86
6	Guinea-Bissau	129	31	Gabon	85
7	Guinea	124	32	Congo	83
8	Burkina Faso	123	33	Tanzania	81
9	Gambia, The	122	34	Benin	79
10	Niger	114	35	Haiti	77
11	Liberia	113		Nigeria	77
12	Angola	112		Togo	77
	Chad	112	38	Pakistan	74
	Somalia	112	39	Ghana	73
15	Uganda	111	40	India	72
16	Yemen	109		Myanmar	72
17	Bhutan	107	42	Sudan	71
	Ethiopia	107	43	Lesotho	69
19	Rwanda	105	44	Bolivia	66
20	Cambodia	102		Kenya	66
21	Zambia	99	46	Swaziland	65
22	Bangladesh	96		Zimbabwe	65
	Burundi	96	48	Senegal	62
	CAR	96	49	Papua New Guinea	61
25	Madagascar	93	50	Peru	59

Lowest death rates[a]
Number of deaths per 1,000 pop.

1	Kuwait	2.2
2	UAE	2.9
3	Brunei	3.5
4	Qatar	3.7
5	Bahrain	3.8
	Costa Rica	3.8
7	Saudi Arabia	4.2
8	Oman	4.3
9	Fiji	4.6
10	Venezuela	4.7

Notes: The data for the number of deaths per 1,000 population are crude rates, i.e. not adjusted for differences in age structure. Thus a country with a high proportion of older people will have a higher rate than one with a younger population. This explains why a number of developed countries have apparently high death rates.

Both death and, in particular, infant mortality rates can be underestimated in certain countries where not all deaths are officially recorded.

Lowest infant mortality[a]
Number of deaths per 1,000 pop

1	Japan	4
2	Finland	5
	Iceland	5
	Singapore	5
	Sweden	5
6	Australia	6
	Austria	6
	Belgium	6
	Canada	6
	Germany	6
	Hong Kong	6
	Luxembourg	6
	Netherlands	6
	Switzerland	6
	United Kingdom	6

a 1995-2000.

Death: *the causes*

Cancer[a]
%

1	Netherlands	26.2
2	France	25.4
3	Canada	25.1
4	Switzerland	25.0
	United Kingdom	25.0
6	Denmark	24.7
7	Belgium	24.6
	Hong Kong	24.6
9	Italy	24.3
10	New Zealand	23.6
11	Ireland	23.4
12	Australia	23.3
	Germany	23.3
14	Austria	23.2
15	Czech Republic	23.0
16	United States	22.6
17	Japan	22.1
18	Uruguay	21.9
19	Slovenia	21.6
20	Norway	21.2

Heart attack[a]
%

1	Armenia	43.7
2	Uzbekistan	42.8
3	Lithuania	39.7
4	Estonia	36.4
5	Austria	35.8
	Iceland	35.8
7	Malta	35.0
	Sweden	35.0
9	Bahrain	34.6
	United States	34.6
	Ex-Yugoslavia	34.6
12	Belarus	34.4
13	Latvia	34.3
14	Finland	33.6
15	Australia	33.4
16	Germany	32.7
17	Argentina	32.5
18	New Zealand	32.4
19	Bulgaria	32.2
	Ireland	32.2

Infectious disease[a]
%

1	Guatemala	16.5
2	Venezuela	4.6
3	Mexico	4.5
4	Sri Lanka	3.9
5	Hong Kong	3.8
	Suriname	3.8
7	Kuwait	3.4
	Tajikistan	3.4
9	Argentina	3.3
	Brazil	3.3
	Chile	3.3
12	Jamaica	3.2
13	Bahamas	2.7
14	Puerto Rico	2.5
15	Barbados	2.4
	Singapore	2.4
17	China	2.3
	Israel	2.3
19	Mauritius	2.2
	Uzbekistan	2.2

Motor accident[a]
%

1	Kuwait	2.8
2	Suriname	2.4
3	Venezuela	2.0
4	Brazil	1.9
	Kirgizstan	1.9
	Latvia	1.9
	Lithuania	1.9
8	Portugal	1.8
9	Slovenia	1.7
10	Estonia	1.6
	Luxembourg	1.6
	Mexico	1.6
	Russia	1.6
14	Costa Rica	1.5
	Greece	1.5
	Mauritius	1.5
	Spain	1.5
18	New Zealand	1.4
	Puerto Rico	1.4
20	Italy	1.3
	Poland	1.3

a   Latest available.

Notes: Data refer to the chances a newborn baby has of eventually dying from one of the causes shown. Statistics are available for only a limited number of countries and many less developed countries are excluded.

Stroke[a]

%

1	Ukraine	28.4
2	Portugal	24.5
3	Bulgaria	22.3
4	Kirgizstan	20.7
5	China	20.0
6	Russia	19.7
7	Greece	19.5
8	Jamaica	19.3
	Latvia	19.3
10	Estonia	18.6
11	Tajikistan	18.1
12	Kazakhstan	17.3
	Uzbekistan	17.3
14	Czech Republic	17.1
15	Romania	16.3
16	Luxembourg	16.1
17	Armenia	16.0
18	Mauritius	15.9
19	Italy	15.5
	Ex-Yugoslavia	15.5

Injury and poisoning[a]

%

1	Russia	14.3
2	Latvia	13.6
3	Estonia	12.2
4	Lithuania	11.7
5	Kazakhstan	9.6
6	Belarus	9.2
7	Suriname	8.7
8	Ukraine	8.5
9	France	8.4
10	Hungary	8.1
11	Cuba	7.9
12	Kirgizstan	7.8
	Slovenia	7.8
14	Mexico	7.4
15	Chile	7.2
16	Finland	6.9
17	Brazil	6.5
	Czech Republic	6.5
19	Sri Lanka	6.4
	Switzerland	6.4

AIDS

Cases per 100,000 inhabitants[a]

1	Bahamas	689.7	21	Gabon	95.7
2	Bermuda	461.9	22	Ghana	93.8
3	Zimbabwe	375.4	23	Martinique	91.7
4	Malawi	368.8	24	Netherlands Antilles	89.8
5	Zambia	353.3	25	Spain	87.5
6	Namibia	340.1	26	Honduras	80.5
7	Congo	308.9	27	Haiti	70.6
8	Uganda	258.8	28	Guinea-Bissau	67.3
9	Barbados	224.5		Switzerland	67.3
10	Kenya	217.4	30	France	66.5
11	Botswana	215.5	31	Zaire	66.1
12	United States	192.4	32	Swaziland	65.1
13	Tanzania	184.6	33	Chad	55.9
14	Côte d'Ivoire	183.1	34	Italy	53.3
15	Guadeloupe	148.3	35	Jamaica	52.6
16	Trinidad & Tobago	146.4	36	Suriname	50.0
17	Togo	139.9	37	Brazil	44.7
18	Rwanda	138.1	38	Cameroon	41.8
19	CAR	138.0	39	Canada	41.6
20	Burundi	113.1	40	Dominican Republic	38.4

a   AIDS data refer to the total number of cases reported to the World Health Organisation up to the 15th December 1995. The number of cases diagnosed and reported depends on the quality of medical practice and administration and is likely to be under-recorded in a number of countries.

Health

Highest population per doctor
1988–91

1	Malawi	50,000		Somalia		14,290
2	Burkina Faso	33,330	22	Benin		14,286
	Chad	33,330		Zaire		14,286
	Ethiopia	33,330	24	Bangladesh		12,500
	Mozambique	33,330		Cameroon		12,500
	Tanzania	33,330		Myanmar		12,500
7	Angola	25,000		Papua New Guinea		12,500
	Cambodia	25,000	28	Gambia, The		11,690
	CAR	25,000	29	Bhutan		11,110
	Ghana	25,000		Côte d'Ivoire		11,110
	Lesotho	25,000		Sudan		11,110
	Rwanda	25,000		Togo		11,110
	Uganda	25,000		Zambia		11,110
14	Kenya	20,000	34	Liberia		9,340
	Mali	20,000	35	Madagascar		8,333
16	Burundi	16,667		Philippines		8,333
	Mauritania	16,667	37	Afghanistan		7,692
	Nepal	16,667		Guinea		7,692
	Senegal	16,667		Zimbabwe		7,692
20	Sierra Leone	14,290	40	Guinea-Bissau		7,260

Lowest population per doctor
1988–91

1	Georgia	170	21	Hungary	312
2	Latvia	200	22	Greece	313
3	Estonia	210	23	Bulgaria	315
	Russia	210	24	Argentina	329
5	Italy	211	25	Cuba	332
6	Lithuania	220	26	France	333
7	Austria	230	27	Israel	350
8	Vietnam	247		Tajikistan	350
9	Armenia	250		Uruguay	350
	Azerbaijan	250	30	Portugal	352
	Kazakhstan	250	31	Denmark	360
	Moldova	250	32	Germany	370
13	Ukraine	259		North Korea	370
14	Spain	262	34	Mongolia	389
15	Kirgizstan	280	35	Sweden	395
	Uzbekistan	280	36	Netherlands	398
17	Belarus	282	37	Finland	405
18	Turkmenistan	290	38	Lebanon	413
19	Belgium	298	39	United States	420
20	Norway	309	40	Australia	440

Highest calorie intake

Calories per person, per day, latest available year

1	Ireland	3,847	31	Mexico	3,181
2	Greece	3,815	32	Australia	3,179
3	Cyprus	3,782	33	Syria	3,175
4	United States	3,732	34	Czech Republic	3,156
5	Spain	3,708	35	Hong Kong	3,144
6	Belgium	3,681	36	Canada	3,094
	Luxembourg	3,681	37	Fiji	3,092
8	New Zealand	3,669	38	Iceland	3,058
9	Denmark	3,664	39	Romania	3,051
10	Portugal	3,634	40	Israel	3,050
11	France	3,633	41	Taiwan	3,048
	Germany	3,633	42	Jordan	3,031
13	Italy	3,561	43	Finland	3,018
14	Serbia, Montenegro	3,551	44	Morocco	2,985
15	Hungary	3,503	45	Sweden	2,972
16	Austria	3,497	46	Japan	2,903
17	Malta	3,486	47	Algeria	2,897
18	Turkey	3,429	48	Costa Rica	2,889
19	Switzerland	3,379	49	Malaysia	2,884
20	Egypt	3,336	50	Argentina	2,880
21	Tunisia	3,333	51	Iran	2,861
22	Lebanon	3,319	52	North Korea	2,834
23	United Kingdom	3,317	53	Cuba	2,833
24	Libya	3,310	54	Bulgaria	2,831
25	Poland	3,301	55	Martinique	2,829
26	South Korea	3,298	56	Brazil	2,824
27	Norway	3,244	57	Indonesia	2,755
28	Barbados	3,223	58	Saudi Arabia	2,751
29	Netherlands	3,222	59	Uruguay	2,750
30	Belarus	3,207	60	Brunei	2,745

Highest health spending

As % of GDP, 1991

1	United States	13.3
2	Canada	9.9
3	France	9.1
	Germany	9.1
5	Finland	8.9
6	Sweden	8.8
7	Netherlands	8.7
8	Australia	8.6
9	Austria	8.5
10	Norway	8.4

Lowest health spending

As % of GDP, 1991

1	Syria	0.4
2	Sudan	0.5
3	Indonesia	0.7
4	Zaire	0.8
5	Morocco	0.9
	Somalia	0.9
7	Cameroon	1.0
	Egypt	1.0
	Laos	1.0
	Philippines	1.0

Till death us do part

Highest marriage rates[a]
Number of marriages per 1,000 population

1	Cuba	17.7	31	Albania	7.5
2	Bermuda	14.2	32	Mongolia	7.5
3	Uzbekistan	11.0		South Korea	7.5
4	Bangladesh	10.9	34	Indonesia	7.4
5	Mauritius	10.6		Iran	7.4
6	Azerbaijan	10.1	36	Mexico	7.3
7	Turkmenistan	9.8	37	Latvia	7.2
8	Fiji	9.6	38	Brunei	7.1
	Puerto Rico	9.6		Canada	7.1
10	Tajikistan	9.2		Macedonia, FYR	7.1
11	Bahamas	9.1		Portugal	7.1
	Kirgizstan	9.1	42	Georgia	7.0
	Macao	9.1		Romania	7.0
14	Moldova	9.0	44	Malta	6.9
	Sri Lanka	9.0		Tunisia	6.9
	United States	9.0	46	Cyprus	6.8
17	Singapore	8.8	47	Netherlands Antilles	6.7
18	Kazakhstan	8.6	48	Australia	6.6
	Russia	8.6		Chile	6.6
20	Iraq	8.5		Switzerland	6.6
21	Egypt	8.4		Uruguay	6.6
	Thailand	8.4	52	Costa Rica	6.4
23	Syria	8.2		Czech Republic	6.4
	Ukraine	8.2		Ecuador	6.4
25	Jordan	8.1		Japan	6.4
26	Turkey	8.0		Lithuania	6.4
27	Barbados	7.9		New Zealand	6.4
	Hong Kong	7.9		Slovakia	6.4
29	Belarus	7.7	59	Israel	6.2
	Kuwait	7.7		Réunion	6.2

Lowest marriage rates[a]
Number of marriages per 1,000 population

1	Colombia	2.4	11	Bulgaria	4.7
2	Qatar	3.0		Finland	4.7
3	El Salvador	3.2		France	4.7
	Malaysia	3.2		Greece	4.7
5	Paraguay	3.7		Guadeloupe	4.7
6	Slovenia	3.8	16	Iceland	4.8
7	Sweden	4.3		Italy	4.8
8	Ireland	4.5	18	Suriname	4.9
	Norway	4.5	19	Estonia	5.0
10	Croatia	4.6	20	Libya	5.1

a Latest available year.

Note: Marriage rates refer to registered marriages only and, therefore, reflect the customs surrounding registry and efficiency of administration. The data are based on latest available figures and hence will be affected by the population age structure at the time.

Highest divorce rates[a]
Number of divorces per 1,000 population

1	Latvia	5.5		Netherlands	2.0
2	United States	4.6	32	France	1.9
3	Russia	4.3	33	Kirgizstan	1.8
4	Cuba	4.2		Kuwait	1.8
	Ukraine	4.2	35	Germany	1.7
6	Puerto Rico	4.0	36	Azerbaijan	1.6
7	Belarus	3.9		Tunisia	1.6
8	Estonia	3.7	38	Slovakia	1.5
	Lithuania	3.7		Tajikistan	1.5
10	Moldova	3.4		Uzbekistan	1.5
11	Bermuda	3.2	41	Barbados	1.4
	Uruguay	3.2		Egypt	1.4
13	United Kingdom	3.0		Georgia	1.4
14	Canada	2.9		Japan	1.4
	Czech Republic	2.9		Romania	1.4
16	Kazakhstan	2.7		Turkmenistan	1.4
	New Zealand	2.7	47	Bahrain	1.3
18	Australia	2.6		Bulgaria	1.3
19	Denmark	2.5		Israel	1.3
	Suriname	2.5		Portugal	1.3
	Sweden	2.5		Réunion	1.3
22	Finland	2.4		Singapore	1.3
	Norway	2.4	53	Bahamas	1.2
24	Netherlands Antilles	2.2		Jordan	1.2
	Switzerland	2.2	55	Brunei	1.1
26	Austria	2.1		Costa Rica	1.1
	Belgium	2.1		Guadeloupe	1.1
	Hungary	2.1	58	Hong Kong	1.0
29	Iceland	2.0		Martinique	1.0
	Luxembourg	2.0		South Korea	1.0

Lowest divorce rates[a]
Number of divorces per 1,000 population

1	Iraq	0.1		Ecuador	0.6
2	Nicaragua	0.2		Jamaica	0.6
3	Macedonia, FYR	0.3		Mexico	0.6
4	Chile	0.4		Spain	0.6
	Italy	0.4	18	Albania	0.7
	South Africa	0.4		Greece	0.7
7	Brazil	0.5		Iran	0.7
	El Salvador	0.5		Mauritius	0.7
	Libya	0.5		Poland	0.7
	Macao	0.5		Slovenia	0.7
	Mongolia	0.5		Syria	0.7
	Turkey	0.5		Thailand	0.7
13	Cyprus	0.6		Serbia, Montenegro	0.7

Households and prices

Biggest households[a]
Population per dwelling

1	Gabon	8.3		Sudan	5.6
2	Iraq	7.1	25	India	5.5
3	Algeria	7.0		Mauritania	5.5
4	Yemen	6.8		Tunisia	5.5
5	Guinea	6.7	28	Benin	5.4
	Jordan	6.7		Zaire	5.4
	Pakistan	6.7	30	Congo	5.3
8	Bahrain	6.6		Philippines	5.3
9	Kuwait	6.5		Tanzania	5.3
10	Niger	6.4	33	Cameroon	5.2
11	Syria	6.3		Colombia	5.2
12	Burkina Faso	6.2		Guatemala	5.2
	Liberia	6.2		Iran	5.2
14	Côte d'Ivoire	5.8		Malaysia	5.2
15	Afghanistan	5.9		Myanmar	5.2
	Morocco	5.9		Paraguay	5.2
17	Brunei	5.8		Sri Lanka	5.2
	Fiji	5.8		Turkey	5.2
	Nepal	5.8	42	Ecuador	5.1
20	Bangladesh	5.7		Kenya	5.1
	Togo	5.7		Peru	5.1
22	Mali	5.6		Venezuela	5.1
	Qatar	5.6			

Highest cost of living[b]
December 1995=100 USA=100

1	Japan	199	17	Congo	116
2	Libya	184	18	Russia	115
3	Switzerland	156	19	Luxembourg	114
4	Norway	147	20	Taiwan	113
5	France	137	21	Côte d'Ivoire	111
6	Austria	133	22	United Kingdom	109
7	Denmark	130	23	Israel	107
8	Gabon	124	24	China	104
9	Belgium	122		Spain	104
10	Germany	121	26	Ireland	103
11	Hong Kong	120	27	Greece	101
12	Finland	119	28	United States	100
	Sweden	119	29	Australia	95
14	Netherlands	118		Brazil	95
	South Korea	118		Portugal	95
16	Singapore	117			

a Latest available year.
b The cost of living index shown is compiled by The Economist Inteligence Unit for
   use by companies in determining expatriate compensation: it is a comparison of the
   cost of maintaining a typical international lifestyle in the country rather than a
   comparison of the purchasing power of a citizen of the country. The index is based
   on typical urban prices an international executive and family will face abroad. The

Smallest households[a]
Population per dwelling

1	Denmark	2.2	24	Australia	3.0
	Sweden	2.2		Japan	3.0
3	Western Germany	2.3	26	Greece	3.1
4	Latvia	2.4		Poland	3.1
	Norway	2.4		Romania	3.1
6	Finland	2.6	29	Malta	3.2
	Netherlands	2.6		Ukraine	3.2
	Switzerland	2.6	31	Puerto Rico	3.3
9	Bermuda	2.6		Uruguay	3.3
	France	2.6	33	Hong Kong	3.4
	United States	2.6		Gambia, The	3.4
12	Austria	2.7	35	Cyprus	3.7
	Belgium	2.7		Israel	3.7
	Canada	2.7		Spain	3.7
	Hungary	2.7	38	Barbados	3.6
16	Ex-Czechoslovakia	2.8		Ireland	3.6
	Italy	2.8		Macao	3.6
	Luxembourg	2.8		Ex-Yugoslavia	3.6
	New Zealand	2.8	42	Bahamas	3.8
	United Kingdom	2.8		Belorussia	3.8
21	Bulgaria	2.9		Bolivia	3.8
	Portugal	2.9		South Korea	3.8
	Russia	2.9			

Lowest cost of living[b]
December 1995=100 USA=100

1	Iran	35	17	Costa Rica	67
2	India	44		Venezuela	67
3	Serbia, Montenegro	51	19	Philippines	68
4	Algeria	54	20	Colombia	69
	Zimbabwe	54	21	Paraguay	70
6	Kenya	56		Poland	70
	Pakistan	56		South Africa	70
8	Hungary	57	24	Kuwait	71
	Nigeria	57	25	Peru	74
10	Romania	60	26	Chile	75
11	Mexico	62		Panama	75
12	Czech Republic	63	28	Saudi Arabia	76
13	Bangladesh	65	29	Guatemala	77
	Sri Lanka	65		Papua New Guinea	77
	Vietnam	65		Tunisia	77
16	Ecuador	66			

prices are for products of international comparable quality found in a supermarket or department store. Prices found in local markets and bazaars are not used unless the available merchandise is of the specified quality and the shopping area itself is safe for executive and family members. New York City prices are used as the base, so USA = 100.

Consumer goods: *ownership*

TV

Number of people per receiver

1	Bermuda	0.9		Malta	2.5
2	United States	1.3		Switzerland	2.5
3	Oman	1.4	28	Singapore	2.6
4	Canada	1.5		Russia	2.6
5	Japan	1.6		Czech Republic	2.6
6	France	1.7	31	Estonia	2.8
7	Germany	1.8		Hong Kong	2.8
8	Denmark	1.9	33	Lithuania	2.9
	Hungary	1.9		Luxembourg	2.9
	Uruguay	1.9	35	Netherlands Antilles	3.0
11	New Zealand	2.0	36	South Korea	3.1
	Finland	2.0		Argentina	3.1
	Netherlands	2.0		Ireland	3.1
14	Australia	2.1		Brunei	3.1
	Austria	2.1		Iceland	3.1
	Sweden	2.1	41	Trinidad & Tobago	3.2
	Latvia	2.1	42	Puerto Rico	3.3
18	Belgium	2.2		Poland	3.3
	United Kingdom	2.2	44	Slovenia	3.4
20	Italy	2.3		Jamaica	3.4
	Qatar	2.3		Israel	3.4
	Spain	2.3		UAE	3.4
23	Norway	2.4	48	Slovakia	3.6
	Bahrain	2.4		Macao	3.6
25	Kuwait	2.5		Moldova	3.6

Telephone

Number of people per telephone line

1	Bermuda	1.4		Belgium	2.2
2	Sweden	1.5		Malta	2.2
3	Denmark	1.7	25	Italy	2.3
	United States	1.7	26	Taiwan	2.5
	Switzerland	1.7		South Korea	2.5
	Canada	1.7		Israel	2.5
7	Iceland	1.8	29	Spain	2.7
	Norway	1.8		Macao	2.7
	Luxembourg	1.8	31	Puerto Rico	2.8
	Finland	1.8	32	Ireland	2.9
	France	1.8		Portugal	2.9
12	Hong Kong	1.9	34	Bulgaria	3.0
13	Netherlands	2.0		Barbados	3.0
	Australia	2.0		UAE	3.0
	United Kingdom	2.0	37	Slovenia	3.4
16	Germany	2.1	38	Bahamas	3.5
	Japan	2.1	39	Croatia	3.7
	Greece	2.1	40	Netherlands Antilles	3.9
	Singapore	2.1	41	Bahrain	4.0
	New Zealand	2.1	42	Estonia	4.1
21	Austria	2.2		Lithuania	4.1
	Cyprus	2.2	44	Kuwait	4.4

Home computer
Computers per 100 people

1	United States	31.9	11	Switzerland	16.2
2	Australia	22.1	12	Ireland	15.9
	Canada	22.1	13	Germany	15.2
4	Norway	22.0	14	Singapore	15.1
5	Finland	20.3	15	France	14.7
6	Denmark	19.5	16	Belgium/Luxembourg	13.3
7	Sweden	18.2	17	Hong Kong	12.0
	United Kingdom	18.2	18	Japan	11.8
9	Netherlands	17.0	19	Austria	10.9
	New Zealand	17.0	20	Israel	9.9

Video cassette recorder[a]
% of households owning

1	Japan	75	10	Finland	63
2	United Kingdom	74	11	Denmark	62
	United States	74	12	Austria	61
4	Ireland	73	13	Italy	60
5	Canada	70	14	Spain	59
6	Sweden	69	15	Switzerland	56
7	Netherlands	68	16	Norway	55
8	France	66	17	Belgium	54
9	Germany	65		Portugal	54

Dishwasher[a]
% of households owning

1	Luxembourg	55	11	Belgium	26
2	Norway	48	12	Slovenia	22
3	Finland	46	13	Ireland	20
	Sweden	46		Spain	20
	Switzerland	46	15	United Kingdom	19
6	United States	45	16	Italy	18
7	France	43		Netherlands	18
8	Denmark	42		Portugal	18
9	Germany	41	19	Turkey	17
10	Austria	36	20	Greece	11

Microwave[a]
% of households owning

1	Japan	81	11	Netherlands	35
2	United States	79	12	Austria	34
3	Finland	71	13	Luxembourg	33
4	United Kingdom	66	14	Switzerland	27
5	Sweden	58	15	Hungary	24
6	Germany	52	16	Belgium	21
7	Ireland	51	17	Czech Republic	12
8	France	50		Slovenia	12
9	Norway	43	19	Slovakia	10
10	Denmark	37		Spain	10

a Latest available year up to 1994.
Note: A number of difficulties arise when dealing with household penetration data. Definitions of articles may vary.

Culture and crime

Books published[a]
Per year

1	United Kingdom	95,015
2	China	92,972
3	Germany	67,206
4	United States	49,276
5	France	41,234
6	Spain	40,758
7	Japan	35,496
8	South Korea	30,861
9	Italy	30,110
10	Russia	29,017
11	Brazil	27,557
12	Canada	22,208
13	Switzerland	14,870
14	Belgium	13,913
15	Sweden	12,895
16	India	12,768
17	Netherlands	11,844
18	Finland	11,785
19	Denmark	11,492
20	Australia	10,723

National libraries[a]
Acquisitions per year

1	Russia	1,002,599
2	Germany	757,382
3	United Kingdom	542,606
4	Latvia	518,100
5	China	476,796
6	Canada	207,297
7	Singapore	164,520
8	Peru	163,165
9	Thailand	138,129
10	Spain	137,265
11	Brazil	129,707
12	Argentina	115,419
13	Netherlands	112,000
14	Belgium	109,900
15	Italy	98,478
16	Norway	97,802
17	Venezuela	97,713
18	Kazakhstan	94,000
19	Austria	83,520
20	Malaysia	81,033

Cinema attendances[a]
Per head per year

1	China	12.3
2	Hong Kong	10.3
3	Mongolia	9.5
4	Georgia	5.6
5	India	5.0
6	Iceland	4.7
7	Latvia	4.3
8	United States	3.9
9	Vietnam	3.8
10	Ex-Czechoslovakia	3.2
11	Mexico	3.0
	Australia	3.0
13	Belarus	2.9
14	Canada	2.8
15	Russia	2.6
16	Norway	2.5
	Ukraine	2.5
18	Kazakhstan	2.3
	France	2.3
	Switzerland	2.3

Daily newspapers
Circulation per '000 pop., 1993

1	Hong Kong	822
2	Norway	607
3	Japan	577
4	Iceland	519
5	Finland	512
6	Sweden	511
7	Macao	510
8	South Korea	412
9	Austria	398
10	Russia	387
11	United Kingdom	383
12	Switzerland	377
13	Luxembourg	372
14	Singapore	336
15	Denmark	332
16	Romania	324
17	Germany	323
18	Belgium	310
19	New Zealand	305
20	Netherlands	303

---

a Data for books, libraries and cinemas are for 1993 or the latest available year.

Biggest drinkers

Average annual consumption of litres of pure alcohol per head

1	Luxembourg	12.5
2	France	11.4
3	Portugal	10.7
4	Germany	10.3
	Hungary	10.3
6	Czech Republic	10.1
7	Austria	9.9
	Denmark	9.9
9	Spain	9.7
	Switzerland	9.7
11	Belgium	9.0
12	Greece	8.9
13	Ireland	8.8
14	Italy	8.7
15	Bulgaria	8.3
16	Netherlands	7.9
17	Cyprus	7.8
18	Australia	7.5
	Slovakia	7.5
	United Kingdom	7.5

Biggest smokers

Average annual consumption of cigarettes per head, per day

1	Greece	7.7
2	Japan	7.3
3	Poland	6.7
4	Estonia	6.4
5	Bulgaria	6.3
6	Switzerland	6.2
7	Hungary	5.9
	South Korea	5.9
9	Latvia	5.6
	Spain	5.6
11	United States	5.1
	Czech Republic	5.1
13	Belarus	5.0
14	Australia	4.9
15	Austria	4.8
	Taiwan	4.8
17	Israel	4.6
	Romania	4.6
19	Ireland	4.5
	Germany	4.5

Murders[a]

Number per 100,000 pop., 1992

1	Colombia[b]	81.89
2	Swaziland	71.64
3	Lesotho	33.87
4	Botswana	29.15
5	Jamaica	25.56
6	Netherlands	24.88
7	Zimbabwe[b]	17.40
8	Venezuela	16.62
9	Estonia	15.93
10	Rwanda	15.63
11	Russia	15.47
12	Malta	14.40
13	Zambia	9.76
14	Armenia	9.75
15	Azerbaijan	9.55
16	Bulgaria	9.54
17	Uganda	9.46
18	United States	9.31
19	Peru	9.28
20	Thailand	8.85

Drug offences[a]

Number per 100,000 pop., 1992

1	Benin	852.66
2	New Zealand	597.97
3	Switzerland	446.95
4	Sweden	353.53
5	Denmark	346.00
6	Luxembourg	273.95
7	Norway	263.05
8	Jamaica	255.94
9	Canada[b]	219.31
10	Israel	197.19
11	Trinidad & Tobago	185.04
12	Thailand	178.73
13	Germany	154.35
14	Mauritius	123.78
15	Ireland	118.18
16	France	116.08
17	Brunei	108.85
18	Austria	107.98
19	Belgium	102.44
20	Botswana	88.65

a Crime statistics are based on offences recorded by the police. The number will therefore depend partly on the efficiency of police administration systems, the definition of offences, and the proportion of crimes reported, and therefore may not be strictly comparable.
b 1991.

Environment: *trees and disasters*

Top deforesters

Average annual rate, km² 1981–90

1	Brazil	-36,710		21	Ghana	-1,380
2	Indonesia	-12,120		22	Vietnam	-1,370
3	Zaire	-7,320		23	Madagascar	-1,350
4	Mexico	-6,780			Mozambique	-1,350
5	Bolivia	-6,250		25	Cambodia	-1,310
6	Venezuela	-5,990		26	CAR	-1,290
7	Thailand	-5,150			Laos	-1,290
8	Sudan	-4,820		27	Nicaragua	-1,240
9	Tanzania	-4,380		28	Cameroon	-1,220
10	Paraguay	-4,030		29	Côte d'Ivoire	-1,190
11	Myanmar	-4,010			Nigeria	-1,190
12	Malaysia	-3,960		31	Gabon	-1,160
13	Columbia	-3,670		32	Papua New Guinea	-1,130
14	Zambia	-3,630		33	Honduras	-1,120
15	India	-3,390		34	Mali	-1,060
16	United States	-3,170		35	Chad	-890
17	Philippines	-3,160		36	Guinea	-870
18	Peru	-2,710		37	Guatemala	-810
19	Ecuador	-2,380		38	Botswana	-770
20	Angola	-1,740			Pakistan	-770
				40	Benin	-700

Top reafforesters

Average annual rate, km² 1980s

1	China	45,520		6	Japan	2,400
2	Ex-Soviet Union	45,400		7	Sweden	2,070
3	United States	17,750		8	North Korea	2,000
4	Canada	7,200		9	Finland	1,580
5	Brazil	4,490		10	India	1,380

Fastest forest depletion

% average annual decrease in forested area, 1981–90

1	Jamaica	7.2		15	Ecuador	1.8
2	Haiti	4.8		16	Guatemala	1.7
3	Bangladesh	3.9			Paraguay	1.7
4	Pakistan	3.4		18	Togo	1.5
5	Philippines	3.3			Vietnam	1.5
	Thailand	3.3		20	Malawi	1.4
7	Costa Rica	2.9			Sri Lanka	1.4
8	Dominican Rep	2.8		22	Benin	1.3
9	El Salvador	2.2			Ghana	1.3
10	Bahamas	2.1			Mexico	1.3
	Honduras	2.1			Myanmar	1.3
12	Malaysia	2.0		26	Bolivia	1.2
13	Nicaragua	1.9			Guinea	1.2
	Panama	1.9			Tanzania	1.2

Most forested countries
% of total area covered with forest, 1992

1	Suriname	90.6	13	Guinea	58.8
2	Papua New Guinea	82.5	14	Malaysia	58.7
3	North Korea	74.4	15	CAR	57.4
4	Gabon	74.2	16	Brazil	57.3
5	Zaire	74.1	17	Indonesia	57.0
6	Finland	68.7	18	Bhutan	54.5
7	Japan	66.8	19	Senegal	53.1
8	South Korea	65.3	20	Peru	52.9
9	Fiji	64.9	21	Laos	52.8
10	Cambodia	64.1	22	Cameroon	51.2
11	Sweden	62.3	23	Bolivia	50.5
12	Congo	61.8	24	Slovenia	50.2

Oil tanker spills

	Country affected	Oil spilled ('000 tonnes)	Name	Flag	Year
1	Trinidad & Tobago	276	Atlantic Express	Greece	1979
2	South Africa	256	Castello de Belvar	Spain	1983
3	France	228	Amoco Cadiz	Liberia	1978
4	Canada	140	Odyssey	Liberia	1988
5	United Kingdom	121	Torrey Canyon	Liberia	1967
6	Oman	120	Sea Star	South Korea	1972
7	Greece	102	Irenes Serenade	Greece	1980
8	Spain	101	Urquiola	Spain	1976
9	United States	99	Hawaiian Patriot	Liberia	1977
10	Turkey	95	Independenta	Romania	1979
11	United Kingdom	85	Braer	Liberia	1993

Industrial disasters, 1984–95[a]

	Location	Origin of accident	Deaths
1984	St J Ixhuatepec	gas explosion	503
	Bhopal, India	chemical leakage	2,800
	Cubatao, Brazil	pipeline explosion	508
1986	Chernobyl, Soviet Union	reactor explosion	31
1988	Islamabad, Pakistan	explosives	100
	Arzamas, Soviet Union	explosives	73
	North Sea, UK	oil explosion	167
	Sverdlosk, Soviet Union	explosives	5
1989	Ionava, Soviet Union	chemical explosion	6
	Acha Ufa, Soviet Union	gas explosion	575
1990	Ufa, Soviet Union	chemical explosion	...
	Bangkok, Thailand	explosion (lorry)	54
	Patna, India	explosion (train)	100
1991	Thailand	explosives	171
	Livorno, Italy	oil explosion	140
	Sterlington, USA	gas explosion	8
1992	Kozlu, Turkey	gas explosion	270
1993	Shenzhen, China	fire (toy factory)	84
	Thailand	fire (toy factory)	189

a Not ranked due to difficulties in comparing the effects of each.

Environment: *pollution and waste*

Carbon dioxide emissions
Kg per head

1	Qatar	44,700	21	Ireland	9,230
2	UAE	36,490		Netherlands	9,230
3	Iraq[a]	27,860	23	Libya	9,120
4	Luxembourg	27,500	24	Japan	8,790
5	United States	19,530	25	Poland	8,060
6	Bahrain	19,400	26	Austria	7,800
7	Canada	15,210	27	Oman	7,400
8	Australia	15,100	28	Israel	7,290
9	Singapore	15,060	29	Greece	7,180
10	Trinidad & Tobago	14,730		South Africa	7,180
11	Saudi Arabia	13,960	31	Iceland	7,000
12	Norway	13,740	32	Italy	6,960
13	North Korea	12,960		New Zealand	6,960
14	Finland	12,410	34	France	6,560
15	Ex-Soviet Union	12,310	35	Bulgaria	6,300
16	Denmark	12,240	36	Sweden	6,230
17	Ex-Czechoslovakia	12,200	37	Switzerland	6,160
18	Germany	12,130		Venezuela	6,160
19	Belgium	10,220	39	Hungary	6,050
20	United Kingdom	10,000		South Korea	6,050

Nitrogen oxide emissions
Kg per head

1	United States	73.4	11	Ireland	36.2
2	Canada	69.1	12	Italy[a]	34.5
3	Luxembourg	56.6	13	Belgium	29.9
4	Finland	56.5	14	Austria	27.3
5	Denmark	54.8	15	France	26.3
6	Norway	50.9	16	Switzerland	25.5
7	United Kingdom	47.6	17	Spain	23.4
8	Sweden	44.7	18	Portugal	14.4
9	Germany	40.1	19	Japan	10.5
10	Netherlands	36.3			

Sulphur dioxide emissions
Kg per head

1	Canada	118.7	11	Luxembourg	25.7
2	United States	81.2	12	France	22.9
3	Germany	70.7	13	Portugal	21.4
4	United Kingdom	61.8	14	Netherlands	13.5
5	Spain	56.1	15	Sweden	12.2
6	Ireland	52.9	16	Norway	10.7
7	Belgium	41.8	17	Austria	10.6
8	Finland	38.3	18	Switzerland	8.9
9	Denmark	35.0	19	Japan	7.0
10	Italy[a]	34.4			

Solid hazardous waste generated
Kg per head

1	Belgium	2,731	11	Poland	90
2	United States	1,059	12	Austria	84
3	Czech Republic	808		Mexico	84
4	Slovakia	507	14	Germany	82
5	Canada	267	15	Hungary	78
6	Luxembourg	214	16	France	69
7	Portugal	139	17	Italy	59
8	Switzerland	117	18	Sweden	57
9	Finland	110	19	Greece	43
10	Netherlands	93		Spain	43

Industrial waste generated
Kg per head

1	United States	485.4	11	Ireland	18.5
2	Canada	138.0	12	Norway	16.6
3	Hungary	61.6	13	Austria	16.1
4	Japan	52.6	14	Finland	14.9
5	Switzerland	42.6	15	France	12.3
6	Germany	32.5	16	Greece	10.0
7	Luxembourg	31.4	17	Australia	8.4
8	Netherlands	30.3	18	Spain	8.3
9	Iceland	21.4	19	Mexico	6.1
10	New Zealand	19.9	20	Poland	4.6

Solid municipal waste generated
Kg per head

1	United States	730	11	Austria	430
2	Australia	690	12	Japan	410
3	Canada	660	13	Belgium	400
4	Finland	620		Switzerland	400
5	Iceland	560	15	Hungary	390
6	Norway	510		Turkey	390
7	Netherlands	500	17	Sweden	370
8	Luxembourg	490	18	Germany	360
9	France	470		Slovakia	360
10	Denmark	460		Spain	360

a Excluding emissions from industrial processes.

The statistics for all tables (including those on page 86) except carbon dioxide emissions, fresh water resources and water use cover OECD and emerging Eastern European countries only. They normally refer to various years in the late 1980s to early 1990s, though some refer to an earlier period.

Environment: *recycling and water*

Glass recycling
Recovery rates, %

1	Switzerland	84		Sweden	56
2	Netherlands	77	12	Italy	54
3	Austria	76	13	Finland	50
4	Canada[a]	75	14	France	48
	Germany	75	15	Australia[a]	36
	Iceland[a]	75	16	Portugal	32
7	Norway	72	17	Ireland	31
8	Belgium	67		Spain	31
	Denmark	67	19	Greece	29
10	Japan[a]	56	20	United Kingdom	28

Paper recycling
Recovery rates, %, 1993

1	Austria[b]	78	11	France	42
	Spain	78	12	Portugal[a]	41
3	Switzerland	54	13	Turkey[a]	39
4	Netherlands[c]	53	14	Denmark[a]	36
5	Japan[a]	51	15	United States	34
6	Australia[c]	50	16	Canada[a]	32
	Sweden	50		Norway	32
8	Italy[c]	47		United Kingdom	32
9	Germany	46	19	Greece	30
10	Finland[a]	45		Iceland[c]	30

Freshwater resources
Cubic metres per head, '000

1	Iceland	653.9	11	Bhutan	58.9
2	Suriname	456.6	12	Panama	57.3
3	Papua New Guinea	197.5	13	CAR	44.4
4	Gabon	132.6	14	Nicaragua	44.3
5	New Zealand	114.9	15	Venezuela	42.4
6	Canada	106.0	16	Bolivia	39.9
7	Norway	94.5	17	Fiji	38.6
8	Liberia	84.3	18	Guinea	37.0
9	Congo	76.4	19	Sierra Leone	36.6
10	Laos	64.4	20	Chile	34.4

Water use
Cubic metres per head, latest year

1	Turkmenistan	6,390	11	Afghanistan	1,830
2	Iraq	4,575	12	Chile	1,626
3	Uzbekistan	4,121	13	Canada	1,602
4	Kirgizstan	2,729	14	Madagascar	1,584
5	Tajikistan	2,455	15	Bulgaria	1,544
6	Kazakhstan	2,294	16	Iran	1,362
7	Azerbaijan	2,248	17	Lithuania	1,190
8	Estonia	2,097	18	Suriname	1,189
9	Pakistan	2,053	19	Armenia	1,145
10	United States	1,870	20	Romania	1,134

a 1992.
b 1990.
c 1991.

=Part II=
COUNTRY PROFILES

ALGERIA

Area	2,381,741 sq km	Currency	Algerian dinar (AD)
Capital	Algiers		

People

Population	27.3m	Life expectancy: men	68 yrs
Pop. per sq km	12	women	70 yrs
Av. ann. growth		Adult literacy	60.6%
in pop. 1985–94	2.5%	Fertility rate (per woman)	3.4
Pop. under 15	38.7%		
Pop. over 65	3.6%		*per 1,000 pop.*
No. of men per 100 women	102.4	Crude birth rate	27.4
Human Development Index	73	Crude death rate	5.6

The economy

GDP	AD1,613bn	GDP per head	$1,688
GDP	$46bn	GDP per head in purchasing	
Av. ann. growth in real		power parity (USA=100)	20
GDP 1985–94	nil		

Origins of GDP		**Components of GDP**	
	% of total		*% of total*
Agriculture	9.6	Private consumption	64.3
Industry, of which:	66.6	Public consumption	4.5
manufacturing	…	Investment	33.8
Services	23.8	Exports	26.0
		Imports	-28.6

Structure of manufacturing

	% of total		*% of total*
Agric. & food processing	22	Other	48
Textiles & clothing	19	Av. ann. increase in industrial	
Metal products & machinery	11	output 1980–93	0.8%

Energy

	'000 TCE		
Total output	156,426	% output exported	71.8
Total consumption	40,380	% consumption imported	4.5
Consumption per head,			
kg coal equivalent	1,511		

Inflation and finance

Consumer price		*av. ann. increase 1989–94*	
inflation 1994	22.5%	Narrow money (M1)	10.9%
Av. ann. inflation 1989–94	26.1%	Broad money	15.0%

Exchange rates

	end 1995		*June 1995*
		Effective rates	*1990 = 100*
AD per $	52.18	Effective rates	1990 = 100
AD per SDR	77.56	– nominal	…
AD per Ecu	68.36	– real	…

Principal exports

	$bn fob		$bn fob
Energy & products	8.1	Total including others	**9.7**

Main export destinations

	% of total		% of total
United States	16.4	Germany	10.2
Italy	15.9	Spain	8.2
France	14.2	Netherlands	6.2

Principal imports[a]

	$bn cif		$bn cif
Food	2.7		
Hydrocarbon sector	1.0	Total incl. others	**9.2**

Main origins of imports

	% of total		% of total
France	28.8	Spain	10.1
United States	14.2	Germany	5.5
Italy	11.1	Belgium-Luxembourg	3.4

Balance of payments[a], reserves and debt, $bn

Visible exports fob	12.3	Overall balance	1.0
Visible imports fob	-6.9	Change in reserves	1.2
Trade balance	5.5	Level of reserves	
Invisibles inflows	0.5	end Dec.	4.8
Invisibles outflows	-3.8	No. months of import cover	4.5
Net transfers	0.2	Foreign debt	29.9
Current account balance	2.4	– as % of GDP	74.3
– as % of GDP	4.5	Debt service paid	5.4
Capital balance	-1.0	Debt service ratio	55.3

Family life

No. of households	3.3m	Divorces per 1,000 pop.	...
Av. no. per household	7.0	Cost of living, Dec. 1995	
Marriages per 1,000 pop.	5.7	New York = 100	54

a 1991.
  1990.

ARGENTINA

Area	2,766,889 sq km	Currency	Peso (F
Capital	Buenos Aires		

People

Population	34.2m	Life expectancy: men	70yr
Pop. per sq km	13	women	77yr
Av. ann. growth		Adult literacy	95.5°
in pop. 1985–94	1.4%	Fertility rate (per woman)	2
Pop. under 15	28.7%		
Pop. over 65	9.5%		*per 1,000 po*
No. of men per 100 women	96.4	Crude birth rate	19
Human Development Index	88	Crude death rate	8.

The economy

GDP	P276bn	GDP per head	$8,06
GDP	$276bn	GDP per head in purchasing	
Av. ann. growth in real		power parity (USA=100)	3
GDP 1985–94	3.5%		

Origins of GDP		Components of GDP	
	% of total		*% of tota*
Agriculture	6.9	Private consumption[a]	81
Industry, of which:	36.5	Public consumption	.
manufacturing	25.9	Investment	23.
Services	56.6	Exports	10.
		Imports	-15.

Structure of manufacturing

	% of total		*% of tota*
Food & agric.	21	Other	5
Textiles & clothing	10	Av. ann. increase in industrial	
Machinery & transport	13	output 1980–93	0.4°

Energy

	'000 TCE		
Total output	82,273	% output exported	14.
Total consumption	68,888	% consumption imported	7.
Consumption per head			
kg coal equivalent	2,039		

Inflation and finance

Consumer price			*av. ann. increase 1989–9*
inflation 1995	3.4%	Narrow money (M1)	319°
Av. ann. inflation 1989–94	215.5%	Broad money	287°

Exchange rates

	end 1995		*June 199*
P per $	1.00	Effective rates	1990 = 10
P per SDR	1.49	– nominal	
P per Ecu	1.31	– real	

Principal exports

	$bn fob		$bn fob
Vegetable products	3.0	Live animals	1.6
Processed foods	2.2	Oils	1.5
Minerals	1.7	Total incl. others	**15.7**

Main export destinations

	% of total		% of total
Brazil	23.2	Chile	6.3
United States	10.9	Italy	4.2
Netherlands	7.5		

Principal imports

	$bn cif		$bn cif
Machinery & industrial		Metals	1.3
equipment	7.4	Plastics	1.1
Transport equipment	3.8	Total incl. others	**21.5**
Chemicals	2.6		

Main origins of imports

	% of total		% of total
United States	22.7	Germany	6.4
Brazil	19.9	France	5.0
Italy	6.6		

Balance of payments[b], reserves and debt, $bn

Visible exports fob	13.1	Overall balance	0.03
Visible imports fob	-15.5	Change in reserves	0.5
Trade balance	-2.4	Level of reserves	
Invisibles inflows	4.2	end Dec.	16.0
Invisibles outflows	-9.6	No. months of import cover	6.1
Net transfers	0.4	Foreign debt	77.4
Current account balance	-7.5	– as % of GDP	27.8
– as % of GDP	-3.1	Debt service paid	6.7
Capital balance	7.4	Debt service ratio	31.8

Family life

No. of households	7.1m	Divorces per 1,000 pop.	…
Av. no. per household	3.9	Cost of living, Dec. 1995	
Marriages per 1,000 pop.	5.7	New York = 100	92

Including public consumption.
1993.

AUSTRALIA

Area	7,682,300 sq km	Currency	Australian dollar (A$
Capital	Canberra		

People

Population	17.8m	Life expectancy: men	75 yr
Pop. per sq km	2	women	81 yr
Av. ann. growth		Adult literacy	99.0%
in pop. 1985–94	1.5%	Fertility rate (per woman)	1.
Pop. under 15	21.6%		
Pop. over 65	11.6%		*per 1,000 po*
No. of men per 100 women	99.7	Crude birth rate	14
Human Development Index	93	Crude death rate	7

The economy

GDP	A$439bn	GDP per head	$17,97
GDP	$321bn	GDP per head in purchasing	
Av. ann. growth in real		power parity (USA=100)	7
GDP 1985–94	2.9%		

Origins of GDP[a]		Components of GDP[a]	
	% of total		*% of total*
Agriculture & mining	7.5	Private consumption	59
Industry, of which:	24.9	Public consumption	17
manufacturing	18.6	Investment	22
Services	67.6	Exports	21
		Imports	-20

Structure of manufacturing

	% of total		*% of tota*
Agric. & food processing	18	Other	5
Textiles & clothing	6	Av. ann. increase in industrial	
Machinery & transport	20	output 1980–93	2.1

Energy

	'000 TCE		
Total output	227,179	% output exported	57
Total consumption	133,649	% consumption imported	20
Consumption per head,			
kg coal equivalent	7,586		

Inflation and finance

		av. ann. increase 1989–9	
Consumer price			
inflation 1995	4.6%	Narrow money (M1)	13.7%
Av. ann. inflation 1989–95	3.9%	Broad money	1.4%

Exchange rates

	end 1995		*June 199*
A$ per $	1.34	Effective rates	*1990 = 10*
A$ per SDR	2.00	– nominal	102
A$ per Ecu	1.76	– real	80

Principal exports[a]

	$bn fob		$bn fob
Ores & minerals	10.4	Gold	3.7
Coal & oil	8.0	Wool	3.1
Machinery	4.5	Total incl. others	**49.4**

Main export destinations

	% of total		% of total
Japan	24.3	United States	6.9
Asean[b]	15.3	Developing countries	42.3
EU	11.2		

Principal imports[a]

	$bn cif		$bn cif
Machinery	15.3	Energy & products	2.7
Consumer goods	14.4	Chemicals	1.8
Motor vehicles & other transport equipment	9.5	Total incl. others	**55.5**

Main origins of imports

	% of total		% of total
EU	24.4	Asean[b]	8.2
United States	21.5	Developing countries	28.8
Japan	17.1		

Balance of payments, reserves and aid, $bn

Visible exports fob	47.1	Capital balance	11.6
Visible imports fob	-50.3	Overall balance	-1.0
Trade balance	-3.2	Change in reserves	0.1
Invisibles inflows	18.6	Level of reserves	
Invisibles outflows	-30.2	end Dec.	14.3
Net transfers	-0.4	No. months of import cover	2.1
Current account balance	-15.2	Aid given	1.1
– as % of GDP	-4.7	– as % of GDP	0.35

Family life

No. of households	5.3m	Divorces per 1,000 pop.	2.6
Av. no. per household	3.0	Cost of living, Dec. 1995	
Marriages per 1,000 pop.	6.6	New York = 100	95

a Year ending June 30, 1995.
b Brunei, Indonesia, Malaysia, Philippines, Singapore, Thailand.

AUSTRIA

Area	83,855 sq km	Currency	Schilling (ASch)
Capital	Vienna		

People

Population	7.9m	Life expectancy: men	74 yrs
Pop. per sq km	95	women	80 yrs
Av. ann. growth		Adult literacy	99.0%
in pop. 1985–94	0.5%	Fertility rate (per woman)	1.6
Pop. under 15	17.8%		
Pop. over 65	14.9%		*per 1,000 pop.*
No. of men per 100 women	95.5	Crude birth rate	11.4
Human Development Index	93	Crude death rate	10.1

The economy

GDP	ASch2,250bn	GDP per head	$24,949
GDP	$197bn	GDP per head in purchasing	
Av. ann. growth in real		power parity (USA=100)	79
GDP 1985–94	2.5%		

Origins of GDP		**Components of GDP**	
	% of total		*% of total*
Agriculture	2.3	Private consumption	55.0
Industry, of which:	35.2	Public consumption	19.0
manufacturing	...	Investment	24.6
Services	63.5	Exports	37.9
		Imports	-37.7

Structure of manufacturing

	% of total		*% of total*
Agric. & food processing	15	Other	51
Textiles & clothing	6	Av. ann. increase in industrial	
Machinery & transport	28	output 1980–93	2.2%

Energy

	'000 TCE		
Total output	8,960	% output exported	20.6
Total consumption	32,955	% consumption imported	80.9
Consumption per head,			
kg coal equivalent	4,191		

Inflation and finance

			av. ann. increase 1989–94
Consumer price			
inflation 1995	2.2%	Narrow money (M1)	6.5%
Av. ann. inflation 1989–95	3.1%	Broad money	7.1%

Exchange rates

	end 1995		*June 1995*
ASch per $	10.09	Effective rates	*1990 = 100*
ASch per SDR	15.00	– nominal	107.3
ASch per Ecu	13.22	– real	96.3

Principal exports

	$bn fob		$bn fob
Machinery & transport		Chemicals	4.1
equipment	17.6	Raw materials	1.9
Manufactured goods	13.0	Food, drink & tobacco	1.3
Consumer goods	6.6	Total incl. others	**45.0**

Main export destinations

	% of total		% of total
Germany	38.1	France	4.6
Italy	8.1	Hungary	3.9
Switzerland	6.4	United States	3.5

Principal imports

	$bn cif		$bn cif
Machinery & transport		Chemicals	5.8
equipment	21.0	Food, drink & tobacco	2.7
Manufactured products	10.6	Fuel & energy	2.4
Consumer goods	10.2	Total incl. others	**55.3**

Main origins of imports

	% of total		% of total
Germany	40.0	Japan	4.3
Italy	8.8	United States	4.4
France	4.7	Switzerland	4.1

Balance of payments, reserves and aid, $bn

Visible exports fob	44.6	Capital balance	3.1
Visible imports fob	-55.4	Overall balance	0.8
Trade balance	-8.9	Change in reserves	2.0
Invisibles inflows	37.7	Level of reserves	
Invisibles outflows	-30.4	end Dec.	23.9
Net transfers	-0.9	No. months of import cover	3.4
Current account balance	-2.5	Aid given	0.7
– as % of GDP	-1.2	– as % of GDP	0.33

Family life

No. of households	2.8m	Divorces per 1,000 pop.	2.1
Av. no. per household	2.7	Cost of living, Dec. 1995	
Marriages per 1,000 pop.	5.7	New York = 100	133

BANGLADESH

Area	143,998 sq km	Currency	Taka (Tk)
Capital	Dhaka		

People

Population	117.8m	Life expectancy: men	58 yrs
Pop. per sq km	836	women	58 yrs
Av. ann. growth		Adult literacy	36.6%
in pop. 1985–94	2.0%	Fertility rate (per woman)	3.9
Pop. under 15	39.5%		
Pop. over 65	3.1%		*per 1,000 pop*
No. of men per 100 women	106.5	Crude birth rate	32.9
Human Development Index	36	Crude death rate	10.2

The economy

GDP	Tk1,086bn	GDP per head	$226
GDP	$27bn	GDP per head in purchasing	
Av. ann. growth in real		power parity (USA=100)	5
GDP 1985–94	4.5%		

Origins of GDP[a]		Components of GDP[a]	
	% of total		*% of total*
Agriculture	30.4	Private consumption	78.9
Industry, of which:	15.7	Public consumption	13.8
manufacturing	9.9	Investment	12.7
Services	53.9	Exports	11.2
		Imports	-16.7

Structure of manufacturing

	% of total		*% of total*
Agric. & food processing	24	Other	31
Textiles & clothing	38	Av. ann. increase in industrial	
Metal products & machinery	7	output 1980–93	5.2%

Energy

	'000 TCE		
Total output	7,411	% output exported	0.0
Total consumption	10,666	% consumption imported	47.1
Consumption per head,			
kg coal equivalent	93		

Inflation and finance

Consumer price		*av. ann. increase 1989–94*	
inflation 1994	3.2%	Narrow money (M1)	13.4%
Av. ann. inflation 1989–93	5.4%	Broad money	14.2%

Exchange rates

	end 1995		*June 1995*
Tk per $	40.75	Effective rates	*1990 = 100*
Tk per SDR	60.57	– nominal	...
Tk per Ecu	53.38	– real	...

Principal exports[b]

	$m fob		$m fob
Textiles & clothing	1,851	Leather	218
Jute goods	340	Raw jute	64
Fish & fish products	329	Total incl. others	**3,269**

Main export destinations[a]

	% of total		% of total
United States	36.4	France	5.1
Germany	8.2	Italy	4.9
United Kingdom	7.2	Belgium	3.6

Principal imports

	$m cif		$m cif
Textiles	1,321	Chemicals	344
Machinery & transport		Food	246
equipment	724		
Energy products	356	Total incl. others	**5,838**

Main origins of imports[c]

	% of total		% of total
South Korea	8.9	Japan	6.9
Hong Kong	7.2	India	6.4
Singapore	7.2	China	6.3

Balance of payments, reserves and debt, $bn

Visible exports fob	2.9	Overall balance	0.7
Visible imports fob	-4.4	Change in reserves	0.7
Trade balance	-1.4	Level of reserves	
Invisibles inflows	0.8	end Dec.	3.2
Invisibles outflows	-1.2	No. months of import cover	7.9
Net transfers	2.1	Foreign debt	16.6
Current account balance	0.2	– as % of GDP	63.4
– as % of GDP	0.9	Debt service paid	0.7
Capital balance	0.8	Debt service ratio	15.1

Family life

No. households	14.8m	Divorces per 1,000 pop.	...
Av. no. per household	5.7	Cost of living, Dec. 1995	
Marriages per 1,000 pop.	10.9	New York = 100	65

a 1992.
b Fiscal year ending June 30 1995.
c Fiscal year ending June 30 1993.

BELGIUM

Area	30,520 sq km	Currency	Belgian franc (BFr)
Capital	Brussels		

People

Population	10.1m	Life expectancy: men		74 yrs
Pop. per sq km	331	women		81 yrs
Av. ann. growth		Adult literacy		99.0%
in pop. 1985–94	0.2%	Fertility rate (per woman)		1.7
Pop. under 15	17.9%			
Pop. over 65	15.8%			per 1,000 pop.
No. of men per 100 women	96.0	Crude birth rate		11.8
Human Development Index	93	Crude death rate		10.5

The economy

GDP	BFr7,728bn	GDP per head	$22,735
GDP	$231bn	GDP per head in purchasing	
Av. ann. growth in real		power parity (USA=100)	78
GDP 1985–94	2.2%		

Origins of GDP[b]		Components of GDP[a]	
	% of total		% of total
Agriculture	1.8	Private consumption	61.7
Industry, of which:	31.7	Public consumption	15.3
manufacturing	23.6	Investment	17.9
Services	66.5	Exports	70.7
		Imports	-65.0

Structure of manufacturing

	% of total		% of total
Agric. & food processing	17	Other	53
Textiles & clothing	8	Av. ann. increase in industrial	
Machinery & transport	22	output 1980–93	2.2%

Energy

	'000 TCE		
Total output	16,040	% output exported[c]	167.6
Total consumption	67,419	% consumption imported[c]	129.8
Consumption per head,			
kg coal equivalent	6,711		

Inflation and finance

			av. ann. increase 1989–93
Consumer price			
inflation 1995	1.5%	Narrow money (M1)	4.4%
Av. ann. inflation 1989–94	2.7%	Broad money	8.6%

Exchange rates

	end 1995		June 1995
			1990 = 100
BFr per $	29.42	Effective rates	
BFr per SDR	43.73	– nominal	109.9
BFr per Ecu	38.54	– real	104.3

Principal exports[a]

	$bn fob		$bn fob
Machinery & transport equipment	38.6	Precious stones & jewellery	9.4
		Textiles & clothing	9.0
Chemicals	23.3	Petroleum & products	3.8
Metals & products	13.9		
Agric. products & foodstuffs	12.5	Total incl. others	**137.4**

Main export destinations

	% of total		% of total
Germany	21.0	United Kingdom	8.5
France	19.0	United States	5.1
Netherlands	13.2	Italy	5.1

Principal imports[a]

	$bn cif		$bn cif
Machinery & transport equipment	32.1	Metals & products	9.1
		Precious stones & jewellery	9.0
Chemicals	16.6	Textiles & clothing	7.5
Agric. products & foodstuffs	11.1	Energy & products	7.2
		Total incl. others	**125.8**

Main origins of imports

	% of total		% of total
Germany	20.2	United Kingdom	9.4
Netherlands	17.6	United States	5.3
France	16.1	Italy	4.2

Balance of payments[a], reserves and aid, $bn

Visible exports fob	117.9	Capital balance	-10.4
Visible imports fob	-111.1	Overall balance	0.2
Trade balance	6.7	Change in reserves	2.3
Invisibles inflows	127.9	Level of reserves	
Invisibles outflows	-118.4	end Dec.	23.5
Net transfers	-3.5	No. months of import cover	1.2
Current account balance	12.8	Aid given	0.7
– as % of GDP	5.5	– as % of GDP	0.32

Family life

No. of households	3.6m	Divorces per 1,000 pop.	2.1
Av. no. per household	2.7	Cost of living, Dec. 1995	
Marriages per 1,000 pop.	5.4	New York = 100	122

a Including Luxembourg.
b 1992.
c Energy trade data are distorted by transitory and oil refining activities.

BRAZIL

Area	8,511,965 sq km	Currency	Real (F
Capital	Brasilia		

People

Population	159.1m	Life expectancy: men	66 yr
Pop. per sq km	19	women	70 yr
Av. ann. growth		Adult literacy	82.1
in pop. 1985–94	1.8%	Fertility rate (per woman)	2
Pop. under 15	32.3%		
Pop. over 65	5.2%		*per 1,000 po*
No. of men per 100 women	99.5	Crude birth rate	22
Human Development Index	80	Crude death rate	7

The economy

GDP	R343bn	GDP per head	$3,37
GDP	$536bn	GDP per head in purchasing	
Av. ann. growth in real		power parity (USA=100)	2
GDP 1985–94	2.2%		

Origins of GDP[a]		Components of GDP[b]	
	% of total		*% of tota*
Agriculture	10.8	Private consumption	62
Industry, of which:	33.8	Public consumption	15
manufacturing	25.0	Investment	19
Services	55.4	Exports	9
		Imports	-6

Structure of manufacturing

	% of total		*% of tota*
Agric. & food processing	15	Other	5
Textiles & clothing	11	Av. ann. increase in industrial	
Machinery & transport	22	output 1980–93	0.7

Energy

	'000 TCE		
Total output	84,983	% output exported	8
Total consumption	129,671	% consumption imported	51
Consumption per head,			
kg coal equivalent	829		

Inflation and finance

		av. ann. increase 1989–9	
Consumer price			
inflation 1995	66%	Narrow money (M1)	1,48
Av. ann. inflation 1988–93	1,025%	Broad money	.

Exchange rates

	end 1995		*June 199*
R per $	0.97	Effective rates	1990 = 10
R per SDR	1.45	– Nominal	.
R per Ecu	1.27	– Real	.

Principal exports[c]

	$bn fob		$bn fob
Metallurgical products	6.1	Chemical products	2.6
Transport equipment		Metallic ore	2.5
& parts	4.2		
Soya beans	3.1	Total incl. others	**38.8**

Main export destinations[e]

	% of total		% of total
EU	29.6	Latin America	20.8
United States	10.6	Asia	15.5

Principal imports[c]

	$bn cif		$bn cif
Raw materials	9.5	Oil & oil products	4.4
Capital goods	8.8	Total incl. others	**25.7**

Main origins of imports[e]

	% of total		% of total
United States	23.4	Middle East	12.3
EU	22.6	Japan	5.9
Aladi[d]	16.7		

Balance of payments, reserves and debt, $bn

Visible exports fob	44.1	Overall balance	-4.7
Visible imports fob	-33.2	Change in reserves	6.7
Trade balance	10.9	Level of reserves	
Invisibles inflows	7.1	end Dec.	38.5
Invisibles outflows	-21.5	No. months of import cover	8.5
Net transfers	2.4	Foreign debt	151.1
Current account balance	-1.2	– as % of GDP	27.9
– as % of GDP	-0.2	Debt service paid	16.1
Capital balance	0.9	Debt service ratio	31.8

Family life

No. of households	26.8m	Divorces per 1,000 pop.	0.5
Av. no. per household	4.4	Cost of living, Dec. 1995	
Marriages per 1,000 pop.	5.4	New York = 100	95

a 1991.
b 1992.
c 1993.
d Argentina, Bolivia, Brazil, Chile, Colombia, Ecuador, Mexico, Paraguay, Peru, Uruguay, Venezuela.

BULGARIA

Area	110,994 sq km	Currency	Lev (BGL)
Capital	Sofia		

People

Population	8.8m	Life expectancy: men	68 yrs
Pop. per sq km	79	women	75 yrs
Av. ann. growth		Adult literacy	94.0%
in pop. 1985–94	-0.2%	Fertility rate (per woman)	1.5
Pop. under 15	18.3%		
Pop. over 65	14.5%		*per 1,000 pop.*
No. of men per 100 women	96.1	Crude birth rate	10.6
Human Development Index	80	Crude death rate	13.3

The economy

GDP	BGL680bn	GDP per head	$1,163
GDP	$10.3bn	GDP per head in purchasing	
Av. ann. growth in real		power parity (USA=100)	18
GDP 1985–94	-2.1%		

Origins of GDP		Components of GDP	
	% of total		*% of total*
Agriculture	12.6	Private consumption	83.3
Industry, of which:	35.7	Public consumption	7.5
manufacturing	...	Investment	8.5
Services	51.7	Net exports	1.7
		Statistical discrepancy	-1.1

Structure of manufacturing

	% of total		*% of total*
Agric. & food processing	...	Other	...
Textiles & clothing	...	Av. ann. increase in industrial	
Machinery & transport	...	output 1980–93	1.1

Energy

	'000 TCE		
Total output	12,829	% output exported	0.7
Total consumption	32,919	% consumption imported	73.0
Consumption per head,			
kg coal equivalent	3,711		

Inflation and finance

			av. ann increase 1989–94
Consumer price			
inflation 1995	68%	Narrow money (M1)	...
Av. ann. inflation 1989–95	79.7%	Broad money	-2.1

Exchange rates

	end 1995		*June 1995*
BGL per $	70.66	Effective rates	*1990 = 100*
BGL per SDR	105.28	– Nominal	...
BGL per Ecu	92.56	– Real	...

Principal exports

	$bn fob		$bn fob
Agricultural goods	0.9	Machinery & equipment	0.5
Metals & metal products	0.8	Total incl. others	**4.2**

Main export destinations

	% of total		% of total
Russia	12.1	Greece	7.1
Macedonia, FYR	9.3	Italy	7.0
Germany	8.4	United States	4.8

Principal imports

	$bn cif		$bn cif
Mineral products & fuels	1.3	Chemicals & plastics	0.5
Machinery & equipment	1.0	Total incl. others	**4.3**

Main origins of imports

	% of total		% of total
Russia	26.2	Italy	5.7
Germany	13.2	Greece	4.8

Balance of payments, reserves and debt, $bn

Visible exports fob	4.2	Overall balance	-0.0
Visible imports fob	-4.0	Change in reserves	...
Trade balance	0.2	Level of reserves	
Invisibles inflows	1.4	end Dec.[a]	2.4
Invisibles outflows	-1.5	No. months of import cover[a]	4.7
Net transfers	0.2	Foreign debt	10.5
Current account balance	0.1	– as % of GDP	105.7
– as % of GDP	1.4	Debt service paid	0.8
Capital balance	-0.2	Debt service ratio	13.8

Family life

No. of households	3.0m	Divorces per 1,000 pop.	1.3
Av. no. per household	2.9	Cost of living, Dec. 1995	
Marriages per 1,000 pop.	4.7	New York = 100	...

[a] 1993.

CAMEROON

Area	475,442 sq km	Currency	CFA franc (CFAfr
Capital	Yaoundé		

People

Population	12.9m	Life expectancy: men		57 yr
Pop. per sq km	28		women	60 yr
Av. ann. growth		Adult literacy		56.5%
in pop. 1985–94	2.8%	Fertility rate (per woman)		5.
Pop. under 15	44.0%			
Pop. over 65	3.6%			*per 1,000 pop*
No. of men per 100 women	98.6	Crude birth rate		39.
Human Development Index	50	Crude death rate		10.

The economy

GDP	CFAfr4,830bn	GDP per head	$67
GDP	$8.7bn	GDP per head in purchasing	
Av. ann. growth in real		power parity (USA=100)	1
GDP 1985–94	-3.5%		

Origins of GDP		**Components of GDP**	
	% of total		*% of total*
Agriculture	28.6	Private consumption	71.
Industry, of which:	24.9	Public consumption	7.
manufacturing	11.3	Investment	15.
Services	46.5	Exports	27.
		Imports	-22

Structure of manufacturing[a]

	% of total		*% of total*
Agric. & food processing	61	Other	4
Textiles & clothing	-13	Av. ann. increase in industrial	
Metal products & machinery	5	output 1980–92	0.5%

Energy

	'000 TCE		
Total output	9,196	% output exported	85.
Total consumption	1,220	% consumption imported	2.
Consumption per head,			
kg coal equivalent	97		

Inflation and finance

		av. ann. change 1989–9	
Consumer price			
inflation 1994	12.7%	Narrow money (M1)	-4.5%
Av. ann. inflation 1989–94	2.1%	Broad money	-2.1%

Exchange rates

	end 1995		*June 199.*
CFAfr per $	490.0	Effective rates	*1990 = 10*
CFAfr per SDR	728.4	– nominal	71.
CFAfr per Ecu	641.9	– real	65.

Principal exports

	$m fob		$m fob
Crude oil	402	Cocoa	100
Timber	282	Coffee	64
		Total incl. others	**1,246**

Main export destinations

	% of total		% of total
France	19	Italy	11
Spain	16	Netherlands	7

Principal imports[c]

	$m fob		$m fob
Manufactures	1,181	Fuel	21
Primary products	246	Total incl. others	**1,585**

Main origins of imports[c]

	% of total		% of total
France	37	Japan	5
Belgium/Luxembourg	8	United States	5

Balance of payments[b], reserves and debt, $bn

Visible exports fob	1.5	Overall balance	-0.9
Visible imports fob	-1.0	Change in reserves	0.00
Trade balance	0.5	Level of reserves	
Invisibles inflows	0.4	end Dec.	0.01
Invisibles outflows	-1.4	No. months of import cover	0.1
Net transfers	-0.1	Foreign debt	7.3
Current account balance	-0.6	– as % of GDP	107.0
– as % of GDP	-5.3	Debt service paid	0.4
Capital balance	-0.3	Debt service ratio	16.5

Family life

No. of households	1.4m	Divorces per 1,000 pop.	…
Av. no. per household	5.2	Cost of living, Dec. 1995	
Marriages per 1,000 pop.	…	New York = 100	…

a 1985.
b 1993.
c 1991.

CANADA

Area[a]	9,970,610 sq km	Currency	Canadian dollar (C$)
Capital	Ottawa		

People

Population	29.1m	Life expectancy: men	75 yrs
Pop. per sq km	3	women	81 yrs
Av. ann. growth		Adult literacy	99.0%
in pop. 1985–94	1.3%	Fertility rate (per woman)	1.9
Pop. under 15	20.8%		
Pop. over 65	11.8%		*per 1,000 pop.*
No. of men per 100 women	98.1	Crude birth rate	14.1
Human Development Index	95	Crude death rate	7.7

The economy

GDP	C$782bn	GDP per head	$19,572
GDP	$570bn	GDP per head in purchasing	
Av. ann. growth in real		power parity (USA=100)	86
GDP 1985–94	2.3%		

Origins of GDP		Components of GDP	
	% of total		*% of total*
Agriculture	3.1	Private consumption	60.7
Industry, of which:	30.7	Public consumption	20.2
manufacturing	22.1	Investment	18.5
Services	66.2	Exports	33.3
		Imports	-32.5

Structure of manufacturing

	% of total		*% of total*
Agric. & food processing	17	Other	52
Textiles & clothing	5	Av. ann. increase in industrial	
Machinery & transport	26	output 1980–93	2.2%

Energy

	'000 TCE		
Total output	450,209	% output exported	43.1
Total consumption	313,843	% consumption imported	18.3
Consumption per head,			
kg coal equivalent	10,891		

Inflation and finance

Consumer price			*av. ann. increase 1989–94*
inflation 1995	2.2%	Narrow money (M1)	5.3%
Av. ann. inflation 1989–95	3.0%	Broad money	9.3%

Exchange rates

	end 1995		*June 1995*
C$ per $	1.37	Effective rates	*1990 = 100*
C$ per SDR	2.03	– nominal	82.1
C$ per Ecu	1.79	– real	76.3

Principal exports

	$bn fob		$bn fob
Motor vehicles & other transport equipment	41.4	Forest products	20.9
		Energy products	14.5
Machinery & industrial equipment	34.1	Agric. products & foodstuffs	13.1
Industrial supplies	27.5	Total incl. others	**163.5**

Main export destinations

	% of total		% of total
United States	81.7	United Kingdom	1.4
Japan	4.3		

Principal imports

	$bn cif		$bn cif
Machinery & industrial equipment	48.0	Consumer goods	17.2
		Agric. products & foodstuffs	9.2
Motor vehicles & other transport equipment	35.4	Energy products	5.1
Industrial supplies	28.1	Total incl. others	**151.3**

Main origins of imports

	% of total		% of total
United States	74.8	United Kingdom	2.4
Japan	4.1		

Balance of payments, reserves and aid, $bn

Visible exports fob	163.5	Capital balance	9.3
Visible imports fob	-151.3	Overall balance	-5.1
Trade balance	12.2	Change in reserves	-1.1
Invisibles inflows	27.6	Level of reserves	
Invisibles outflows	-56.9	end Dec.	13.8
Net transfers	-0.3	No. months of import cover	0.8
Current account balance	-17.4	Aid given	2.25
– as % of GDP	-3.1	– as % of GDP	0.43

Family life

No. of households	10.0m	Divorces per 1,000 pop.	2.9
Av. no. per household	2.7	Cost of living, Dec. 1995	
Marriages per 1,000 pop.	7.1	New York = 100	83

a Including freshwater.

CHILE

Area	756,945 sq km	Currency	Chilean peso (peso
Capital	Santiago		

People

Population	14.0m	Life expectancy: men	71 yrs
Pop. per sq km	19	women	78 yr
Av. ann. growth		Adult literacy	93.8%
in pop. 1985–94	1.7%	Fertility rate (per woman)	2.4
Pop. under 15	29.6%		
Pop. over 65	6.6%		*per 1,000 pop*
No. of men per 100 women	97.5	Crude birth rate	20.
Human Development Index	88	Crude death rate	5.

The economy

GDP	21,004bn pesos	GDP per head	$3,56
GDP	$50bn	GDP per head in purchasing	
Av. ann. growth in real		power parity (USA=100)	3
GDP 1985–94	6.8%		

Origins of GDP		Components of GDP	
	% of total		*% of tota*
Agriculture	9.0	Private consumption	66.
Industry, of which:	36.2	Public consumption	9.
manufacturing	18.5	Investment	28.
Services	54.8	Exports	36.
		Imports	-41.

Structure of manufacturing[a]

	% of total		*% of tota*
Agric. & food processing	25	Other	6
Textiles & clothing	8	Av. ann. increase in industrial	
Metal products & machinery	5	output 1980–93	4.5%

Energy

	'000 TCE		
Total output	7,562	% output exported	0.
Total consumption	18,390	% consumption imported	61.
Consumption per head,			
kg coal equivalent	1,330		

Inflation and finance

Consumer price		*av. ann. increase 1989–9*	
inflation 1995	8.2%	Narrow money (M1)	21.6%
Av. ann. inflation 1989–95	15.9%	Broad money	23.3%

Exchange rates

	end 1995		*June 199.*
Peso per $	406.9	Effective rates	*1990 = 10*
Peso per SDR	604.9	– nominal	251.
Peso per Ecu	533.0	– real	122.

Principal exports

	$bn fob		*$bn fob*
Industrial products incl. other mining prods.	6.1	Agric. products & foodstuffs	1.2
Copper	4.2	Total incl. others	**11.5**

Main export destinations

	% of total		*% of total*
Japan	17.0	South Korea	5.0
United States	17.3	Germany	5.0
Argentina	5.5	Taiwan	4.6
Brazil	5.2		

Principal imports

	$bn cif		*$bn cif*
Industrial supplies	6.1	Consumer goods	2.2
Capital goods	3.5	Total incl. others	**11.8**

Main origins of imports

	% of total		*% of total*
United States	23.2	Germany	4.9
Japan	8.9	France	3.2
Brazil	8.8	Italy	3.1
Argentina	8.4		

Balance of payments, reserves and debt, $bn

Visible exports fob	11.5	Overall balance	3.2
Visible imports fob	-10.9	Change in reserves	3.4
Trade balance	0.7	Level of reserves	
Invisibles inflows	3.3	end Dec.	13.8
Invisibles outflows	-5.1	No. months of import cover	10.4
Net transfers	0.3	Foreign debt	22.9
Current account balance	-0.8	– as % of GDP	45.5
– as % of GDP	-1.5	Debt service paid	2.9
Capital balance	4.4	Debt service ratio	19.2

Family life

No. of households	3.3m	Divorces per 1,000 pop.	0.4
Av. no. per household	4.1	Cost of living, Dec. 1995	
Marriages per 1,000 pop.	6.6	New York = 100	75

a 1992.

CHINA

Area	9,560,900 sq km	Currency	Yuan
Capital	Beijing		

People

Population	1,190.9m	Life expectancy: men	68 yrs
Pop. per sq km	127	women	72 yrs
Av. ann. growth		Adult literacy	80.0%
in pop. 1985–94	1.4%	Fertility rate (per woman)	2.0
Pop. under 15	26.4%		
Pop. over 65	6.1%		*per 1,000 pop.*
No. of men per 100 women	106.0	Crude birth rate	17.3
Human Development Index	59	Crude death rate	7.1

The economy

GDP	Yuan5,430bn	GDP per head	$529
GDP	$630bn	GDP per head in purchasing	
Av. ann. growth in real		power parity (USA=100)	8
GDP 1985–94	9.4%		

Origins of GDP[a]		**Components of GDP**[a]	
	% of total		*% of total*
Agriculture	20.5	Private consumption	51.2
Industry, of which:	49.2	Public consumption	9.1
manufacturing	...	Investment	33.9
Services	30.3	Exports	26.2
		Imports	-20.3

Structure of manufacturing

	% of total		*% of total*
Agric. & food processing	13	Other	47
Textiles & clothing	13	Av. ann. increase in industrial	
Metal products & machinery	27	output 1980–93	11.5%

Energy

	'000 TCE		
Total output	1,069,992	% output exported	4.9
Total consumption	1,012,679	% consumption imported	3.5
Consumption per head,			
kg coal equivalent	861		

Inflation and finance

		av. ann. increase 1989–93	
Consumer price			
inflation 1995	14.7%	Narrow money (M1)	20.9%
Av. ann. inflation 1989–95	10.8%	Broad money	25.1%

Exchange rates

	end 1995		*June 1995*
			1990 = 100
Yuan per $	8.32	Effective rates	
Yuan per SDR	12.36	– nominal	...
Yuan per Ecu	10.89	– real	...

Principal exports

	$bn fob		$bn fob
Clothing & footwear	29.8	Food	10.0
Machinery	19.3	Chemicals	6.2
Textiles	11.8	Total incl. others	**121.0**

Main export destinations

	% of total		% of total
Hong Kong	26.8	Germany	3.9
Japan	17.8	South Korea	3.6
United States	17.8	Singapore	2.1

Principal imports

	$bn fob		$bn fob
Machinery	41.8	Textiles	9.3
Chemicals	12.1	Fuels	3.6
Transport equipment	9.6		
Iron & steel	9.4	Total incl. others	**115.7**

Main origins of imports

	% of total		% of total
Japan	22.8	South Korea	6.3
Taiwan	12.2	Germany	6.2
United States	12.1	Russia	3.0
Hong Kong	8.2		

Balance of payments, reserves and debt, $bn

Visible exports fob	102.6	Overall balance	30.5
Visible imports fob	-95.3	Change in reserves	30.4
Trade balance	7.3	Level of reserves	
Invisibles inflows	22.4	end Dec.	57.8
Invisibles outflows	-23.1	No. months of import cover	5.9
Net transfers	-0.04	Foreign debt	100.5
Current account balance	6.5	- as % of GDP	19.3
- as % of GDP	1.0	Debt service paid	11.1
Capital balance	33.0	Debt service ratio	8.9

Family life

No. of households	220.1m	Divorces per 1,000 pop.	...
Av. no. per household	4.4	Cost of living, Dec. 1995	
Marriages per 1,000 pop.	...	New York = 100	104

a 1995 estimates.

COLOMBIA

Area	1,141,748 sq km	Currency	Colombian peso (peso)
Capital	Bogota		

People

Population	36.3m	Life expectancy: men	67 yrs
Pop. per sq km	31	women	73 yrs
Av. ann. growth		Adult literacy	87.4%
in pop. 1985–94	2.2%	Fertility rate (per woman)	2.5
Pop. under 15	32.9%		
Pop. over 65	4.5%		*per 1,000 pop.*
No. of men per 100 women	98.3	Crude birth rate	22.0
Human Development Index	84	Crude death rate	5.8

The economy

GDP	49,846bn pesos	GDP per head	$1,622
GDP	$59bn	GDP per head in purchasing	
Av. ann. growth in real		power parity (USA=100)	23
GDP 1985–94	4.4%		

Origins of GDP		**Components of GDP**	
	% of total		*% of total*
Agriculture	19.7	Private consumption	70.9
Industry, of which:	27.9	Public consumption	14.7
manufacturing	20.0	Investment	24.6
Services	52.4	Exports	21.9
		Imports	-32.1

Structure of manufacturing

	% of total		*% of total*
Agric. & food processing	29	Other	47
Textiles & clothing	14	Av. ann. increase in industrial	
Machinery & transport	10	output 1980–93	4.5%

Energy

	'000 TCE		
Total output	61,837	% output exported	59.6
Total consumption	28,296	% consumption imported	13.2
Consumption per head,			
kg coal equivalent	833		

Inflation and finance

Consumer price		*av. ann. increase 1991–94*	
inflation 1995	20.9%	Narrow money (M1)	34.3
Av. ann. inflation 1989–95	25.4%	Broad money	21.9

Exchange rates

	end 1995		*June 1995*
Peso per $	988	Effective rates	*1990 = 100*
Peso per SDR	1,468	– nominal	135.2
Peso per Ecu	1,294	– real	136.3

Principal exports

	$bn fob		$bn fob
Coffee	2.0	Bananas	0.5
Petroleum & products	1.3	Flowers	0.4
Coal	0.6	Total incl. others	**8.7**

Main export destinations

	% of total		% of total
United States	36.5	Andean Pact[a]	13.2
EU	28.2	Japan	4.2

Principal imports

	$bn fob		$bn fob
Industrial supplies	4.6	Consumer goods	2.0
Capital goods	4.4	Total	**11.0**

Main origins of imports

	% of total		% of total
United States	38.1	Andean Pact[a]	13.0
EU	16.6	Japan	8.2

Balance of payments[b], reserves and debt, $bn

Visible exports fob	7.3	Overall balance	1.2
Visible imports fob	-6.0	Change in reserves	0.2
Trade balance	1.2	Level of reserves	
Invisibles inflows	2.4	end Dec.	7.9
Invisibles outflows	-4.5	No. months of import cover	6.0
Net transfers	1.7	Foreign debt	19.4
Current account balance	0.9	– as % of GDP	30.9
– as % of GDP	2.0	Debt service paid	3.7
Capital balance	0.3	Debt service ratio	29.8

Family life

No. of households	5.3m	Divorces per 1,000 pop.	...
Av. no. per household	5.2	Cost of living, Dec. 1995	
Marriages per 1,000 pop.	2.4	New York = 100	69

a   Bolivia, Colombia, Ecuador, Peru, Venezuela.
b   1992.

CÔTE D'IVOIRE

Area	322,463 sq km	Currency	CFA franc (CFAfr)
Capital	Abidjan/Yamoussoukro		

People

Population	13.8m	Life expectancy: men	49 yrs
Pop. per sq km	44	women	51 yrs
Av. ann. growth		Adult literacy	55.8%
in pop. 1985–94	3.6%	Fertility rate (per woman)	6.9
Pop. under 15	49.1%		
Pop. over 65	2.6%		*per 1,000 pop.*
No. of men per 100 women	102.8	Crude birth rate	47.6
Human Development Index	37	Crude death rate	15.3

The economy

GDP	CFAfr3,886bn	GDP per head	$513
GDP	$7bn	GDP per head in purchasing	
Av. ann. growth in real		power parity (USA=100)	7
GDP 1985–94	-0.4%		

Origins of GDP[a]		Components of GDP[a]	
	% of total		*% of total*
Agriculture	33.7	Private consumption	67.9
Industry, of which:	28.8	Public consumption	18.2
manufacturing	...	Investment	8.9
Services	37.5	Exports	33.6
		Imports	-28.6

Structure of manufacturing

	% of total		*% of total*
Agric. & food processing	...	Other	...
Textiles & clothing	...	Av. ann. increase in industrial	
Metal products & machinery	...	output 1980–93	2.5%

Energy

	'000 TCE		
Total output	598	% output exported	64.0
Total consumption	3,726	% consumption imported	129.5
Consumption per head,			
kg coal equivalent	280		

Inflation and finance

Consumer price		*av. ann. change 1989–94*	
inflation 1994	26%	Narrow money (M1)	1.7%
Av. ann. inflation 1989–94	5.3%	Broad money	1.5%

Exchange rates

	end 1995		*June 1995*
CFAfr per $	490.0	Effective rates	*1990 = 100*
CFAfr per SDR	728.4	– nominal	96.4
CFAfr per Ecu	641.9	– real	70.4

Principal exports

	$m fob		$m fob
Cocoa beans & products	884	Canned fish	117
Timber & products	303	Raw cotton	116
Coffee & products	199	Total incl. others	**2,734**

Main export destinations

	% of total		% of total
France	16	Netherlands	9
Germany	10	Italy	7

Principal imports

	$m cif		$m cif
Petroleum products	367	Rice	79
Machinery & equipment	122	Pharmaceuticals	79
Fish & products	98	Total incl. others	**1,662**

Main origins of imports

	% of total		% of total
France	28	United States	6
Nigeria	27	Italy	5

Balance of payments, reserves and debt, $bn

Visible exports fob	2.9	Overall balance	0.04
Visible imports fob	-1.6	Change in reserves	0.2
Trade balance	1.3	Level of reserves	
Invisibles inflows	0.4	end Dec.	0.22
Invisibles outflows	-1.7	No. months of import cover	0.7
Net transfers	-0.04	Foreign debt	18.5
Current account balance	0.01	– as % of GDP	338.9
– as % of GDP	0.2	Debt service paid	1.3
Capital balance	0.3	Debt service ratio	40.1

Family life

No. of households	1.8m	Divorces per 1,000 pop.	...
Av. no. per household	6.0	Cost of living, Dec. 1995	
Marriages per 1,000 pop.	...	New York = 100	111

a 1992.

CZECH REPUBLIC

Area	78,864 sq km	Currency	Koruna (Kc)
Capital	Prague		

People

Population	10.3m	Life expectancy: men	68 yrs
Pop. per sq km	131	women	75 yrs
Av. ann. growth		Adult literacy[a]	99.0%
in pop. 1985–94	nil	Fertility rate (per woman)	1.8
Pop. under 15	19.4%		
Pop. over 65	12.5%		per 1,000 pop
No. of men per 100 women[a]	95.2	Crude birth rate	13.8
Human Development Index[a]	87	Crude death rate	12.1

The economy

GDP	Kcs950bn	GDP per head	$3,210
GDP	$33bn	GDP per head in purchasing	
Av. ann. growth in real		power parity (USA=100)	32
GDP 1990–94	-4.9%		

Origins of GDP		Components of GDP	
	% of total		% of total
Agriculture	5.8	Private consumption	54.9
Industry, of which:	40.7	Public consumption	21.6
manufacturing	...	Investment	29.2
Services	53.5	Net exports	-5.8
		Imports	..

Structure of manufacturing[a]

	% of total		% of total
Agric. & food processing	10	Other	44
Textiles & clothing	11	Av. ann. increase in industrial	
Metal products & machinery	35	output 1980–92	0.4%

Energy

	'000 TCE		
Total output	49,087	% output exported	23.4
Total consumption	56,619	% consumption imported	37.9
Consumption per head,			
kg coal equivalent	5,032		

Inflation and finance

		av. ann. increase 1993–94	
Consumer price			
inflation 1995	9.2%	Narrow money (M1)	8.3%
Av. ann. inflation 1991–95	20.4%	Broad money	20.3%

Exchange rates

	end 1995		June 1995
Kc per $	26.60	Effective rates	1990 = 100
Kc per SDR	39.54	– nominal	..
Kc per Ecu	34.85	– real	..

Principal exports

	$bn fob		$bn fob
Manufactured goods	4.3	Raw materials & fuels	1.8
Machinery & industrial		Chemicals	1.4
equipment	3.7	Total incl. others	**14.0**

Main export destinations

	% of total		% of total
EU	45.9	Ex-Soviet Union	9.4
Slovakia	16.3	Other ex-communist countries	9.6

Principal imports

	$bn fob		$bn fob
Machinery & industrial		Raw materials & fuels	2.2
equipment	5.2		
Manufactured goods	2.5	Total incl. others	**15.0**

Main origins of imports

	% of total		% of total
EU	45.1	Ex-Soviet Union	9.9
Slovakia	10.2	Other ex-communist countries	5.2

Balance of payments, reserves and debt, $bn

Visible exports fob	14.0	Overall balance	3.5
Visible imports fob	-15.0	Change in reserves	2.4
Trade balance	-0.9	Level of reserves	
Invisibles inflows	5.7	end Dec.	6.9
Invisibles outflows	-5.0	No. months of import cover	4.2
Net transfers	0.1	Foreign debt	10.7
Current account balance	-0.08	– as % of GDP	29.7
– as % of GDP	-0.2	Debt service paid	2.5
Capital balance	4.5	Debt service ratio	12.6

Family life[a]

No. of households	5.4m	Divorces per 1,000 pop.	2.9
Av. no. per household	2.8	Cost of living, Dec. 1995	
Marriages per 1,000 pop.	6.4	New York = 100	63

a 1992.

DENMARK

Area	43,075 sq km	Currency	Danish krone (DKr)
Capital	Copenhagen		

People

Population	5.2m	Life expectancy: men	73 yrs
Pop. per sq km	120	women	79 yrs
Av. ann. growth		Adult literacy	99.0%
in pop. 1985–94	0.1	Fertility rate (per woman)	1.7
Pop. under 15	17.1%		
Pop. over 65	15.2%		*per 1,000 pop.*
No. of men per 100 women	97.7	Crude birth rate	12.0
Human Development Index	92	Crude death rate	11.8

The economy

GDP	DKr922bn	GDP per head	$28,104
GDP	$145bn	GDP per head in purchasing	
Av. ann. growth in real		power parity (USA=100)	80
GDP 1985–94	1.7%		

Origins of GDP		Components of GDP	
	% of total		*% of total*
Agriculture	3.6	Private consumption	53.7
Industry, of which:	28.1	Public consumption	25.3
manufacturing	20.6	Investment	14.6
Services	68.3	Exports	34.9
		Imports	-28.4

Structure of manufacturing

	% of total		*% of total*
Agric. & food processing	23	Other	50
Textiles & clothing	4	Av. ann. increase in industrial	
Machinery & transport	23	output 1980–93	2.3%

Energy

	'000 TCE		
Total output	17,918	% output exported	88.0
Total consumption	25,988	% consumption imported	91.6
Consumption per head,			
kg coal equivalent	5,032		

Inflation and finance

Consumer price		*av. ann. increase 1989–94*	
inflation 1995	2.1%	Narrow money (M1)	6.3%
Av. ann. inflation 1989–95	2.5%	Broad money	5.4%

Exchange rates

	end 1995		*June 1995*
DKr per $	5.55	Effective rates	*1990 = 100*
DKr per SDR	8.24	– nominal	110.4
DKr per Ecu	7.27	– real	107.6

Principal exports

	$bn fob		$bn fob
Machinery & equipment	9.6	Energy & products	1.2
Agric. products & foodstuffs	5.4		
Animals & products	4.5	Total incl. others	**41.4**

Main export destinations

	% of total		% of total
Germany	21.6	Norway	6.2
Sweden	10.0	United States	5.3
United Kingdom	7.9	France	5.3

Principal imports

	$bn cif		$bn cif
Consumer goods	9.1	Fuels	1.8
Capital goods	3.8	Agricultural products	1.2
Building & construction	2.5	Total incl. others	**23.2**

Main origins of imports

	% of total		% of total
Germany	20.9	United Kingdom	6.3
Sweden	11.2	France	5.2
Netherlands	6.4	Norway	4.9

Balance of payments, reserves and aid, $bn

Visible exports fob	41.8	Capital balance	-2.3
Visible imports fob	-34.1	Overall balance	-2.0
Trade balance	7.7	Change in reserves	-1.3
Invisibles inflows	25.7	Level of reserves	
Invisibles outflows	-39.6	end Dec.	9.8
Net transfers	-1.2	No. months of import cover	1.6
Current account balance	2.7	Aid given	1.45
– as % of GDP	1.8	– as % of GDP	1.03

Family life

No. of households	2.3m	Divorces per 1,000 pop.	2.5
Av. no. per household	2.2	Cost of living, Dec. 1995	
Marriages per 1,000 pop.	6.1	New York = 100	130

EGYPT

Area	1,000,250 sq km	Currency	Egyptian pound (£E)
Capital	Cairo		

People

Population	57.6m	Life expectancy: men		65 yrs
Pop. per sq km	63		women	67 yrs
Av. ann. growth		Adult literacy		50.0%
in pop. 1985–94	2.0%	Fertility rate (per woman)		3.4
Pop. under 15	38.1%			
Pop. over 65	4.2%			*per 1,000 pop.*
No. of men per 100 women	103.7	Crude birth rate		26.4
Human Development Index	61	Crude death rate		7.1

The economy

GDP	£E139bn	GDP per head	$711
GDP	$41bn	GDP per head in purchasing	
Av. ann. growth in real		power parity (USA=100)	15
GDP 1985–94	2.9%		

Origins of GDP[b]		**Components of GDP**[b]	
	% of total		*% of total*
Agriculture	16.5	Private consumption	72.7
Industry, of which:	33.4	Public consumption	10.9
manufacturing	...	Investment	20.8
Services	50.1	Exports	30.2
		Imports	-34.6

Structure of manufacturing

	% of total		*% of total*
Agric. & food processing	15	Other	56
Textiles & clothing	23	Av. ann. increase in industrial	
Machinery & transport	6	output 1980–93	1.6%

Energy

	'000 TCE		
Total output	83,087	% output exported	45.1
Total consumption	41,839	% consumption imported	5.1
Consumption per head,			
kg coal equivalent	694		

Inflation and finance

Consumer price		*av. ann. increase 1989–94*	
inflation 1995	5.8%	Narrow money (M1)	10.8%
Av. ann. inflation 1989–95	13.8%	Broad money	18.5%

Exchange rates

	end 1995		*June 1995*
		Effective rates	*1990 = 100*
£E per $	3.39	– nominal	...
£E per SDR	5.04	– real	...
£E per Ecu	4.44		

Principal exports[b]

	$m fob		$m fob
Petroleum & products	1,499	Other agric. products	193
Cotton yarn & textiles	496	Raw cotton	45
Industrial goods	329	Total incl. others	**3,065**

Main export destinations

	% of total		% of total
Italy	19.8	United Kingdom	6.3
United States	9.7	Spain	4.8
Greece	8.8	Germany	4.7

Principal imports[b]

	$m cif		$m cif
Machinery & transport		Chemicals & rubber	1,169
equipment	2,943	Base metals & manufactures	1,011
Agric. products &		Wood, paper & textiles	1,002
foodstuffs	1,940	Total incl. others	**10,716**

Main origins of imports

	% of total		% of total
United States	20.4	France	6.1
Italy	9.7	Japan	5.1
Germany	9.2	United Kingdom	4.1

Balance of payments, reserves and debt, $bn

Visible exports fob	4.0	Overall balance	-1.2
Visible imports fob	-10.0	Change in reserves	0.6
Trade balance	-6.0	Level of reserves	
Invisibles inflows	9.4	end Dec.	14.4
Invisibles outflows	-7.8	No. months of import cover	10.7
Net transfers	4.3	Foreign debt	33.4
Current account balance	0.03	– as % of GDP	78.9
– as % of GDP	0.1	Debt service paid	2.3
Capital balance	-1.5	Debt service ratio	14.6

Family life

No. of households	9.7m	Divorces per 1,000 pop.	1.4
Av. no. per household	4.9	Cost of living, Dec. 1995	
Marriages per 1,000 pop.	8.4	New York = 100	89

a   1991.
b   Year ending June 30, 1994.

FINLAND

Area	338,145 sq km	Currency	Markka (Fmk)
Capital	Helsinki		

People

Population	5.1m	Life expectancy: men	73 yrs
Pop. per sq km	15	women	80 yrs
Av. ann. growth		Adult literacy	99%
in pop. 1985–94	0.4%	Fertility rate (per woman)	1.9
Pop. under 15	19.1%		
Pop. over 65	14.1%		*per 1,000 pop.*
No. of men per 100 women	94.8	Crude birth rate	12.5
Human Development Index	93	Crude death rate	10.2

The economy

GDP	Fmk501bn	GDP per head	$18,850
GDP	$96bn	GDP per head in purchasing	
Av. ann. growth in real		power parity (USA=100)	69
GDP 1985–94	0.9%		

Origins of GDP		**Components of GDP**	
	% of total		*% of total*
Agriculture	6.0	Private consumption	51.3
Industry, of which:	32.3	Public consumption	21.7
manufacturing	26.6	Investment	20.1
Services	61.7	Exports	33.9
		Imports	-27.1

Structure of manufacturing

	% of total		*% of total*
Agric. & food processing	14	Other	60
Textiles & clothing	3	Av. ann. increase in industrial	
Machinery & transport	23	output 1980–93	2.2%

Energy

	'000 TCE		
Total output	11,056	% output exported[a]	43.5
Total consumption	34,586	% consumption imported[a]	77.3
Consumption per head,			
kg coal equivalent	6,838		

Inflation and finance

Consumer price			*av. ann. increase 1989–94*
inflation 1995	1.0%	Narrow money (M1)	28.1%
Av. ann. inflation 1989–95	3.5%	Broad money	4.2%

Exchange rates

	end 1995		*June 1995*
Fmk per $	4.36	Effective rates	*1990 = 100*
Fmk per SDR	6.48	– nominal	87.3
Fmk per Ecu	5.71	– real	71.0

Principal exports

	$bn fob		$bn fob
Metals & engineering		Chemicals	3.0
equipment	10.6	Wood & products	2.7
Paper & products	7.9	Total incl. others	**29.5**

Main export destinations

	% of total		% of total
Germany	13.4	Russia	5.2
Sweden	10.9	France	5.1
United Kingdom	10.3	Netherlands	5.1
United States	7.2		

Principal imports

	$bn cif		$bn cif
Raw materials	12.6	Energy & products	2.2
Consumer goods	4.7		
Capital goods	3.3	Total incl. others	**23.0**

Main origins of imports

	% of total		% of total
Germany	14.7	United States	7.6
Sweden	10.4	Japan	6.5
Russia	8.9	Norway	4.8
United Kingdom	8.3		

Balance of payments, reserves and aid, $bn

Visible exports fob	29.3	Capital balance	4.3
Visible imports fob	-21.7	Overall balance	4.7
Trade balance	7.7	Change in reserves	5.2
Invisibles inflows	7.2	Level of reserves	
Invisibles outflows	-13.3	end Dec.	11.4
Net transfers	-0.4	No. months of import cover	3.9
Current account balance	1.1	Aid given	0.29
– as % of GDP	1.1	– as % of GDP	0.31

Family life

No. of households	2.0m	Divorces per 1,000 pop.	2.4
Av. no. per household	2.5	Cost of living, Dec. 1995	
Marriages per 1,000 pop.	4.7	New York = 100	119

a Energy trade data are distorted by transitory and oil refinery activities.

FRANCE

Area	543,965 sq km	Currency	Franc (FFr)
Capital	Paris		

People

Population	57.7m	Life expectancy: men	74 yrs
Pop. per sq km	105	women	81 yrs
Av. ann. growth		Adult literacy	99.0%
in pop. 1985–94	0.5%	Fertility rate (per woman)	1.7
Pop. under 15	19.6%		
Pop. over 65	14.9%		*per 1,000 pop*
No. of men per 100 women	95.1	Crude birth rate	12.4
Human Development Index	93	Crude death rate	9.0

The economy

GDP	FFr7,523bn	GDP per head	$23,474
GDP	$1,355bn	GDP per head in purchasing	
Av. ann. growth in real		power parity (USA=100)	82
GDP, 1985–94	2.2%		

Origins of GDP		Components of GDP	
	% of total		*% of total*
Agriculture	2.6	Private consumption	60.1
Industry, of which:	28.7	Public consumption	19.8
manufacturing	...	Investment	17.1
Services	68.7	Exports	22.8
		Imports	-20.0

Structure of manufacturing

	% of total		*% of total*
Agric. & food processing	14	Other	50
Textiles & clothing	6	Av. ann. increase in industrial	
Metal products & machinery	30	output 1980–93	1.2%

Energy

	'000 TCE		
Total output	161,946	% output exported	18.1
Total consumption	312,325	% consumption imported	62.4
Consumption per head,			
kg coal equivalent	5,428		

Inflation and finance

Consumer price		*av. ann. increase 1989–95*	
inflation 1995	1.7%	Narrow money (M1)	1.8%
Av. ann. inflation 1989–95	2.6%	Broad money	2.6%

Exchange rates

	end 1995		*June 1995*
FFr per $	4.90	Effective rates	*1990 = 100*
FFr per SDR	7.28	– nominal	108.1
FFr per Ecu	6.42	– real	99.1

Principal exports

	$bn fob		$bn fob
Capital equipment	61.1	Motor vehicles & other	
Non-durable consumer		transport equipment	32.1
goods	36.5	Steel & other metals	19.6
Agric. products & foodstuffs	36.2		
Chemicals	35.8	Total incl. others	**235.0**

Main export destinations

	% of total		% of total
Germany	17.1	Spain	7.1
United Kingdom	9.9	United States	7.0
Italy	9.4	Netherlands	4.6
Belgium/Luxembourg	8.8		

Principal imports

	$bn cif		$bn cif
Capital equipment	54.3	Motor vehicles & other	
Non-durable consumer		transport equipment	26.5
goods	37.9	Steel & other metals	20.0
Chemicals	36.3	Energy products	17.4
Agric. products			
& foodstuffs	28.1	Total incl. others	**229.3**

Main origins of imports

	% of total		% of total
Germany	17.8	United Kingdom	8.0
Italy	10.1	Spain	6.1
Belgium/Luxembourg	9.1	Netherlands	5.0
United States	8.5		

Balance of payments, reserves and aid, $bn

Visible exports fob	223.5	Capital balance	-7.2
Visible imports fob	-215.6	Overall balance	5.0
Trade balance	7.9	Change in reserves	3.0
Invisibles inflows	201.3	Level of reserves	
Invisibles outflows	-192.7	end Dec.	57.6
Net transfers	-8.3	No. months of import cover	1.7
Current account balance	8.1	Aid given[a]	8.5
– as % of GDP	0.6	– as % of GDP	0.64

Family life

No. of households	21.5m	Divorces per 1,000 pop.	1.9
Av. no. per household	2.6	Cost of living, Dec. 1995	
Marriages per 1,000 pop.	4.7	New York = 100	137

a Including aid to French overseas territories.

GERMANY

Area	357,868 sq km	Currency	Deutschemark (DM)
Capital	Berlin		

People

Population	81.1m	Life expectancy: men		74 yrs
Pop. per sq km	229		women	80 yrs
Av. ann. growth		Adult literacy		99.0%
in pop. 1985–94	0.5%	Fertility rate (per woman)		1.3
Pop. under 15	16.0%			
Pop. over 65	15.2%			*per 1,000 pop.*
No. of men per 100 women	95.3	Crude birth rate		9.2
Human Development Index	92	Crude death rate		10.9

The economy

GDP	DM3,367bn	GDP per head	$25,578
GDP	$2,075bn	GDP per head in purchasing	
Av. ann. growth in real		power parity (USA=100)	89
GDP 1985–94[a]	2.8%		

Origins of GNP		**Components of GNP**	
	% of total		*% of total*
Agriculture	1.0	Private consumption	57.3
Industry, of which:	33.9	Public consumption	19.6
manufacturing	…	Investment	22.6
Services	65.1	Exports	22.7
		Imports	-22.0

Structure of manufacturing[a]

	% of total		*% of total*
Agric. & food processing	10	Other	45
Textiles & clothing	4	Av. ann. increase in industrial	
Machinery & transport	41	output 1980–92	1.1

Energy

	'000 TCE		
Total output	210,799	% output exported	12.8
Total consumption	468,270	% consumption imported	62.9
Consumption per head,			
kg coal equivalent	5,791		

Inflation[a] and finance

			av. ann. increase 1989–94
Consumer price			
inflation 1995	1.8%	Narrow money (M1)	10.3%
Av. ann. inflation 1989–95	3.1%	Broad money	9.0%

Exchange rates

	end 1995		*June 1995*
DM per $	1.43	Effective rates	*1990 = 100*
DM per SDR	2.13	– nominal	112.4
DM per Ecu	1.87	– real	119.9

Principal exports

	$bn fob		$bn fob
Non-electrical machinery	74.8	Food, drink & tobacco	20.4
Road vehicles & aircraft	70.9	Iron & steel	12.1
Chemicals	53.7		
Electrical machinery			
& appliances	43.0	Total incl. others	**422.8**

Main export destinations

	% of total		% of total
France	12.0	Italy	7.6
United Kingdom	8.0	United States	7.9
Netherlands	7.7	Belgium/Luxembourg	6.8

Principal imports

	$bn cif		$bn cif
Road vehicles & aircraft	44.1	Non-electrical machinery	34.8
Chemicals	40.3	Food, drink & tobacco	34.6
Electrical machinery &		Textiles & clothing	29.2
appliances	35.3	Total incl. others	**377.2**

Main origins of imports

	% of total		% of total
France	11.0	United Kingdom	6.3
Italy	8.4	Belgium/Luxembourg	6.0
Netherlands	8.2	United States	5.3

Balance of payments, reserves and aid, $bn

Visible exports fob	430.3	Capital balance	25.1
Visible imports fob	-379.8	Overall balance	-2.1
Trade balance	50.5	Change in reserves	-1.0
Invisibles inflows	136.4	Level of reserves	
Invisibles outflows	-170.7	end Dec.	113.8
Net transfers	-37.9	No. months of import cover	2.5
Current account balance	-21.7	Aid given	6.8
– as % of GDP	-1.0	– as % of GDP	0.34

Family life

No. of households	32.7m	Divorces per 1,000 pop.	1.7
Av. no. per household[a]	2.3	Cost of living, Dec. 1995	
Marriages per 1,000 pop.	5.5	New York = 100	121

[a] Western Germany.

GREECE

Area	131,957 sq km	Currency	Drachma (Dr)
Capital	Athens		

People

Population	10.4m	Life expectancy: men	76 yrs
Pop. per sq km	79	women	81 yrs
Av. ann. growth		Adult literacy	93.8%
in pop. 1985–94	0.5%	Fertility rate (per woman)	1.4
Pop. under 15	16.7%		
Pop. over 65	15.9%		*per 1,000 pop*
No. of men per 100 women	97.0	Crude birth rate	9.8
Human Development Index	91	Crude death rate	10.1

The economy

GDP	Dr19,408bn	GDP per head	$7,705
GDP	$80bn	GDP per head in purchasing	
Av. ann. growth in real		power parity (USA=100)	35
GDP 1985–94	1.5%		

Origins of GDP		Components of GDP	
	% of total		*% of total*
Agriculture	13.7	Private consumption	71.8
Industry, of which:	35.0	Public consumption	19.8
manufacturing	25.8	Investment	18.1
Services	51.3	Exports	23.2
		Imports	-33.1

Structure of manufacturing

	% of total		*% of total*
Agric. & food processing	26	Other	45
Textiles & clothing	17	Av. ann. increase in industrial	
Metal products & machinery	12	output 1980–93	1.2%

Energy

	'000 TCE		
Total output	12,010	% output exported[a]	41.2
Total consumption	33,745	% consumption imported[a]	88.2
Consumption per head,			
kg coal equivalent	2,357		

Inflation and finance

Consumer price			*av. ann. increase 1989–94*
inflation 1995	9.3%	Narrow money (M1)	17.8%
Av. ann. inflation 1989–95	14.8%	Broad money[b]	14.6%

Exchange rates

	end 1995		*June 1995*
Dr per $	237	Effective rates	1990 = 100
Dr per SDR	352	– nominal	66.2
Dr per Ecu	310	– real	108.2

Principal exports

	$bn fob		$bn fob
Manufactured products	2.4	Minerals	0.2
Food & beverages	1.6		
Petroleum products	0.6		
Raw materials & industrial supplies	0.3	Total incl. others	**9.4**

Main export destinations

	% of total		% of total
Germany	24.4	United Kingdom	5.9
Italy	12.0	United States	4.6
France	6.4	Cyprus	3.2

Principal imports

	$bn cif		$bn cif
Manufactured consumer goods	7.5	Petroleum	1.2
		Chemicals & products	0.8
Machinery equipment	3.5	Iron & steel	0.6
Foodstuffs	2.8	Total incl. others	**21.5**

Main origins of imports[b]

	% of total		% of total
Germany	16.9	Japan	6.8
Italy	14.0	Netherlands	6.6
France	7.9	United Kingdom	6.1

Balance of payments, reserves and debt, $bn

Visible exports fob	5.3	Overall balance	6.3
Visible imports fob	-16.6	Change in reserves	6.7
Trade balance	-11.3	Level of reserves	
Invisibles inflows	10.4	end Dec.	15.8
Invisibles outflows	-6.1	No. months of import cover	8.3
Net transfers	6.9	Aid given	...
Current account balance	-0.1	– as % of GDP	...
– as % of GDP	-0.2		
Capital balance	6.9		

Family life

No. of households	3.0m	Divorces per 1,000 pop.	0.7
Av. no. per household	3.1	Cost of living, Dec. 1995	
Marriages per 1,000 pop.	4.7	New York = 100	101

a   Energy trade figures are distorted by transitory and oil refining activities.
b   1993.

HONG KONG

Area	1,075 sq km	Currency	Hong Kong dollar (HK$)
Capital	Victoria		

People

Population	5.8m	Life expectancy: men	76 yrs
Pop. per sq km	5,612	women	82 yrs
Av. ann. growth		Adult literacy	90.0%
in pop. 1985–94	0.7%	Fertility rate (per woman)	1.2
Pop. under 15	19.2%		
Pop. over 65	10.2%		*per 1,000 pop.*
No. of men per 100 women	104.6	Crude birth rate	9.8
Human Development Index	91	Crude death rate	6.3

The economy

GDP	HK$983bn	GDP per head	$21,650
GDP	$126bn	GDP per head in purchasing	
Av. ann. growth in real		power parity (USA=100)	86
GDP 1985–94	6.7%		

Origins of GDP[a]		Components of GDP	
	% of total		*% of total*
Agriculture	0.2	Private consumption	58.7
Industry, of which:	18.4	Public consumption	8.1
manufacturing	11.1	Investment	31.3
Services	81.4	Exports	139.2
		Imports	-137.4

Structure of manufacturing

	% of total		*% of total*
Agric. & food processing	11	Other	33
Textiles & clothing	35	Av. ann. increase in industrial	
Machinery & transport	21	output 1980–89	6.5%

Energy

	'000 TCE		
Total output	nil	% output exported	nil
Total consumption	13,182	% consumption imported	200.3
Consumption per head,			
kg coal equivalent	2,269		

Inflation and finance

Consumer price			*av. ann. increase 1988–92*
inflation 1995	8.7%	Narrow money (M1)	...
Av. ann. inflation 1989–95	9.4%	Broad money	...

Exchange rates

	end 1995		*June 1995*
HK$ per $	7.73	Effective rates	*1990 = 100*
HK$ per SDR	11.52	– nominal	...
HK$ per Ecu	10.13	– real	...

Principal exports[b]

	$bn fob		$bn fob
Clothing	9.4	Watches, clocks &	
Electrical machinery		photographic equipment	1.7
& apparatus	3.2	Total incl. others	**28.7**
Textiles	1.9		

Main export destinations[c]

	% of total		% of total
China	32.8	Germany	4.7
United States	23.2	United Kingdom	3.2
Japan	5.6		

Principal imports

	$bn cif		$bn cif
Consumer goods	66.5	Agric. products & foodstuffs	6.9
Raw materials & semi-		Fuels	2.9
manufactured products	55.9	Total incl. others	**161.8**
Capital goods	29.6		

Main origins of imports

	% of total		% of total
China	37.6	United States	7.1
Japan	15.6	Singapore	5.0
Taiwan	8.6	South Korea	4.6

Balance of payments, reserves and debt, $bn

Visible exports fob	151.4	Overall balance	...
Visible imports cif	-161.8	Change in reserves	6.3
Trade balance	-10.4	Level of reserves	
Invisibles inflows	32.1	end Dec.	49.3
Invisibles outflows	-19.0	No. months of import cover	3.3
Net transfers	...	Foreign debt	17.5
Current account balance	2.7	– as % of GDP	13.2
– as % of GDP	2.1	Debt service paid	2.0
Capital balance	...	Debt service ratio	1.1

Family life

No. of households	1.6m	Divorces per 1,000 pop.	1.0
Av. no. per household	3.4	Cost of living, Dec. 1995	
Marriages per 1,000 pop.	7.9	New York = 100	120

a 1993.
b Domestic.
c Including re-exports.

HUNGARY

Area	93,030 sq km	Currency	Forint (Ft)
Capital	Budapest		

People

Population	10.2m	Life expectancy: men	65 yrs
Pop. per sq km	109	women	74 yrs
Av. ann. growth		Adult literacy	99.0%
in pop. 1985–94	-0.4%	Fertility rate (per woman)	1.7
Pop. under 15	18.1%		
Pop. over 65	14.0%		*per 1,000 pop.*
No. of men per 100 women	91.9	Crude birth rate	12.4
Human Development Index	86	Crude death rate	14.5

The economy

GDP	Ft4,101bn	GDP per head	$3,839
GDP	$39bn	GDP per head in purchasing	
Av. ann. growth in real		power parity (USA=100)	28
GDP 1985–94	-1.0%		

Origins of GDP

	% of total
Agriculture	7.3
Industry, of which:	37.5
manufacturing	…
Services	55.2

Components of GDP

	% of total
Private consumption	74.1
Public consumption	13.1
Investment	23.0
Exports	34.6
Imports	-44.8

Structure of manufacturing

	% of total		*% of total*
Agric. & food processing	11	Other	53
Textiles & clothing	9	Av. ann. increase in industrial	
Machinery & transport	27	output 1980–93	-1.6%

Energy

	'000 TCE		
Total output	18,195	% output exported	9.6
Total consumption	33,785	% consumption imported	58.6
Consumption per head,			
kg coal equivalent	3,309		

Inflation and finance

Consumer price		*av. ann. increase 1989–94*	
inflation 1995	28.2%	Narrow money (M1)	17.6%
Av. ann. inflation 1989–95	24.5%	Broad money	21.5%

Exchange rates

	end 1995		*June 1995*
Ft per $	139.5	Effective rates	*1990 = 100*
Ft per SDR	207.3	– nominal	56.1
Ft per Ecu	182.7	– real	127.9

Principal exports

	$bn fob		*$bn fob*
Machinery & transport		Clothing & footwear	1.3
equipment	2.7	Chemicals	1.2
Food & food products	1.8	Total incl. others	**10.7**

Main export destinations

	% of total		*% of total*
Germany	28.2	Italy	8.5
Austria	10.9	Russia	7.5

Principal imports

	$bn cif		*$bn cif*
Machinery & transport		Fuels	1.5
equipment	5.0	Food & food products	0.8
Chemicals	1.8	Total incl. others	**14.6**

Main origins of imports

	% of total		*% of total*
Germany	23.4	Russia	11.9
Austria	12.0	Italy	7.0

Balance of payments, reserves and debt, $bn

Visible exports fob	7.6	Overall balance	-0.5
Visible imports fob	-11.4	Change in reserves	0.04
Trade balance	-3.7	Level of reserves	
Invisibles inflows	3.8	end Dec.	6.9
Invisibles outflows	-5.0	No. months of import cover	5.2
Net transfers	0.9	Foreign debt	28.0
Current account balance	-4.1	– as % of GDP	70.1
– as % of GDP	-10.4	Debt service paid	5.7
Capital balance	3.4	Debt service ratio	52.2

Family life

No. of households	3.9m	Divorces per 1,000 pop.	2.1
Av. no. per household	2.7	Cost of living, Dec. 1995	
Marriages per 1,000 pop.	5.5	New York = 100	57

a 1990.

INDIA

Area	3,287,263 sq km	Currency	Indian rupee (Rs)
Capital	New Delhi		

People

Population	913.6m	Life expectancy: men	63 yrs
Pop. per sq km	285	women	63 yrs
Av. ann. growth		Adult literacy	49.8%
in pop. 1985–94	2.0%	Fertility rate (per woman)	3.4
Pop. under 15	35.2%		
Pop. over 65	4.6%		*per 1,000 pop.*
No. of men per 100 women	106.9	Crude birth rate	26.6
Human Development Index	44	Crude death rate	8.9

The economy

GDP	Rs8,753bn	GDP per head	$305
GDP	$279bn	GDP per head in purchasing	
Av. ann. growth in real		power parity (USA=100)	5
GDP 1985–94	5.0%		

Origins of GDP[a]		Components of GDP[a]	
	% of total		*% of total*
Agriculture	31.8	Private consumption	69.5
Industry, of which:	26.9	Public consumption	11.0
manufacturing	…	Investment	20.2
Services	41.3	Exports	8.8
		Imports	-9.5

Structure of manufacturing

	% of total		*% of total*
Agric. & food processing	12	Other	48
Textiles & clothing	15	Av. ann. increase in industrial	
Machinery & transport	25	output 1980–93	6.2%

Energy

	'000 TCE		
Total output	275,954	% output exported	0.2
Total consumption	318,620	% consumption imported	21.0
Consumption per head,			
kg coal equivalent	353		

Inflation and finance

Consumer price		*av. ann. increase 1989–94*	
inflation 1995	10.2%	Narrow money (M1)	17.8%
Av. ann. inflation 1989–95	9.6%	Broad money	17.3%

Exchange rates

	end 1995		*June 1995*
Rs per $	35.18	Effective rates	*1990 = 100*
Rs per SDR	52.30	– nominal	…
Rs per Ecu	46.09	– real	…

Principal exports

	$bn fob		$bn fob
Gems & jewellery	4.0	Textiles	1.5
Engineering products[b]	3.0	Leather goods	1.3
Clothing	2.6	Total incl. others	**22.2**

Main export destinations

	% of total		% of total
United States	18.0	United Kingdom	6.2
Japan	7.8	OPEC	10.7
Germany	6.9		

Principal imports

	$bn cif		$bn cif
Crude oil & products	5.8	Chemicals	2.3
Capital goods	5.3		
Gems	2.6	Total incl. others	**23.9**

Main origins of imports

	% of total		% of total
United States	11.7	Japan	6.6
Belgium	8.0	United Kingdom	6.6
Germany	7.7	OPEC	22.4

Balance of payments[c], reserves and debt, $bn

Visible exports fob	20.0	Overall balance	1.1
Visible imports fob	-22.2	Change in reserves	9.5
Trade balance	-2.1	Level of reserves	
Invisibles inflows	5.3	end Dec.	24.2
Invisibles outflows	-10.6	No. months of import cover	6.7
Net transfers	3.3	Foreign debt	99.0
Current account balance	-4.1	– as % of GDP	34.2
– as % of GDP	-1.5	Debt service paid	10.5
Capital balance	4.1	Debt service ratio	26.3

Family life

No. of households	118.6m	Divorces per 1,000 pop.	...
Av. no. per household	5.5	Cost of living, Dec. 1995	
Marriages per 1,000 pop.	...	New York = 100	45

a Year ending March 31, 1994.
b Including electronics and computer software.
c 1992.

INDONESIA

Area	1,919,445 sq km	Currency	Rupiah (Rp)
Capital	Jakarta		

People

Population	189.9m	Life expectancy: men		63 yrs
Pop. per sq km	104		women	67 yrs
Av. ann. growth		Adult literacy		84.4%
in pop. 1985–94	1.6%	Fertility rate (per woman)		2.6
Pop. under 15	33.0%			
Pop. over 65	4.3%			*per 1,000 pop.*
No. of men per 100 women	99.5	Crude birth rate		23.1
Human Development Index	64	Crude death rate		7.6

The economy

GDP	Rp363,014bn	GDP per head	$883
GDP	$168bn	GDP per head in purchasing	
Av. ann. growth in real		power parity (USA=100)	12
GDP 1985–94	6.5%		

Origins of GDP		**Components of GDP**	
	% of total		*% of total*
Agriculture	17.4	Private consumption	56.5
Industry, of which:	39.5	Public consumption	8.2
manufacturing	23.9	Investment	34.0
Services	43.1	Exports	25.1
		Imports	-23.8

Structure of manufacturing

	% of total		*% of total*
Agric. & food processing	23	Other	47
Textiles & clothing	16	Av. ann. increase in industrial	
Machinery & transport	14	output 1980–93	6.3%

Energy

	'000 TCE		
Total output	243,796	% output exported	54.0
Total consumption	90,679	% consumption imported	19.8
Consumption per head,			
kg coal equivalent	473		

Inflation and finance

Consumer price		*av. ann. increase 1989–92*	
inflation 1995	9.4%	Narrow money (M1)	20.1%
Av. ann. inflation 1989–95	9.0%	Broad money	29.9%

Exchange rates

	end 1995		*June 1995*
Rp per $	2,380	Effective rates	*1990 = 100*
Rp per SDR	3,431	– nominal	...
Rp per Ecu	3,118	– real	...

Principal exports

	$bn fob		$bn fob
Petroleum & products	6.0	Natural gas	3.7
Textiles & clothing	5.8	Rubber & products	1.4
Timber	3.7	Total incl. others	**40.1**

Main export destinations

	% of total		% of total
Japan	27.3	Taiwan	4.1
United States	14.6	Netherlands	3.3
Singapore	10.4	China	3.3
South Korea	6.5		

Principal imports

	$bn cif		$bn cif
Machinery & transport equipment	13.5	Raw materials	2.7
		Fuels	2.4
Other manufactures	5.2	Food, drink & tobacco	2.0
Chemicals	4.9	Total incl. others	**32.0**

Main origins of imports

	% of total		% of total
Japan	24.2	Singapore	6.0
United States	11.2	Australia	4.8
Germany	7.7	Taiwan	4.5
South Korea	6.8		

Balance of payments, reserves and debt, $bn

Visible exports fob	40.2	Overall balance	0.8
Visible imports fob	-32.3	Change in reserves	0.8
Trade balance	7.9	Level of reserves	
Invisibles inflows	6.1	end Dec.	13.3
Invisibles outflows	-17.4	No. months of import cover	3.0
Net transfers	0.6	Foreign debt	96.5
Current account balance	-2.8	– as % of GDP	57.4
– as % of GDP	-1.7	Debt service paid	14.8
Capital balance	3.8	Debt service ratio	30.0

Family life

No. of households	39.7m	Divorces per 1,000 pop.	0.8
Av. no. per household	4.5	Cost of living, Dec. 1995	
Marriages per 1,000 pop.	7.4	New York = 100	88

IRAN

Area	1,648,000 sq km	Currency	Rial (IR)
Capital	Tehran		

People

Population	65.8m	Life expectancy: men		69 yrs
Pop. per sq km	41		women	70 yrs
Av. ann. growth		Adult literacy		56.0%
in pop. 1985–94	3.3%	Fertility rate (per woman)		4.5
Pop. under 15	43.5%			
Pop. over 65	3.9%			*per 1,000 pop.*
No. of men per 100 women	103.4	Crude birth rate		32.5
Human Development Index	77	Crude death rate		5.8

The economy

GDP	IR103,128bn	GDP per head	$896
GDP	$59bn	GDP per head in purchasing	
Av. ann. growth in real		power parity (USA=100)	23
GDP 1985–94	1.4%		

Origins of GDP[a]		Components of GDP[a]	
	% of total		*% of total*
Agriculture	23.9	Private consumption	55.0
Industry, of which:	38.2	Public consumption	14.5
manufacturing	...	Investment	29.1
Services	37.9	Exports	24.1
		Imports	-22.8

Structure of manufacturing

	% of total		*% of total*
Agric. & food processing	14	Other	43
Textiles & clothing	17	Av. ann. increase in industrial	
Metal products & machinery	26	output 1980–93	4.6%

Energy

	'000 TCE		
Total output	288,259	% output exported	66.3
Total consumption	111,368	% consumption imported	7.1
Consumption per head,			
kg coal equivalent	1,736		

Inflation and finance

Consumer price		*av. ann. increase 1989–94*	
inflation 1994	35.2%	Narrow money (M1)	21.9%
Av. ann. inflation 1989–94	21.4%	Broad money	24.8%

Exchange rates

	end 1995		*June 1995*
IR per $	1,478	Effective rates	*1990 = 100*
IR per SDR	2,598	– nominal	...
IR per Ecu	1,936	– real	...

Principal exports[a]

	$bn fob		$bn fob
Oil & gas	14.3	Fruit	0.7
Carpets	1.4	Total incl. others	**18.1**

Main export destinations

	% of total		% of total
Japan	13.0	France	4.7
South Korea	6.1	Greece	4.3
Italy	4.8	Germany	3.9
Netherlands	4.8		

Principal imports[a]

	$bn cif		$bn cif
Raw materials & intermediate goods	12.6	Consumer goods	2.2
Capital goods	5.1	Total incl. others	**20.0**

Main origins of imports

	% of total		% of total
Germany	14.4	Italy	6.5
UAE	8.9	United Kingdom	4.0
Japan	8.3	United States	3.0
France	7.5		

Balance of payments[a], reserves and debt, $bn

Visible exports fob	18.1	Overall balance	0.2
Visible imports fob	-19.3	Change in reserves	…
Trade balance	-1.2	Level of reserves	
Invisibles inflows	1.2	end Dec.	…
Invisibles outflows	-5.7	No. months of import cover	…
Net transfers	1.5	Foreign debt	22.7
Current account balance	-4.2	– as % of GDP[b]	14.7
– as % of GDP	-7.2	Debt service paid	4.3
Capital balance	5.6	Debt service ratio	21.8

Family life

No. of households	10.8m	Divorces per 1,000 pop.	0.7
Av. no. per household	5.2	Cost of living, Dec. 1995	
Marriages per 1,000 pop.	7.4	New York = 100	35

a   Iranian year ending March 20, 1994.
b   1992.

IRAQ

Area	438,317 sq km	Currency	Iraqi dinar (ID)
Capital	Baghdad		

People

Population	20.0m	Life expectancy: men	67 yrs
Pop. per sq km	47	women	70 yrs
Av. ann. growth		Adult literacy	62.5%
in pop. 1985–94	2.9%	Fertility rate (per woman)	5.3
Pop. under 15	43.6%		
Pop. over 65	3.0%		*per 1,000 pop.*
No. of men per 100 women	103.7	Crude birth rate	35.8
Human Development Index	62	Crude death rate	5.9

The economy

GDP[a]	ID5.6bn	GDP per head[a]	$902
GDP[a]	$18bn	GDP per head in purchasing	
Av. ann. growth in real		power parity (USA=100)[a]	14
GDP 1985–94	-9.3%		

Origins of GDP[b]		Components of GDP[c]	
	% of total		*% of total*
Agriculture	5.1	Private consumption	52.7
Industry, of which:	72.9	Public consumption	30.0
manufacturing	11.6	Investment	21.9
Services	22.0	Exports	24.6
		Imports	-29.1

Structure of manufacturing

	% of total		*% of total*
Agric. & food processing	...	Other	...
Textiles & clothing	...	Av. ann. increase in industrial	
Machinery & transport	...	output 1980–92	4.4

Energy

	'000 TCE		
Total output	50,350	% output exported	15.4
Total consumption	31,827	% consumption imported	0.0
Consumption per head,			
kg coal equivalent	1,636		

Inflation and finance[a]

Consumer price			*av. ann. increase 1988–92*
inflation 1994	60%	Narrow money (M1)	...
Av. ann. inflation 1989–94	48.8%	Broad money	...

Exchange rates

	end 1995		*June 1995*
ID per $	0.31	Effective rates	*1990 = 100*
ID per SDR	0.46	– nominal	93.8
ID per Ecu	0.41	– real	...

Principal exports[abe]

	$bn fob		$bn fob
Crude oil	14.5	Total incl. others	**14.6**

Main export destinations[ad]

	% of total		% of total
United States	28.5	Netherlands	7.4
Brazil	9.9	Spain	4.6
Turkey	9.8	France	3.5
Japan	7.8		

Principal imports[a]

	$bn cif		$bn cif
Civilian goods	5.0		
Military goods	2.7	Total incl. others	**7.7**

Main origins of imports[ad]

	% of total		% of total
Germany	13.3	United Kingdom	8.4
United States	10.7	Japan	4.5
Turkey	9.2	Italy	4.5
France	8.7	Brazil	3.1

Balance of payments[be], reserves and debt[e], $bn

Visible exports fob	9.5	Overall balance	...
Visible imports fob	-5.1	Change in reserves	...
Trade balance	4.4	Level of reserves	
Invisibles inflows	...	end Dec.	...
Invisibles outflows	...	No. months of import cover	...
Net transfers	...	Foreign debt	82.9
Current account balance	-0.9	– as % of GDP	...
– as % of GDP	...	Debt service	161
Capital balance	...	Debt service ratio	...

Family life

No. of households	2.1m	Divorces per 1,000 pop.	0.1
Av. no. per household	7.1	Cost of living, Dec. 1995	
Marriages per 1,000 pop.	8.5	New York = 100	...

a Estimate.
b 1989.
c 1985.
d 1990.
e Trade, balance of payments and debt data for Iraq are estimates based on limited
   and inconsistent information.

IRELAND

Area	70,282 sq km	Currency	Punt (I£)
Capital	Dublin		

People

Population	3.5m	Life expectancy: men	73 yrs
Pop. per sq km	51	women	79 yrs
Av. ann. growth		Adult literacy	99.0%
in pop. 1985–94	nil	Fertility rate (per woman)	2.1
Pop. under 15	24.4%		
Pop. over 65	11.2%		*per 1,000 pop.*
No. of men per 100 women	99.7	Crude birth rate	15.1
Human Development Index	92	Crude death rate	8.8

The economy

GDP	I£32bn	GDP per head	$13,625
GDP	$48bn	GDP per head in purchasing	
Av. ann. growth in real		power parity (USA=100)	54
GDP 1985–94	4.2%		

Origins of GDP		**Components of GDP**	
	% of total		*% of total*
Agriculture	9.0	Private consumption	56.0
Industry, of which:	38.0	Public consumption	16.0
manufacturing	...	Investment	14.0
Services	53.0	Exports	72.0
		Imports	-58.0

Structure of manufacturing

	% of total		*% of total*
Agric. & food processing	27	Other	41.3
Textiles & clothing	3	Av. ann. increase in industrial	
Machinery & transport	27	output 1980–89	-4.3%

Energy

	'000 TCE		
Total output	5,170	% output exported	21.4
Total consumption	14,621	% consumption imported	74.6
Consumption per head,			
kg coal equivalent	3,309		

Inflation and finance

Consumer price		*av. ann. increase 1989–94*	
inflation 1995	2.5%	Narrow money (M1)	7.1%
Av. ann. inflation 1989–95	2.8%	Broad money	11.1%

Exchange rates

	end 1995		*June 1995*
I£ per $	0.62	Effective rates	*1990 = 100*
I£ per SDR	0.93	– nominal	97.4
I£ per Ecu	0.82	– real	...

Principal exports

	$bn fob		$bn fob
Machinery & transport equipment	10.2	Agric. products & foodstuffs	6.3
Chemicals	7.1	Total incl. others	**34.1**

Main export destinations

	% of total		% of total
United Kingdom	27.5	Netherlands	5.5
Germany	14.1	Belgium/Luxembourg	3.9
France	9.2	Italy	3.8
United States	8.4		

Principal imports

	$bn cif		$bn cif
Machinery & transport equipment	9.9	Manufactured goods	3.0
Chemicals	3.3	Total incl. others	**25.7**

Main origins of imports

	% of total		% of total
United Kingdom	36.3	France	3.8
United States	18.3	Netherlands	2.8
Germany	7.1	Italy	2.2
Japan	4.8		

Balance of payments, reserves and aid, $bn

Visible exports fob	33.6	Capital balance	-4.2
Visible imports fob	-24.0	Overall balance	-0.2
Trade balance	9.5	Change in reserves	0.2
Invisibles inflows	6.8	Level of reserves	
Invisibles outflows	-15.4	end Dec.	6.3
Net transfers	2.3	No. months of import cover	1.9
Current account balance	3.2	Aid given	0.11
– as % of GDP	6.6	– as % of GDP	0.25

Family life

No. of households	0.9m	Divorces per 1,000 pop.	…
Av. no. per household	3.6	Cost of living, Dec. 1995	
Marriages per 1,000 pop.	4.5	New York = 100	103

ISRAEL

Area	20,770 sq km	Currency	New Shekel (NIS)
Capital	Jerusalem		

People

Population	5.4m	Life expectancy: men		75 yrs
Pop. per sq km	267	women		79 yrs
Av. ann. growth		Adult literacy		95.0%
in pop. 1985–94	2.7%	Fertility rate (per woman)		2.7
Pop. under 15	29.1%			
Pop. over 65	9.5%			*per 1,000 pop.*
No. of men per 100 women	98.3	Crude birth rate		19.6
Human Development Index	91	Crude death rate		6.5

The economy

GDP	NIS235bn	GDP per head	$14,412
GDP	$78bn	GDP per head in purchasing	
Av. ann. growth in real		power parity (USA=100)	62
GDP 1985–94	4.7%		

Origins of NDP		**Components of GDP**	
	% of total		*% of total*
Agriculture	2.6	Private consumption	64.1
Industry, of which:	30.4	Public consumption	27.5
manufacturing	21.5	Investment	21.3
Services	67.0	Exports	32.6
		Imports	-45.5

Structure of manufacturing[a]

	% of total		*% of total*
Agric. & food processing	14	Other	46
Textiles & clothing	9	Av. ann. increase in industrial	
Machinery & transport	31	output 1980–90	…

Energy

	'000 TCE		
Total output	44	% output exported[b]	8,936.4
Total consumption	17,239	% consumption imported[b]	140.3
Consumption per head,			
kg coal equivalent	3,281		

Inflation and finance

			av. ann. increase 1989–94
Consumer price			
inflation 1995	10.0%	Narrow money (M1)	25.0%
Av. ann. inflation 1989–95	14.4%	Broad money	21.6%

Exchange rates

	end 1995		*June 1995*
			1990 = 100
NIS per $	3.14	Effective rates	
NIS per SDR	4.46	– nominal	…
NIS per Ecu	4.11	– real	…

Principal exports

	$bn fob		$bn fob
Metal, machinery & electronics	5.7	Textiles & clothing	1.0
		Agric. products & foodstuffs	0.6
Diamonds	4.4		
Chemicals	2.1	Total incl. others	**16.7**

Main export destinations

	% of total		% of total
United States	31.6	United Kingdom	5.1
Japan	5.9	Germany	5.0
Belgium/Luxembourg	5.5		

Principal imports

	$bn cif		$bn cif
Investment goods	4.5	Durable consumer products	1.5
Diamonds	4.1		
Energy & products	1.7		
Non-durable consumer products	1.5	Total incl. others	**22.5**

Main origins of imports

	% of total		% of total
United States	17.9	United Kingdom	8.7
Belgium/Luxembourg	12.7	Italy	7.8
Germany	10.4		

Balance of payments, reserves and debt[c], $bn

Visible exports fob	16.6	Overall balance	0.1
Visible imports fob	-22.7	Change in reserves	0.4
Trade balance	-6.1	Level of reserves	
Invisibles inflows	7.6	end Dec.	6.8
Invisibles outflows	-11.1	No. months of import cover	2.4
Net transfers	5.7	Foreign debt	26.5
Current account balance	-4.0	– as % of GDP	40.7
– as % of GDP	-5.1	Debt service	3.2
Capital balance	2.4	Debt service ratio	14.4

Family life

No. of households	1.1m	Divorces per 1,000 pop.	1.3
Av. no. per household	3.5	Cost of living, Dec. 1995	
Marriages per 1,000 pop.	6.2	New York = 100	107

a 1992.
b Energy trade data are distorted by transitory and oil refining activities.
c 1993.

ITALY

Area	301,245 sq km	Currency	Lira (L)
Capital	Rome		

People

Population	57.2m	Life expectancy: men	75 yrs
Pop. per sq km	190	women	81 yrs
Av. ann. growth		Adult literacy	97.4%
in pop. 1985–94	0.1%	Fertility rate (per woman)	1.3
Pop. under 15	15.0%		
Pop. over 65	16.0%		*per 1,000 pop.*
No. of men per 100 women	94.6	Crude birth rate	9.6
Human Development Index	91	Crude death rate	9.9

The economy

GDP	L1,775,252bn	GDP per head	$19,268
GDP	$1,101bn	GDP per head in purchasing	
Av. ann. growth in real		power parity (USA=100)	76
GDP 1985–94	2.0%		

Origins of GDP		Components of GDP	
	% of total		*% of total*
Agriculture	3.3	Private consumption	62.8
Industry, of which:	28.2	Public consumption	17.3
manufacturing	23.0	Investment	17.0
Services	68.5	Exports	23.0
		Imports	-20.1

Structure of manufacturing

	% of total		*% of total*
Agric. & food processing	10	Other	43
Textiles & clothing	14	Av. ann. increase in industrial	
Machinery & transport	33	output 1980–93	2.2%

Energy

	'000 TCE		
Total output	41,845	% output exported	75.6
Total consumption	230,277	% consumption imported	87.6
Consumption per head,			
kg coal equivalent	4,029		

Inflation and finance

			av. ann. increase 1989–94
Consumer price			
inflation 1995	5.4%	Narrow money (M1)	7.3%
Av. ann. inflation 1989–95	5.4%	Broad money	7.4%

Exchange rates

	end 1995		*June 1995*
		Effective rates	*1990 = 100*
L per $	1,585		
L per SDR	2,356	– nominal	67.4
L per Ecu	2,083	– real	69.5

Principal exports

	$bn fob		$bn fob
Industrial & agricultural machinery	32.2	Electrical equipment	17.1
		Chemicals	15.0
Textiles & clothing	22.7		
Transport equipment	17.9	Total incl. others	**189.6**

Main export destinations

	% of total		% of total
Germany	19.0	Spain	4.6
France	13.1	Switzerland	3.8
United States	7.8		
United Kingdom	6.5		

Principal imports

	$bn cif		$bn cif
Chemicals	23.5	Metals	15.8
Transport equipment	17.5	Energy	12.0
Electrical equipment	16.4	Total incl. others	**167.4**

Main origins of imports

	% of total		% of total
Germany	19.2	Netherlands	5.7
France	13.6	Switzerland	4.7
United Kingdom	6.1	United States	4.6

Balance of payments, reserves and aid, $bn

Visible exports fob	189.8	Capital balance	-13.0
Visible imports fob	-154.3	Overall balance	1.6
Trade balance	35.5	Change in reserves	4.2
Invisibles inflows	88.3	Level of reserves	
Invisibles outflows	-102.1	end Dec.	57.8
Net transfers	-7.1	No. months of import cover	2.7
Current account balance	14.6	Aid given	2.71
– as % of GDP	1.3	– as % of GDP	0.27

Family life

No. of households	19.8m	Divorces per 1,000 pop.	0.4
Av. no. per household	2.8	Cost of living, Dec. 1995	
Marriages per 1,000 pop.	4.8	New York = 100	91

JAPAN

Area	377,727 sq km	Currency	Yen (¥)
Capital	Tokyo		

People

Population	124.8m	Life expectancy:	men	77 yrs
Pop. per sq km	331		women	83 yrs
Av. ann. growth		Adult literacy		99.0%
in pop. 1985–94	0.4%	Fertility rate (per woman)		1.5
Pop. under 15	16.3%			
Pop. over 65	14.1%		*per 1,000 pop.*	
No. of men per 100 women	96.4	Crude birth rate		10.5
Human Development Index	94	Crude death rate		8.3

The economy

GDP	¥441,649bn	GDP per head	$34,629
GDP	$4,321bn	GDP per head in purchasing	
Av. ann. growth in real		power parity (USA=100)	86
GDP 1985–94	3.1%		

Origins of NDP[a]		Components of GDP	
	% of total		*% of total*
Agriculture	2.2	Private consumption	58.1
Industry, of which:	41.1	Public consumption	9.6
manufacturing	27.9	Investment	29.7
Services	61.1	Exports	9.4
		Imports	-7.1

Structure of manufacturing

	% of total		*% of total*
Agric. & food processing	10	Other	47
Textiles & clothing	5	Av. ann. increase in industrial	
Machinery & transport	38	output 1980–93	5.0%

Energy

	'000 TCE		
Total output	118,252	% output exported[b]	9.1
Total consumption	597,294	% consumption imported[b]	89.1
Consumption per head,			
kg coal equivalent	4,796		

Inflation and finance

Consumer price		*av. ann. increase 1989–94*	
inflation 1995	-0.1%	Narrow money (M1)	4.8%
Av. ann. inflation 1989–95	1.8%	Broad money	5.1%

Exchange rates

	end 1995		*June 1995*
¥ per $	102.8	Effective rates	*1990 = 100*
¥ per SDR	152.9	– nominal	170.0
¥ per Ecu	134.7	– real	163.8

Principal exports

	$bn fob		$bn fob
Motor vehicles	56.9	Iron & steel products	14.8
Office machinery	29.1		
Chemicals	23.7		
Scientific & optical equipment	15.9	Total incl. others	**395.6**

Main export destinations

	% of total		% of total
United States	29.7	Taiwan	6.0
Hong Kong	6.5	Singapore	5.0
South Korea	6.2		

Principal imports

	$bn cif		$bn cif
Energy	47.8	Chemicals	20.2
Agric. products & foodstuffs	46.7	Wood	9.7
Textiles	20.4	Total incl. others	**274.7**

Main origins of imports

	% of total		% of total
United States	22.8	South Korea	4.9
China	10.0	South Korea	4.9
Australia	5.0	Indonesia	4.7

Balance of payments, reserves and aid, $bn

Visible exports fob	384.2	Capital balance	-86.2
Visible imports fob	-238.3	Overall balance	25.3
Trade balance	145.9	Change in reserves	27.2
Invisibles inflows	215.9	Level of reserves	
Invisibles outflows	-225.1	end Dec.	135.1
Net transfers	-7.5	No. months of import cover	3.5
Current account balance	129.2	Aid given	13.24
– as % of GDP	3.0	– as % of GDP	0.29

Family life

No. of households	40.7m	Divorces per 1,000 pop.	1.4
Av. no. per household	3.0	Cost of living, Dec. 1995	
Marriages per 1,000 pop.	6.4	New York = 100	199

a 1992.
b Energy trade data are distorted by transitory and oil refining activities.

KENYA

Area	582,646 sq km	Currency	Kenyan shilling (KSh)
Capital	Nairobi		

People

Population	26.0m	Life expectancy: men		53 yrs
Pop. per sq km	49	women		55 yrs
Av. ann. growth		Adult literacy		70.5%
in pop. 1985–94	2.9%	Fertility rate (per woman)		5.8%
Pop. under 15	47.7%			
Pop. over 65	2.9%			*per 1,000 pop*
No. of men per 100 women	100.3	Crude birth rate		42.8
Human Development Index	48	Crude death rate		11.8

The economy

GDP	KSh370bn	GDP per head	$255
GDP	$6.6bn	GDP per head in purchasing	
Av. ann. growth in real		power parity (USA=100)	6
GDP 1985–94	3.5%		

Origins of GDP		**Components of GDP**	
	% of total		*% of total*
Agriculture	29.1	Private consumption	58.7
Industry, of which:	...	Public consumption	17.5
manufacturing	10.5	Investment	20.6
Other	60.4	Exports	38.0
		Imports	-34.8

Structure of manufacturing

	% of total		*% of total*
Agric. & food processing	39	Other	42
Textiles & clothing	9	Av. ann. increase in industrial	
Machinery & transport	10	output 1980–93	3.8%

Energy

	'000 TCE		
Total output	701	% output exported[a]	124.4
Total consumption	3,068	% consumption imported[a]	125.6
Consumption per head,			
kg coal equivalent	116		

Inflation and finance

		av. ann. increase 1989–94	
Consumer price			
inflation 1994	29.0%	Narrow money (M1)	21.2%
Av. ann. inflation 1989–94	25.0%	Broad money	21.4%

Exchange rates

	end 1995		*June 1995*
KSh per $	55.85	Effective rates	*1990 = 100*
KSh per SDR	83.02	– nominal	...
KSh per Ecu	73.16	– real	...

Principal exports

	$m fob		$m fob
Tea	301	Petroleum products	90
Coffee	233		
Horticultural products	148	Total incl. others	**1,528**

Main export destinations

	% of total		% of total
Uganda	12.7	Tanzania	10.6
United Kingdom	11.6	Germany	7.8

Principal imports

	$m cif		$m cif
Industrial machinery	290	Iron & steel	111
Petroleum & products	257		
Motor vehicles & chassis	170	Total incl. others	**2,053**

Main origins of imports

	% of total		% of total
United Kingdom	13.2	Japan	8.6
UAE	11.2	United States	6.6

Balance of payments[b], reserves and debt, $bn

Visible exports fob	1.3	Overall balance	0.4
Visible imports fob	-1.5	Change in reserves	0.2
Trade balance	-0.2	Level of reserves	
Invisibles inflows	1.1	end Dec.	0.6
Invisibles outflows	-0.9	No. months of import cover	2.5
Net transfers	0.2	Foreign debt	7.3
Current account balance	0.1	– as % of GDP	112.4
– as % of GDP	1.8	Debt service paid	0.9
Capital balance	0.03	Debt service ratio	33.3

Family life

No. of households	3.0m	Divorces per 1,000 pop.	...
Av. no. per household	5.1	Cost of living, Dec. 1995	
Marriages per 1,000 pop.	...	New York = 100	56

a   Energy trade data are distorted by transitory and oil refining activities.
b   1993.

MALAYSIA

Area	332,665 sq km	Currency	Malaysian dollar/ringgit
Capital	Kuala Lumpur		(M$)

People

Population	19.5m	Life expectancy: men		70 yrs
Pop. per sq km	61	women		74 yrs
Av. ann. growth		Adult literacy		80.0%
in pop. 1985–94	2.5%	Fertility rate (per woman)		3.2
Pop. under 15	38.0%			
Pop. over 65	3.9%			*per 1,000 pop.*
No. of men per 100 women	101.8	Crude birth rate		25.2
Human Development Index	82	Crude death rate		4.8

The economy

GDP	M$181bn	GDP per head	$3,522
GDP	$69bn	GDP per head in purchasing	
Av. ann. growth in real		power parity (USA=100)	33
GDP 1985–94	7.5%		

Origins of GDP		**Components of GDP**	
	% of total		*% of total*
Agriculture	14.5	Private consumption	50.1
Industry, of which:	43.3	Public consumption	13.0
manufacturing	31.7	Investment	38.4
Services	42.2	Exports	89.9
		Imports	-91.4

Structure of manufacturing

	% of total		*% of total*
Agric. & food processing	10	Other	50
Textiles & clothing	6	Av. ann. increase in industrial	
Machinery & transport	34	output 1980–93	8.2%

Energy

	'000 TCE		
Total output	73,948	% output exported	73.9
Total consumption	33,973	% consumption imported	46.7
Consumption per head,			
kg coal equivalent	1,765		

Inflation and finance

Consumer price		*av. ann. increase 1989–93*	
inflation 1995	3.4%	Narrow money (M1)	20.7%
Av. ann. inflation 1989–95	3.6%	Broad money	19.5%

Exchange rates

	end 1995		*June 1995*
M$ per $	2.54	Effective rates	*1990 = 100*
M$ per SDR	3.78	– nominal	95.9
M$ per Ecu	3.33	– real	99.2

Principal exports

	$bn fob		$bn fob
Electronics & electrical		Timber & products	2.6
machinery	29.1	Textiles	2.3
Petroleum & products	3.4		
Palm oil	3.2	Total incl. others	**58.7**

Main export destinations

	% of total		% of total
United States	21.2	Hong Kong	4.6
Singapore	20.7	United Kingdom	3.8
Japan	11.9	Thailand	3.8

Principal imports

	$bn cif		$bn cif
Manufacturing supplies	21.6	Consumer durables	2.1
Machinery & transport		Food, beverages & tobacco	1.8
equipment	10.2		
Metal products	3.2	Total incl. others	**59.5**

Main origins of imports

	% of total		% of total
Japan	26.7	Germany	5.5
United States	16.7	Taiwan	5.1
Singapore	14.1	United Kingdom	3.2

Balance of payments, reserves and debt, $bn

Visible exports fob	56.9	Overall balance	-3.2
Visible imports fob	-55.3	Change in reserves	-1.8
Trade balance	1.6	Level of reserves	
Invisibles inflows	8.9	end Dec.	26.3
Invisibles outflows	-14.8	No. months of import cover	4.5
Net transfers	0.2	Foreign debt	24.8
Current account balance	-4.1	as % of GDP	36.9
– as % of GDP	-6.0	Debt service paid	5.0
Capital balance	1.5	Debt service ratio	7.7

Family life

No. households	2.5m	Divorces per 1,000 pop.	...
Av. no. per household	5.2	Cost of living, Dec. 1995	
Marriages per 1,000 pop.	3.2	New York = 100	80

MEXICO

Area	1,972,545 sq km	Currency	Mexican peso (P$
Capital	Mexico City		

People

Population	91.9m	Life expectancy: men	69 y
Pop. per sq km	48	women	75 y
Av. ann. growth		Adult literacy	88.6
in pop. 1985–94	2.2%	Fertility rate (per woman)	2
Pop. under 15	35.9%		
Pop. over 65	4.2%		*per 1,000 po*
No. of men per 100 women	99.5	Crude birth rate	24
Human Development Index	84	Crude death rate	5

The economy

GDP	1,245bn New pesos	GDP per head	$4,0
GDP	$369bn	GDP per head in purchasing	
Av. ann. growth in real		power parity (USA=100)	
GDP 1985–94	1.9%		

Origins of GDP

Components of GDP

	% of total		*% of tot*
Agriculture	7.4	Private consumption	71
Industry, of which:	33.0	Public consumption	11
manufacturing	22.5	Investment	21
Services	59.6	Exports	12
		Imports	-18

Structure of manufacturing

	% of total		*% of tot*
Agric. & food processing	24	Other	
Textiles & clothing	5	Av. ann. increase in industrial	
Machinery & transport	25	output 1980–93	1.7

Energy

	'000 TCE		
Total output	275,260	% output exported	40
Total consumption	168,592	% consumption imported	8
Consumption per head,			
kg coal equivalent	1,873		

Inflation and finance

Consumer price			*av. ann. increase 1989–9*
inflation 1995	35.0%	Narrow money (M1)	42.0
Av. ann. inflation 1989–95	19.2%	Broad money	34.7

Exchange rates

	end 1995		*June 199*
PS per $	7.64	Effective rates	*1990 = 10*
PS per SDR	11.36	– nominal	
PS per Ecu	10.01	– real	

Principal exports

	$bn fob		$bn fob
Manufactured products	50.4	Agric. products & foodstuffs	2.7
Crude oil	6.6	Total incl. others	**60.8**

Main export destinations

	% of total		% of total
United States	84.9	Spain	1.4
Canada	2.4	France	0.7
Japan	1.6		

Principal imports

	$bn cif		$bn cif
Industrial supplies	56.5	Consumer goods	9.5
Capital goods	13.3	Total	**79.4**

Main origins of imports

	% of total		% of total
United States	69.4	Canada	1.9
Japan	4.6	France	1.8
Germany	3.8		

Balance of payments, reserves and debt, $bn

Visible exports fob	60.9	Overall balance	-17.7
Visible imports fob	-79.3	Change in reserves	-18.9
Trade balance	-18.5	Level of reserves	
Invisibles inflows	13.2	end Dec.	6.4
Invisibles outflows	-27.5	No. months of import cover	0.9
Net transfers	4.0	Foreign debt	128.3
Current account balance	-28.8	– as % of GDP	35.2
– as % of GDP	-7.8	Debt service paid	19.0
Capital balance	12.8	Debt service ratio	33.9

Family life

No. of households	16.2m	Divorces per 1,000 pop.	0.6
Av. no. per household	5.0	Cost of living, Dec. 1995	
Marriages per 1,000 pop.	7.3	New York = 100	62

MOROCCO

Area	446,550 sq km	Currency	Dirham (Dh)
Capital	Rabat		

People

Population	26.5m	Life expectancy: men	64 yrs
Pop. per sq km	61	women	68 yrs
Av. ann. growth		Adult literacy	52.5%
in pop. 1985–94	2.2%	Fertility rate (per woman)	3.1
Pop. under 15	36.1%		
Pop. over 65	4.1%		*per 1,000 pop.*
No. of men per 100 women	100.2	Crude birth rate	25.5
Human Development Index	55	Crude death rate	7.1

The economy

GDP	Dh276bn	GDP per head	$1,145
GDP	$30bn	GDP per head in purchasing	
Av. ann. growth in real		power parity (USA=100)	14
GDP 1985–94	3.8%		

Origins of GDP[a]

	% of total
Agriculture	14.3
Industry, of which:	32.4
manufacturing	18.0
Services	53.3

Components of GDP[a]

	% of total
Private consumption	66.0
Public consumption	18.2
Investment	21.2
Exports	22.5
Imports	-27.9

Structure of manufacturing

	% of total		% of total
Agric. & food processing	25	Other	51
Textiles & clothing	18	Av. ann. increase in industrial	
Machinery & transport	6	output 1980–93	2.8%

Energy

	'000 TCE		
Total output	705	% output exported	0.0
Total consumption	10,150	% consumption imported	108.2
Consumption per head,			
kg coal equivalent	391		

Inflation and finance

Consumer price			*av. ann. increase 1989–94*
inflation 1994	5.1%	Narrow money (M1)	11.2%
Av. ann. inflation 1989–94	5.7%	Broad money	12.7%

Exchange rates

	end 1995		June 1995
			1990 = 100
Dh per $	8.47	Effective rates	
Dh per SDR	12.59	– nominal	118.7
Dh per Ecu	11.10	– real	109.6

Principal exports[a]

	$bn fob		$bn fob
Consumer goods	1.1	Mineral ores	0.4
Agricultural products &		Capital goods	0.2
foodstuffs	1.0		
Semi-finished goods	0.9	Total incl. others	**3.7**

Main export destinations

	% of total		% of total
France	33.4	Italy	5.9
Germany	8.8	United Kingdom	4.8
Spain	8.0		

Principal imports[a]

	$bn cif		$bn cif
Industrial equipment	1.8	Energy & fuels	1.0
Semi-manufactured goods	1.5	Consumer goods	0.7
Agric. products & foodstuffs	1.0	Total incl. others	**7.2**

Main origins of imports

	% of total		% of total
France	27.7	Italy	7.7
Germany	9.8	United States	5.2
Spain	8.8		

Balance of payments, reserves and debt, $bn

Visible exports fob	5.5	Overall balance	0.5
Visible imports fob	-7.6	Change in reserves	0.7
Trade balance	-2.1	Level of reserves	
Invisibles inflows	2.2	end Dec.	4.6
Invisibles outflows	-3.1	No. months of import cover	5.6
Net transfers	2.3	Foreign debt	22.5
Current account balance	-0.7	– as % of GDP	76.3
– as % of GDP	-2.4	Debt service paid	2.9
Capital balance	1.2	Debt service ratio	32.1

Family life

No. of households	3.4m	Divorces per 1,000 pop.	...
Av. no. per household	5.9	Cost of living, Dec. 1995	
Marriages per 1,000 pop.	...	New York = 100	...

1993.

NETHERLANDS

Area[a]	41,526 sq km	Currency	Guilder (F
Capital	Amsterdam		

People

Population	15.4m	Life expectancy: men	75 yr
Pop. per sq km	380	women	81 y
Av. ann. growth		Adult literacy	99.0%
in pop. 1985–94	0.7%	Fertility rate (per woman)	1
Pop. under 15	18.4%		
Pop. over 65	13.2%		*per 1,000 po*
No. of men per 100 women	98.1	Crude birth rate	12
Human Development Index	94	Crude death rate	8

The economy

GDP	Fl615bn	GDP per head	$21,97
GDP	$338bn	GDP per head in purchasing	
Av. ann. growth in real		power parity (USA=100)	7
GDP 1985–94	2.5%		

Origins of GDP

	% of total
Agriculture	3.6
Industry, of which:	28.5
manufacturing	22.3
Services	67.9

Components of GDP

	% of tota
Private consumption	60
Public consumption	14
Investment	19.
Exports	51
Imports	-46

Structure of manufacturing

	% of total		% of tota
Agric. & food processing	21	Other	5
Textiles & clothing	3	Av. ann. increase in industrial	
Machinery & transport	24	output 1980–89	1.1%

Energy

	'000 TCE		
Total output	106,194	% output exported[c]	110.
Total consumption	112,816	% consumption imported[c]	117.
Consumption per head,			
kg coal equivalent	7,381		

Inflation and finance

		av. ann. increase 1989–9	
Consumer price			
inflation 1995	1.9%	Narrow money (M1)	5.8%
Av. ann. inflation 1989–95	2.6%	Broad money	6.0%

Exchange rates

	end 1995		June 199
Fl per $	1.60	Effective rates	1990 = 10
Fl per SDR	2.38	– nominal	109
Fl per Ecu	2.06	– real	108.

Principal exports

	$bn fob		$bn fob
Machinery & transport equipment	36.5	Fuels	10.8
		Raw materials, oils & fats	6.1
Food, drink & tobacco	29.2		
Chemicals & plastics	25.3	Total incl. others	**146.1**

Main export destinations

	% of total		% of total
Germany	24.2	United Kingdom	8.0
Belgium/Luxembourg	11.2	Italy	4.4
France	9.0	United States	3.6

Principal imports

	$bn cif		$bn cif
Machinery & transport equipment	41.0	Fuels	9.0
		Raw materials, oils & fats	8.1
Chemicals & plastics	16.4		
Food, drink & tobacco	15.8	Total incl. others	**130.5**

Main origins of imports

	% of total		% of total
Germany	18.3	United Kingdom	7.2
Belgium/Luxembourg	9.3	France	5.9
United States	7.4	Japan	3.3

Balance of payments, reserves and aid, $bn

Visible exports fob	137.6	Capital balance	-8.2
Visible imports fob	-123.1	Overall balance	0.6
Trade balance	14.5	Change in reserves	2.8
Invisibles inflows	96.1	Level of reserves	
Invisibles outflows	-93.8	end Dec.	47.9
Net transfers	-5.3	No. months of import cover	2.6
Current account balance	11.5	Aid given	2.52
– as % of GDP	3.4	– as % of GDP	0.76

Family life

No. of households	5.9m	Divorces per 1,000 pop.	2.0
Av. no. per household	2.5	Cost of living, Dec. 1995	
Marriages per 1,000 pop.	5.8	New York = 100	118

a Includes water.
b 1992.
c Energy trade data are distorted due to transitory and oil refining activities.

NEW ZEALAND

Area	270,534 sq km	Currency New Zealand dollar (NZ$)	
Capital	Wellington		

People

Population	3.5m	Life expectancy: men	73 yrs
Pop. per sq km	13	women	79 yrs
Av. ann. growth		Adult literacy	99.0%
in pop. 1985–94	0.9%	Fertility rate (per woman)	2.1
Pop. under 15	23.4%		
Pop. over 65	11.3%	*per 1,000 pop.*	
No. of men per 100 women	97.6	Crude birth rate	16.0
Human Development Index	92	Crude death rate	8.2

The economy

GDP	NZ$79bn	GDP per head	$13,191
GDP	$47bn	GDP per head in purchasing	
Av. ann. growth in real		power parity (USA=100)	63
GDP 1985–94	1.0%		

Origins of GDP[a]

	% of total		
		Components of GDP[b]	
			% of total
Agriculture	7.9	Private consumption	59.7
Industry, of which:	25.8	Public consumption	15.4
manufacturing	17.4	Investment	20.9
Services	66.3	Exports	30.8
		Imports	-27.7

Structure of manufacturing

	% of total		% of total
Agric. & food processing	27	Other	51
Textiles & clothing	8	Av. ann. increase in industrial	
Machinery & transport	14	output 1980–93	0.8%

Energy

	'000 TCE		
Total output	16,923	% output exported	16.4
Total consumption	19,273	% consumption imported	29.1
Consumption per head,			
kg coal equivalent	5,530		

Inflation and finance

Consumer price		*av. ann. increase 1989–94*	
inflation 1995	3.8%	Narrow money (M1)	13.5%
Av. ann. inflation 1989–95	3.2%	Broad money	16.1%

Exchange rates

	end 1995		June 1995
NZ$ per $	1.53	Effective rates	1990 = 100
NZ$ per SDR	2.28	– nominal	105.0
NZ$ per Ecu	2.00	– real	100.5

Principal exports

	$bn fob		$bn fob
Dairy produce	2.1	Fish	0.7
Meat	2.0	Fruit & vegetables	0.6
Forest products	1.4		
Wool	0.7	Total incl. others	**11.8**

Main export destinations

	% of total		% of total
Australia	21.4	United States	11.0
Japan	15.3	United Kingdom	6.0

Principal imports

	$bn cif		$bn cif
Intermediate goods	5.0	Vehicles & aircraft	1.7
Consumer goods	2.7	Mineral fuels	0.6
Plant & machinery	1.9	Total incl. others	**11.0**

Main origins of imports

	% of total		% of total
Australia	21.5	Japan	15.3
United States	19.0	United Kingdom	6.2

Balance of payments, reserves and aid, $bn

Visible exports fob	12.0	Capital balance	-0.6
Visible imports fob	-10.6	Overall balance	-1.2
Trade balance	1.3	Change in reserves	0.4
Invisibles inflows	4.0	Level of reserves	
Invisibles outflows	-7.5	end Dec.	3.7
Net transfers	0.1	No. months of import cover	2.5
Current account balance	-2.0	Aid given	0.11
– as % of GDP	-4.3	– as % of GDP	0.24

Family life

No. of households	1.2m	Divorces per 1,000 pop.	2.7
Av. no. per household	2.8	Cost of living, Dec. 1995	
Marriages per 1,000 pop.	6.4	New York = 100	91

a Year ending March 31, 1991.
b Year ending March 31, 1994.

NIGERIA

Area	923,768 sq km	Currency	Naira (N)
Capital	Abuja		

People

Population	107.9m	Life expectancy: men	51 yrs
Pop. per sq km	121	women	54 yrs
Av. ann. growth		Adult literacy	52.0%
in pop. 1985–94	2.9%	Fertility rate (per woman)	6.0
Pop. under 15	45.5%		
Pop. over 65	2.8%		*per 1,000 pop.*
No. of men per 100 women	98.3	Crude birth rate	42.3
Human Development Index	41	Crude death rate	13.9

The economy

GDP	N660bn	GDP per head	$278
GDP	$30bn	GDP per head in purchasing	
Av. ann. growth in real		power parity (USA=100)	7
GDP 1985–94	4.2%		

Origins of GDP		**Components of GDP**	
	% of total		*% of total*
Agriculture	36.6	Private consumption	85.4
Industry, of which:	21.2	Public consumption	3.5
manufacturing	6.9	Investment	9.4
Services	43.8	Exports	21.2
		Imports	-19.5

Structure of manufacturing

	% of total		*% of total*
Agric. & food processing	...	Other	...
Textiles & clothing	...	Av. ann. increase in industrial	
Machinery & transport	...	output 1980–93	0.8%

Energy

	'000 TCE		
Total output	141,275	% output exported	83.8
Total consumption	24,047	% consumption imported	11.5
Consumption per head,			
kg coal equivalent	228		

Inflation and finance

Consumer price			*av. ann. increase 1989–91*
inflation 1995	65.0%	Narrow money (M1)	36.9%
Av. ann. inflation 1989–95	40.4%	Broad money	28.7%

Exchange rates

	end 1995		*June 1995*
N per $	21.89	Effective rates	*1990 = 100*
N per SDR	32.53	– nominal	26.2
N per Ecu	28.68	– real	108.3

Principal exports

	$bn fob		$bn fob
Petroleum	9.1		
Cocoa beans & products	0.1	Total incl. others	**9.4**

Main export destinations

	% of total		% of total
United States	37.8	Germany	7.1
France	8.7	Netherlands	5.4
Spain	8.6		

Principal imports

	$bn cif		$bn cif
Machinery & transport equipment	2.3	Agric products & foodstuffs	0.8
Chemicals	1.8		
Manufactured goods	1.6	Total incl. others	**6.5**

Main origins of imports

	% of total		% of total
United Kingdom	14.1	Germany	9.0
United States	10.3	Netherlands	5.6
France	10.0		

Balance of payments, reserves and debt, $bn

Visible exports fob	9.5	Overall balance	-1.9
Visible imports fob	-6.5	Change in reserves	0.0
Trade balance	2.9	Level of reserves	
Invisibles inflows	0.4	end Dec.	1.6
Invisibles outflows	-6.0	No. months of import cover	1.7
Net transfers	0.5	Foreign debt	33.5
Current account balance	-2.1	– as % of GDP	102.5
– as % of GDP	-7.1	Debt service paid	1.9
Capital balance	0.3	Debt service ratio	19.6

Family life

No. households	...	Divorces per 1,000 pop.	...
Av. no. per household	...	Cost of living, Dec. 1995	
Marriages per 1,000 pop.	...	New York = 100	...

NORWAY

Area	323,878 sq km	Currency	Norwegian krone (Nkr)
Capital	Oslo		

People

Population	4.3m	Life expectancy: men	74 yrs
Pop. per sq km	13	women	81 yrs
Av. ann. growth		Adult literacy	99.0%
in pop. 1985–94	0.4%	Fertility rate (per woman)	2.0
Pop. under 15	19.5%		
Pop. over 65	15.9%		*per 1,000 pop.*
No. of men per 100 women	98.0	Crude birth rate	14.2
Human Development Index	93	Crude death rate	10.8

The economy

GDP	Nkr805bn	GDP per head	$26,477
GDP	$114bn	GDP per head in purchasing	
Av. ann. growth in real		power parity (USA=100)	78
GDP 1985–94	2.4%		

Origins of GDP[a]		Components of GDP	
	% of total		*% of total*
Agriculture	2.7	Private consumption	52.0
Industry, of which:	32.8	Public consumption	21.9
manufacturing	12.9	Investment	19.7
Services	64.5	Exports	43.4
		Imports	-37.0

Structure of manufacturing

	% of total		*% of total*
Agric. & food processing	23	Other	48
Textiles & clothing	2	Av. ann. increase in industrial	
Machinery & transport	27	output 1980–93	5.3%

Energy

	'000 TCE		
Total output	217,180	% output exported	86.4
Total consumption	30,859	% consumption imported	20.6
Consumption per head,			
kg coal equivalent	7,172		

Inflation and finance

			av. ann. increase 1989–94
Consumer price			
inflation 1995	2.5%	Narrow money (M1)	13.5%
Av. ann. inflation 1989–94	2.9%	Broad money	6.1%

Exchange rates

	end 1995		*June 1995*
Nkr per $	6.32	Effective rates	*1990 = 100*
Nkr per SDR	9.39	– nominal	99.3
Nkr per Ecu	8.28	– real	97.2

Principal exports

	$bn fob		$bn fob
Oil, gas & products	17.0	Fish & fish products	2.7
Food, drink & tobacco	3.0	Machinery incl. electrical	2.5
Non-ferrous metals	2.7	Total incl. others	**34.6**

Main export destinations

	% of total		% of total
United Kingdom	20.7	Sweden	9.5
Germany	12.1	France	7.9
Netherlands	9.5		

Principal imports

	$bn cif		$bn cif
Machinery incl. electrical	6.5	Clothing	1.3
Road vehicles	2.1	Iron & steel	1.2
Food, drink & tobacco	1.4	Total incl. others	**27.3**

Main origins of imports

	% of total		% of total
Sweden	15.0	Denmark	7.4
Germany	13.9	United States	7.3
United Kingdom	10.3		

Balance of payments, reserves and aid, $bn

Visible exports fob	34.9	Capital balance	-1.3
Visible imports fob	-26.6	Overall balance	1.5
Trade balance	8.3	Change in reserves	-0.6
Invisibles inflows	15.9	Level of reserves	
Invisibles outflows	-19.0	end Dec.	19.5
Net transfers	-1.6	No. months of import cover	5.1
Current account balance	3.6	Aid given	1.14
– as % of GDP	3.2	– as % of GDP	1.05

Family life

No. households	1.8m	Divorces per 1,000 pop.	2.4
Av. no. per household	2.4	Cost of living, Dec. 1995	
Marriages per 1,000 pop.	4.5	New York = 100	147

a 1992.

PAKISTAN

Area	803,940 sq km	Currency	Pakistan rupee (PRs)
Capital	Islamabad		

People

Population	126.3m	Life expectancy: men	63 yrs
Pop. per sq km	176	women	65 yrs
Av. ann. growth		Adult literacy	36.4%
in pop. 1985–94	2.8%	Fertility rate (per woman)	5.6
Pop. under 15	44.3%		
Pop. over 65	3.0%		*per 1,000 pop.*
No. of men per 100 women	107.2	Crude birth rate	37.3
Human Development Index	48	Crude death rate	7.8

The economy

GDP	PRs1,712bn	GDP per head	$440
GDP	$56bn	GDP per head in purchasing	
Av. ann. growth in real		power parity (USA=100)	12
GDP 1985–94	5.2%		

Origins of GDP[a]		**Components of GDP**[b]	
	% of total		*% of total*
Agriculture	25.6	Private consumption	71.9
Industry, of which:	...	Public consumption	12.1
manufacturing	17.8	Investment	19.0
Services	...	Exports	15.6
		Imports	-18.8

Structure of manufacturing[c]

	% of total		*% of total*
Agric. & food processing	29	Other	45
Textiles & clothing	19	Av. ann. increase in industrial	
Machinery & transport	7	output 1980–93	7.2%

Energy

	'000 TCE		
Total output	26,138	% output exported	2.4
Total consumption	38,722	% consumption imported	37.1
Consumption per head,			
kg coal equivalent	291		

Inflation and finance

Consumer price			*av. ann. increase 1989–94*
inflation 1995	13.2%	Narrow money (M1)	14.2%
Av. ann. inflation 1989–95	10.5%	Broad money	16.2%

Exchange rates

	end 1995		*June 1995*
PRs per $	34.25	Effective rates	*1990 = 100*
PRs per SDR	50.91	– nominal	...
PRs per Ecu	44.87	– real	...

Principal exports[b]

	$bn fob		$bn fob
Cotton yarn	1.3	Raw cotton	0.8
Clothing	1.1	Rice	0.2
Cotton fabrics	0.8	Total incl. others	**6.8**

Main export destinations[d]

	% of total		% of total
United States	12.0	Japan	5.9
Germany	6.7	Hong Kong	5.7
United Kingdom	6.2	South Korea	4.0

Principal imports[b]

	$bn cif		$bn cif
Non-electrical machinery	1.6	Transport equipment	0.8
Petroleum & products	1.4		
Chemicals	0.9	Total incl. others	**8.6**

Main origins of imports[d]

	% of total		% of total
Japan	13.7	Saudi Arabia	4.7
United States	8.1	United Kingdom	4.5
Germany	6.5	France	3.6

Balance of payments[e], reserves and debt, $bn

Visible exports fob	6.8	Overall balance	-0.1
Visible imports fob	-9.3	Change in reserves	1.7
Trade balance	-2.6	Level of reserves	
Invisibles inflows	1.6	end Dec.	3.7
Invisibles outflows	-4.2	No. months of import cover	3.5
Net transfers	2.3	Foreign debt	29.6
Current account balance	-2.9	– as % of GDP	56.6
– as % of GDP	-5.5	Debt service paid	3.4
Capital balance	2.9	Debt service ratio	34.8

Family life

No. households	12.6m	Divorces per 1,000 pop.	...
Av. no. per household	6.7	Cost of living, Dec. 1995	
Marriages per 1,000 pop.	...	New York = 100	56

a Fiscal year ending June 30, 1995.
b Fiscal year ending June 30, 1994.
c 1991.
d Fiscal year ending June 30, 1993.
e 1993.

PERU

Area	1,285,216 sq km	Currency	Nuevo Sol (New Sol)
Capital	Lima		

People

Population	23.3m	Life expectancy: men		66 yrs
Pop. per sq km	19	women		69 yrs
Av. ann. growth		Adult literacy[a]		86.2%
in pop. 1985–94	2.0%	Fertility rate (per woman)		3.1
Pop. under 15	35.1%			
Pop. over 65	4.1%			*per 1,000 pop.*
No. of men per 100 women	101.3	Crude birth rate		25.7
Human Development Index	71	Crude death rate		6.5

The economy

GDP	New Soles 96.6bn	GDP per head	$1,891
GDP	$44bn	GDP per head in purchasing	
Av. ann. growth in real		power parity (USA=100)	14
GDP 1985–94	1.2%		

Origins of GDP[b]		**Components of GDP**	
	% of total		*% of total*
Agriculture	13.6	Private consumption	74.5
Industry, of which:	39.4	Public consumption	7.3
manufacturing	22.3	Investment	21.5
Services	47.0	Exports	11.3
		Imports	-16.6

Structure of manufacturing[b]

	% of total		*% of total*
Agric. & food processing	23	Other	53
Textiles & clothing	14	Av. ann. increase in industrial	
Machinery & transport	10	output 1980–92	-0.5%

Energy

	'000 TCE		
Total output	11,106	% output exported	31.0
Total consumption	10,711	% consumption imported	29.5
Consumption per head,			
kg coal equivalent	468		

Inflation and finance

Consumer price			*av. ann. increase 1989–94*
inflation 1995	10.9%	Narrow money (M1)	421%
Av. ann. inflation 1989–95	365%	Broad money	501%

Exchange rates

	end 1995		*June 1995*
New Soles per $	2.31	Effective rates	*1990 = 100*
New Soles per SDR	3.43	– nominal	...
New Soles per Ecu	3.03	– real	...

Principal exports

	$bn fob		$bn fob
Non-traditional products	1.3	Zinc	0.3
Copper	0.8	Coffee	0.2
Fishmeal	0.7		
Gold	0.3	Total incl. others	**4.6**

Main export destinations

	% of total		% of total
United States	20.9	Germany	6.2
Japan	9.2	Italy	4.8
United Kingdom	8.5		

Principal imports

	$bn fob		$bn fob
Industrial supplies	2.3	Consumer goods	1.4
Capital goods	1.7	Total incl. others	**5.7**

Main origins of imports

	% of total		% of total
United States	27.6	Argentina	6.4
Japan	7.6	Brazil	6.2

Balance of payments, reserves and debt, $bn

Visible exports fob	4.6	Overall balance	1.4
Visible imports fob	-5.7	Change in reserves	3.5
Trade balance	-1.1	Level of reserves	
Invisibles inflows	1.4	end Dec.	7.4
Invisibles outflows	-3.0	No. months of import cover	12.7
Net transfers	0.4	Foreign debt	22.6
Current account balance	-2.3	– as % of GDP	45.8
– as % of GDP	-5.1	Debt service paid	1.1
Capital balance	1.9	Debt service ratio	20.2

Family life

No. of households	4.2m	Divorces per 1,000 pop.	...
Av. no. per household	5.1	Cost of living, Dec. 1995	
Marriages per 1,000 pop.	6.0	New York = 100	74

a Excluding indigenous jungle population.
b 1991.

PHILIPPINES

Area	300,000 sq km	Currency	Philippine peso (P)
Capital	Manila		

People

Population	66.2m	Life expectancy: men	67 yrs
Pop. per sq km	225	women	70 yrs
Av. ann. growth		Adult literacy	90.4%
in pop. 1985–94	2.1%	Fertility rate (per woman)	3.6
Pop. under 15	38.3%		
Pop. over 65	3.4%		*per 1,000 pop.*
No. of men per 100 women	101.3	Crude birth rate	28.0
Human Development Index	68	Crude death rate	5.7

The economy

GDP	P1,664bn	GDP per head	$957
GDP	$63bn	GDP per head in purchasing	
Av. ann. growth in real		power parity (USA=100)	11
GDP 1985–94	3.3%		

Origins of GDP		Components of GDP	
	% of total		*% of total*
Agriculture	22.3	Private consumption	74.6
Industry, of which:	34.9	Public consumption	10.0
manufacturing	24.9	Investment	26.3
Services	42.8	Exports	34.6
		Imports	-42.4

Structure of manufacturing

	% of total		*% of total*
Agric. & food processing	37	Other	39
Textiles & clothing	13	Av. ann. increase in industrial	
Machinery & transport	11	output 1980–93	-0.1%

Energy

	'000 TCE		
Total output	9,409	% output exported	7.3
Total consumption	26,855	% consumption imported	86.8
Consumption per head,			
kg coal equivalent	414		

Inflation and finance

Consumer price		*av. ann. increase 1989–94*	
inflation 1995	8%	Narrow money (M1)	17.2%
Av. ann. inflation 1989–95	11.2%	Broad money	21.5%

Exchange rates

	end 1995		*June 1995*
P per $	26.21	Effective rates	*1990 = 100*
P per SDR	38.97	– nominal	80.5
P per Ecu	34.34	– real	112.7

Principal exports

	$bn fob		$bn fob
Electrical & electronic		Machinery & transport	
equipment	5.0	equipment	0.4
Clothing	2.4	Copper	0.4
Coconut products	0.5	Total incl. others	**11.4**

Main export destinations[a]

	% of total		% of total
United States	38.2	Germany	4.9
Japan	15.0	Hong Kong	4.8
Singapore	5.3	United Kingdom	4.7

Principal imports

	$bn cif		$bn cif
Raw materials		Mineral fuels	2.0
& intermediaries	5.6		
Capital goods	5.0	Total incl. others	**21.2**

Main origins of imports[a]

	% of total		% of total
Japan	22.8	Hong Kong	5.4
United States	19.8	South Korea	4.6
Singapore	5.7	Saudi Arabia	4.3
Taiwan	5.7		

Balance of payments[a], reserves and debt, $bn

Visible exports fob	11.4	Overall balance	0.3
Visible imports fob	-17.6	Change in reserves	1.2
Trade balance	-6.2	Level of reserves	
Invisibles inflows	7.5	end Dec.	7.1
Invisibles outflows	-5.3	No. months of import cover	3.1
Net transfers	0.7	Foreign debt	39.3
Current account balance	-3.3	– as % of GDP	59.3
– as % of GDP	-6.0	Debt service paid	4.5
Capital balance	3.3	Debt service ratio	18.5

Family life

No. of households	11.4m	Divorces per 1,000 pop.	...
Av. no. per household	5.3	Cost of living, Dec. 1995	
Marriages per 1,000 pop.	6.0	New York = 100	68

a 1993.

POLAND

Area	312,683 sq km	Currency	Zloty (Zl)
Capital	Warsaw		

People

Population	38.3m	Life expectancy: men	67 yrs
Pop. per sq km	119	women	76 yrs
Av. ann. growth		Adult literacy	99.0%
in pop. 1985–94	0.3%	Fertility rate (per woman)	1.9
Pop. under 15	22.8%		
Pop. over 65	11.0%		*per 1,000 pop.*
No. of men per 100 women	94.9	Crude birth rate	13.5
Human Development Index	86	Crude death rate	10.7

The economy

GDP	Zl216bn	GDP per head	$2,468
GDP	$95bn	GDP per head in purchasing	
Av. ann. growth in real		power parity (USA=100)	20
GDP 1985–94	0.3%		

Origins of GDP[a]		**Components of GDP**[a]	
	% of total		*% of total*
Agriculture	6.7	Private consumption	63.0
Industry, of which:	38.3	Public consumption	21.3
manufacturing	...	Accumulation	15.7
Services	55.0	Exports	...
		Imports	...

Structure of manufacturing

	% of total		*% of total*
Agric. & food processing	21	Other	44
Textiles & clothing	9	Av. ann. increase in industrial	
Machinery & transport	26	output 1980–93	-3.2

Energy

	'000 TCE		
Total output	132,325	% output exported	17.7
Total consumption	138,404	% consumption imported	20.9
Consumption per head,			
kg coal equivalent	3,614		

Inflation and finance

Consumer price			*av. ann. increase 1989–94*
inflation 1995	28.1%	Narrow money (M1)	98.1%
Av. ann. inflation 1989–95	101.6%	Broad money	107.3%

Exchange rates

	end 1995		*June 1995*
			1990 = 100
Zl per $	2.47	Effective rates	
Zl per SDR	3.67	– nominal	52.3
Zl per Ecu	3.34	– real	182.4

Principal exports

	$bn fob		$bn fob
Machinery & equipment	4.4	Chemicals	1.7
Light industry products	2.5	Paper & wood	1.7
Metals	2.4	Total incl. others	**17.2**

Main export destinations

	% of total		% of total
Germany	35.7	United Kingdom	4.6
Netherlands	5.9	France	4.0
Russia	5.4	United States	3.4
Italy	4.9		

Principal imports

	$bn fob		$bn fob
Machinery & equipment	7.3	Light industry	2.3
Chemicals	4.1	Metals	1.1
Food & agric. products	4.0		
Oil & gas	2.3	Total incl. others	**21.6**

Main origins of imports

	% of total		% of total
Germany	27.5	Netherlands	4.6
Italy	8.4	France	4.5
Russia	6.8	United States	3.9
United Kingdom	5.3		

Balance of payments, reserves and debt, $bn

Visible exports fob	17.1	Overall balance	-0.5
Visible imports fob	-18.9	Change in reserves	1.7
Trade balance	-1.8	Level of reserves	
Invisibles inflows	5.1	end Dec.	6.0
Invisibles outflows	-7.0	No. months of import cover	3.3
Net transfers	1.2	Foreign debt	42.2
Current account balance	-2.5	– as % of GDP	46.8
– as % of GDP	-2.7	Debt service paid	3.1
Capital balance	2.2	Debt service ratio	15.8

Family life

No. of households	12.0m	Divorces per 1,000 pop.	0.7
Av. no. per household	3.1	Cost of living, Dec. 1995	
Marriages per 1,000 pop.	5.4	New York = 100	70

a 1993.

PORTUGAL

Area	88,940 sq km	Currency	Escudo (Esc)
Capital	Lisbon		

People

Population	9.8m	Life expectancy: men	72 yrs
Pop. per sq km	106	women	79 yrs
Av. ann. growth		Adult literacy	86.2%
in pop. 1985–94	-0.1%	Fertility rate (per woman)	1.6
Pop. under 15	18.9%		
Pop. over 65	14.1%		*per 1,000 pop.*
No. of men per 100 women	93.4	Crude birth rate	11.8
Human Development Index	87	Crude death rate	10.5

The economy

GDP	Esc15,271bn	GDP per head	$9,370
GDP	$92bn	GDP per head in purchasing	
Av. ann. growth in real		power parity (USA=100)	42
GDP 1985–94	3.2%		

Origins of GDP		**Components of GDP**	
	% of total		*% of total*
Agriculture	6.0	Private consumption	67.7
Industry, of which:	35.8	Public consumption	19.2
manufacturing	30.3	Investment	24.8
Services	58.2	Exports	24.6
		Imports	-36.3

Structure of manufacturing

	% of total		*% of total*
Agric. & food processing	20	Other	45
Textiles & clothing	23	Av. ann. increase in industrial	
Machinery & transport	12	output 1980–90	…

Energy

	'000 TCE		
Total output	1,195	% output exported[a]	367.7
Total consumption	20,564	% consumption imported[a]	127.5
Consumption per head,			
kg coal equivalent	2,090		

Inflation and finance

Consumer price		*av. ann. increase 1989–94*	
inflation 1995	4.1%	Narrow money (M1)	13.7%
Av. ann. inflation 1989–95	8.8%	Broad money	16.0%

Exchange rates

	end 1995		*June 1995*
Esc per $	149.4	Effective rates	*1990 = 100*
Esc per SDR	222.1	– nominal	93.7
Esc per Ecu	195.7	– real	112.8

Principal exports

	$bn fob		$bn fob
Clothing	3.3	Vehicles & transport	
Machinery	2.8	equipment	1.2
Shoes	1.8		
Textiles	1.4	Total incl. others	**18.3**

Main export destinations

	% of total		% of total
Germany	18.7	United Kingdom	11.7
France	14.7	United States	5.2
Spain	14.4	Netherlands	5.1

Principal imports

	$bn cif		$bn cif
Machinery	5.0	Chemicals	2.2
Food products	2.9	Textiles	1.9
Energy & fuels	2.3	Total incl. others	**25.8**

Main origins of imports

	% of total		% of total
Spain	15.2	Italy	8.5
Germany	13.8	United Kingdom	6.6
France	12.8	Netherlands	4.3

Balance of payments, reserves and debt, $bn

Visible exports fob	18.5	Overall balance	-1.4
Visible imports fob	-25.2	Change in reserves	-0.4
Trade balance	-6.7	Level of reserves	
Invisibles inflows	8.8	end Dec.	21.7
Invisibles outflows	-8.5	No. months of import cover	7.7
Net transfers	5.4	Aid given	0.31
Current account balance	-1.0	– as % of GDP	0.35
– as % of GDP	-1.1		
Capital balance	0.7		

Family life

No. of households	3.4m	Divorces per 1,000 pop.	1.3
Av. no. per household	2.9	Cost of living, Dec. 1995	
Marriages per 1,000 pop.	7.1	New York = 100	95

a Energy trade data are distorted by transitory and oil refining activities.

ROMANIA

˙Area	237,500 sq km	Currency	Leu (L)
Capital	Bucharest		

People

Population	22.7m	Life expectancy: men	67 yrs
Pop. per sq km	96	women	73 yrs
Av. ann. growth		Adult literacy	96.9%
in pop. 1985–94	0.2%	Fertility rate (per woman)	1.5
Pop. under 15	20.5%		
Pop. over 65	11.8%		*per 1,000 pop.*
No. of men per 100 women	97.1	Crude birth rate	11.6
Human Development Index	70	Crude death rate	11.5

The economy

GDP	L46,343bn	GDP per head	$1,228
GDP	$28bn	GDP per head in purchasing	
Av. ann. growth in real		power parity (USA=100)	12
GDP 1985–94	-3.0%		

Origins of GDP		**Components of GDP**	
	% of total		*% of total*
Agriculture	19.6	Private consumption	61.1
Industry, of which:	39.1	Public consumption	14.1
manufacturing	...	Investment	26.6
Services	41.3	Exports	26.0
		Imports	-27.8

Structure of manufacturing

	% of total		*% of total*
Agric. & food processing	19	Other	54
Textiles & clothing	15	Av. ann. increase in industrial	
Machinery & transport	12	output 1980–93	-4.4%

Energy

	'000 TCE		
Total output	45,888	% output exported	8.8
Total consumption	60,117	% consumption imported	36.4
Consumption per head,			
kg coal equivalent	2,611		

Inflation and finance

Consumer price		*av. ann. increase 1989–94*	
inflation 1995	40%	Narrow money (M1)	58.2%
Av. ann. inflation 1989–95	94.3%	Broad money	63.7%

Exchange rates

	end 1995		*June 1995*
		Effective rates	*1990 = 100*
L per $	2,578.0	Effective rates	1990 = 100
L per SDR	3,832.2	– nominal	...
L per Ecu	3,377.2	– real	...

Principal exports

	$bn fob		$bn fob
Textiles & footwear	1.5	Chemicals	0.5
Basic metals & products	1.1		
Machinery & equipment	0.7	Total incl. others	**6.2**

Main export destinations

	% of total		% of total
Germany	15.9	China	4.6
Italy	12.7	Turkey	4.1
France	5.1	Netherlands	3.5

Principal imports

	$bn cif		$bn cif
Fuels, minerals & metals	1.9	Food products	0.4
Machinery & equipment	1.5		
Chemicals	0.6	Total incl. others	**7.1**

Main origins of imports

	% of total		% of total
Germany	19.2	United States	5.5
Russia	13.0	France	5.5
Italy	12.8	Iran	3.7

Balance of payments, reserves and debt, $bn

Visible exports fob	6.0	Overall balance	0.4
Visible imports fob	-6.3	Change in reserves	1.2
Trade balance	-0.3	Level of reserves	
Invisibles inflows	1.2	end Dec.	3.1
Invisibles outflows	-1.4	No. months of import cover	4.6
Net transfers	0.3	Foreign debt	5.5
Current account balance	-0.3	– as % of GDP	18.3
– as % of GDP	-0.9	Debt service paid	0.6
Capital balance	0.9	Debt service ratio	7.9

Family life

No. of households	7.3m	Divorces per 1,000 pop.	1.4
Av. no. per household	3.1	Cost of living, Dec. 1995	
Marriages per 1,000 pop.	7.0	New York = 100	60

RUSSIA[a]

Area	17,075,400 sq km	Currency	Rouble (Rb)
Capital	Moscow		

People

Population	148.4m	Life expectancy: men	62 yrs
Pop. per sq km	9	women	74 yrs
Av. ann. growth		Adult literacy	98.7%
in pop. 1985–94	0.5%	Fertility rate (per woman)	1.5
Pop. under 15	21.0%		
Pop. over 65	12.1%		*per 1,000 pop.*
No. of men per 100 women	88.3	Crude birth rate	10.8
Human Development Index	85	Crude death rate	13.0

The economy

GDP	Rb1,391,600bn	GDP per head	$2,645
GDP	$392bn	GDP per head in purchasing	
Av. ann. growth in real		power parity (USA=100)	26
GDP 1990–94	-14.8%		

Origins of GDP		**Components of GDP**	
	% of total		*% of total*
Agriculture	6.3	Private consumption	46.6
Industry, of which:	43.7	Public consumption	21.8
manufacturing	...	Investment	26.7
Services	50.0	Foreign trade balance	4.9

Structure of manufacturing

	% of total		*% of total*
Agric. & food processing	...	Other	...
Textiles & clothing	...	Av. ann. increase in industrial	
Machinery & transport	...	output 1980–93	0.2%

Energy

	'000 TCE		
Total output	1,485,953	% output exported	31.7
Total consumption	1,025,049	% consumption imported	5.6
Consumption per head,			
kg coal equivalent	6,937		

Inflation and finance

Consumer price			*av. ann. increase 1988–92*
inflation 1995	198%	Narrow money (M1)	...
Av. ann. inflation 1991–95	222.1%	Broad money	...

Exchange rates

	end 1995		*June 1995*
Rb per $	4,640	Effective rates	*1990 = 100*
Rb per SDR	6,897	– nominal	...
Rb per Ecu	6,078	– real	...

Principal exports[bc]

	$ bn		$ bn
Fuels & raw materials	31.0	Timber & paper	1.9
Machinery & equipment	2.9	Food	1.8
Chemicals & rubber	2.7	Total incl. others	**44.3**

Main export destinations

	% of total		% of total
Ukraine	10.5	United States	5.9
Germany	8.5	United Kingdom	5.8
Switzerland	6.0	China	4.5

Principal imports[bc]

	$ bn		$ bn
Machinery & equipment	11.2	Fuels & raw materials	2.4
Food products	7.3	Chemicals & rubber	2.0
Textiles	5.4	Total incl. others	**33.0**

Main origins of imports

	% of total		% of total
Germany	14.6	United States	5.3
Turkmenistan	11.6	Kazakhstan	5.3
Belarus	5.4		

Balance of payments, reserves and debt, $bn

Visible exports fob	67.7	Overall balance	-21.7
Visible imports fob	-48.0	Change in reserves	-2.6
Trade balance	19.7	Level of reserves	
Invisibles inflows	12.5	end Dec.	7.2
Invisibles outflows	-20.7	No. months of import cover	1.5
Net transfers	-0.1	Foreign debt	94.2
Current account balance	11.4	– as % of GDP	25.4
– as % of GDP	2.9	Debt service paid	3.7
Capital balance	0.8	Debt service ratio	6.2

Family life

No. of households	40.5m	Divorces per 1,000 pop.	4.3
Av. no. per household	2.9	Cost of living, Dec. 1995	
Marriages per 1,000 pop.	8.6	New York = 100	115

a For selected data on Ukraine and other ex-Soviet republics, see page 192.
b Outside ex-Soviet Union only.
c 1993.

SAUDI ARABIA

Area	2,200,000 sq km	Currency	Riyal (SR)
Capital	Riyadh		

People

Population	17.5m	Life expectancy: men	70 yrs
Pop. per sq km	8	women	73 yrs
Av. ann. growth		Adult literacy	64.1%
in pop. 1985–94	3.6%	Fertility rate (per woman)	5.9
Pop. under 15	41.8%		
Pop. over 65	2.7%		*per 1,000 pop.*
No. of men per 100 women	125.8	Crude birth rate	34.7
Human Development Index	76	Crude death rate	4.2

The economy

GDP	SR476bn	GDP per head	$7,235
GDP	$127bn	GDP per head in purchasing	
Av. ann. growth in real		power parity (USA=100)	42
GDP 1985–94	3.7%		

Origins of GDP		**Components of GDP**	
	% of total		*% of total*
Agriculture	7.0	Private consumption	43.8
Industry, of which:	50.3	Public consumption	27.0
manufacturing	8.6	Investment	19.7
Services	42.7	Exports	39.3
		Imports	-29.8

Structure of manufacturing

	% of total		*% of total*
Agric. & food processing	7	Other	88
Textiles & clothing	1	Av. ann. increase in industrial	
Machinery & transport	4	output 1980–92	-2.9%

Energy

	'000 TCE		
Total output	654,133	% output exported	78.4
Total consumption	100,076	% consumption imported	0.0
Consumption per head,			
kg coal equivalent	5,846		

Inflation and finance

Consumer price			*av. ann. increase 1989–94*
inflation 1995	5.0%	Narrow money (M1)	4.9%
Av. ann. inflation 1989–95	1.9%	Broad money	3.3%

Exchange rates

	end 1995		*June 1995*
SR per $	3.75	Effective rates	*1990 = 100*
SR per SDR	5.57	– nominal	88.9
SR per Ecu	4.91	– real	85.6

Principal exports

	$bn fob		$bn fob
Crude oil & refined		Petrochemicals	3.0
petroleum	37.6	Total incl. others	**42.2**

Main export destinations

	% of total		% of total
Japan	16.9	Singapore	6.1
United States	16.8	France	5.5
South Korea	8.0	United Kingdom	2.3

Principal imports

	$bn cif		$bn cif
Transport equipment	4.8	Chemical products	2.6
Machinery & equipment	4.8	Textiles & clothing	1.7
Agric. products & foodstuffs	3.0	Total incl. others	**23.3**

Main origins of imports

	% of total		% of total
United States	20.0	Germany	5.3
Japan	10.8	Italy	4.4
United Kingdom	7.7	France	4.4

Balance of payments, reserves and debt[a], $bn

Visible exports fob	41.8	Overall balance	-0.1
Visible imports fob	-21.3	Change in reserves	-0.1
Trade balance	20.5	Level of reserves	
Invisibles inflows	7.5	end Dec.	9.1
Invisibles outflows	-21.4	No. months of import cover	2.6
Net transfers	-15.6	Foreign debt	20.0
Current account balance	-9.1	– as % of GDP	16.0
– as % of GDP	-7.2	Debt service	2.4
Capital balance	8.9	Debt service ratio	4.5

Family life

No. of households	...	Divorces per 1,000 pop.	...
Av. no. per household	...	Cost of living, Dec. 1995	
Marriages per 1,000 pop.	...	New York = 100	76

a 1993.

SINGAPORE

Area	639 sq km	Currency	Singapore dollar (S$)
Capital	Singapore		

People

Population	2.8m	Life expectancy: men	74 yrs
Pop. per sq km	4,608	women	79 yrs
Av. ann. growth		Adult literacy	92.0%
in pop. 1985–94	1.1%	Fertility rate (per woman)	1.7
Pop. under 15	22.7%		
Pop. over 65	6.7%		*per 1,000 pop.*
No. of men per 100 women	102.5	Crude birth rate	13.9
Human Development Index	88	Crude death rate	5.7

The economy

GDP	S$101bn	GDP per head	$23,357
GDP	$66bn	GDP per head in purchasing	
Av. ann. growth in real		power parity (USA=100)	77
GDP 1985–94	8.2%		

Origins of GDP		**Components of GDP**	
	% of total		*% of total*
Agriculture	0.2	Private consumption	40.2
Industry, of which:	36.1	Public consumption	8.5
manufacturing	27.0	Investment	34.2
Services	63.7	Exports less imports	18.9

Structure of manufacturing

	% of total		*% of total*
Agric. & food processing	4	Other	39
Textiles & clothing	3	Av. ann. increase in industrial	
Machinery & transport	54	output 1980–93	6.2%

Energy

	'000 TCE		
Total output	...	% output exported	...
Total consumption	25,422	% consumption imported[a]	412.1
Consumption per head,			
kg coal equivalent	9,102		

Inflation and finance

Consumer price		*av. ann. increase 1989–94*	
inflation 1995	1.8%	Narrow money (M1)	12.2%
Av. ann. inflation 1989–95	2.7%	Broad money	14.6%

Exchange rates

	end 1995		*June 1995*
S$ per $	1.41	Effective rates	*1990 = 100*
S$ per SDR	2.10	– nominal	...
S$ per Ecu	1.85	– real	112.1

Principal exports

	$bn fob		$bn fob
Machinery & equipment	61.7	Agric. products & foodstuffs	2.3
Mineral fuels	9.1	Crude materials	1.4
Manufactured products	5.8		
Chemicals	5.5	Total incl. others	**96.5**

Main export destinations

	% of total		% of total
United States	19.1	Thailand	5.6
Malaysia	18.8	Germany	3.5
Hong Kong	8.7	United Kingdom	2.7
Japan	7.0		

Principal imports

	$bn cif		$bn cif
Machinery & equipment	57.8	Agric. products & foodstuffs	3.4
Manufactured products	10.8	Crude minerals	1.3
Mineral fuels	9.0		
Chemicals	6.6	Total incl. others	**102.4**

Main origins of imports

	% of total		% of total
Japan	22.0	Taiwan	3.8
Malaysia	16.4	South Korea	3.8
United States	15.3	Saudi Arabia	3.5
Thailand	4.8		

Balance of payments, reserves and debt[b], $bn

Visible exports fob	98.7	Overall balance	4.7
Visible imports fob	-96.6	Change in reserves	9.8
Trade balance	2.1	Level of reserves	
Invisibles inflows	31.4	end Dec.	58.2
Invisibles outflows	-20.8	No. months of import cover	5.9
Net transfers	-0.8	Foreign debt	5.5
Current account balance	12.0	– as % of GDP	10.0
– as % of GDP	18.1	Debt service	0.6
Capital balance	1.8	Debt service ratio	0.6

Family life

No. of households	0.6m	Divorces per 1,000 pop.	1.3
Av. no. per household	4.6	Cost of living, Dec. 1995	
Marriages per 1,000 pop.	8.8	New York = 100	117

a   Energy trade data are distorted by transitory and oil refining activities.
b   1993.

SLOVAKIA

Area	49,035 sq km	Currency	Koruna (Kc)
Capital	Bratislava		

People

Population	5.3m	Life expectancy: men	67 yrs
Pop. per sq km	109	women	75 yrs
Av. ann. growth		Adult literacy	...
in pop. 1985–94	0.4%	Fertility rate (per woman)	1.9
Pop. under 15	22.9%		
Pop. over 65	10.8%		*per 1,000 pop.*
No. of men per 100 women	95.1	Crude birth rate	14.8
Human Development Index	87	Crude death rate	10.6

The economy

GDP	Kc385bn	GDP per head	$2,234
GDP	$12bn	GDP per head in purchasing	
Av. ann. growth in real		power parity (USA=100)	28
GDP 1990–94	-5.5%		

Origins of GDP		Components of GDP	
	% of total		*% of total*
Agriculture	5.3	Private consumption	48.1
Industry, of which:	49.7	Public consumption	23.1
manufacturing	...	Investment	14.0
Services	44.9	Exports	76.5
		Imports	-61.7

Structure of manufacturing

	% of total		*% of total*
Agric. & food processing	...	Other	...
Textiles & clothing	...	Av. ann. increase in industrial	
Machinery & transport	...	output 1980–92	...

Energy

	'000 TCE		
Total output	6,343	% output exported	35.4
Total consumption	22,917	% consumption imported	84.3
Consumption per head,			
kg coal equivalent	4,313		

Inflation and finance

Consumer price		*av. ann. increase 1993–94*	
inflation 1995	10%	Narrow money (M1)	9.8
Av. ann. inflation 1991–94	29.7%	Broad money	...

Exchange rates

	end 1995		*June 1995*
Kc per $	29.57	Effective rates	*1990 = 100*
Kc per SDR	43.95	– nominal	...
Kc per Ecu	38.74	– real	...

Principal exports[a]

	$bn fob		$bn fob
Consumer goods	2.7	Chemicals	0.9
Machinery & industrial		Fuels & raw materials	0.6
equipment	2.0	Total incl. others	**6.6**

Main export destinations[a]

	% of total		% of total
EU	37.7	Czech Republic	35.5

Principal imports[a]

	$bn fob		$bn fob
Machinery & industrial		Consumer goods	1.2
equipment	2.3	Chemicals	0.9
Fuels & raw materials	1.5	Total incl. others	**6.5**

Main origins of imports[a]

	% of total		% of total
EU	34.2	Czech Republic	28.3

Balance of payments, reserves and debt, $bn

Visible exports fob	6.7	Overall balance	1.2
Visible imports fob	-6.6	Change in reserves	1.3
Trade balance	0.1	Level of reserves	
Invisibles inflows	2.4	end Dec.	2.2
Invisibles outflows	-1.9	No. months of import cover	3.1
Net transfers	0.1	Foreign debt	4.1
Current account balance	0.7	– as % of GDP	33.2
– as % of GDP	6.0	Debt service paid	0.8
Capital balance	0.1	Debt service ratio	9.1

Family life

No. of households	...	Divorces per 1,000 pop.	1.5
Av. no. per household	...	Cost of living, Dec. 1995	
Marriages per 1,000 pop.	6.4	New York = 100	...

a Estimates.

SOUTH AFRICA

Area	1,225,815 sq km	Currency	Rand (R)
Capital	Pretoria		

People

Population	41.6m	Life expectancy: men	62 yrs
Pop. per sq km	34	women	68 yrs
Av. ann. growth		Adult literacy	80.0%
in pop. 1985–94	2.4%	Fertility rate (per woman)	3.8
Pop. under 15	37.3%		
Pop. over 65	4.4%		*per 1,000 pop.*
No. of men per 100 women	98.7	Crude birth rate	29.5
Human Development Index	71	Crude death rate	7.9

The economy

GDP	R444bn	GDP per head	$3,011
GDP	$125bn	GDP per head in purchasing	
Av. ann. growth in real		power parity (USA=100)	16
GDP 1985–94	0.9%		

Origins of GDP		**Components of GDP**	
	% of total		*% of total*
Agriculture	4.7	Private consumption	59.2
Industry, of which:	35.4	Public consumption	21.1
manufacturing	23.5	Investment	15.0
Services	59.9	Exports	23.7
		Imports	-21.8

Structure of manufacturing

	% of total		*% of total*
Agric. & food processing	17	Other	56
Textiles & clothing	8	Av. ann. increase in industrial	
Machinery & transport	19	output 1980–93	-0.2%

Energy

	'000 TCE		
Total output	141,449	% output exported	30.4
Total consumption	122,093	% consumption imported	19.9
Consumption per head,			
kg coal equivalent	2,697		

Inflation and finance

Consumer price		*av. ann. increase 1992–94*	
inflation 1995	8.6%	Narrow money (M1)	16.2%
Av. ann. inflation 1989–95	12.2%	Broad money	18.6%

Exchange rates

	end 1995		*June 1995*
R per $	3.65	Effective rates	*1990 = 100*
R per SDR	5.42	– nominal	64.1
R per Ecu	4.78	– real	95.3

Principal exports

	$bn fob		$bn fob
Gold	6.4	Food, drink & tobacco	2.1
Base metals	3.0		
Diamonds	2.6	Total incl. others	**25.1**

Main export destinations

	% of total		% of total
Switzerland	6.7	Japan	4.6
United Kingdom	6.6	Germany	4.1
United States	4.9		

Principal imports

	$bn cif		$bn cif
Machinery & transport		Manufactured goods	1.8
equipment	10.0	Food, drink & tobacco	1.0
Chemicals	2.6	Total incl. others	**23.4**

Main origins of imports

	% of total		% of total
Germany	13.4	United Kingdom	8.7
United States	11.3	Italy	3.4
Japan	10.4		

Balance of payments, reserves and debt[a], $bn

Visible exports fob	25.1	Overall balance	0.9
Visible imports fob	-21.4	Change in reserves	0.4
Trade balance	3.7	Level of reserves	
Invisibles inflows	4.5	end Dec.	3.3
Invisibles outflows	-8.8	No. months of import cover	1.3
Net transfers	0.1	Foreign debt	17.3
Current account balance	-0.6	– as % of GDP	14.7
– as % of GDP	-0.5	Debt service	2.9
Capital balance	2.6	Debt service ratio	10.1

Family life

No. of households	...	Divorces per 1,000 pop.	0.4
Av. no. per household	...	Cost of living, Dec. 1995	
Marriages per 1,000 pop.	...	New York = 100	70

a 1993.

SOUTH KOREA

Area	99,274 sq km	Currency	Won (W)
Capital	Seoul		

People

Population	44.6m	Life expectancy: men	69 yrs
Pop. per sq km	454	women	76 yrs
Av. ann. growth		Adult literacy	96.8%
in pop. 1985–94	1.0%	Fertility rate (per woman)	1.8
Pop. under 15	23.6%		
Pop. over 65	5.6%		*per 1,000 pop*
No. of men per 100 women	100.9	Crude birth rate	16.1
Human Development Index	88	Crude death rate	6.3

The economy

GDP	W294,063bn	GDP per head	$8,224
GDP	$366bn	GDP per head in purchasing	
Av. ann. growth in real		power parity (USA=100)	39
GDP 1985–94	8.8%		

Origins of GDP		**Components of GDP**	
	% of total		*% of total*
Agriculture	7.0	Private consumption	53.1
Industry, of which:	43.0	Public consumption	10.6
manufacturing	26.9	Investment	36.6
Services	50.0	Exports	30.1
		Imports	-30.9

Structure of manufacturing

	% of total		*% of total*
Agric. & food processing	10	Other	48
Textiles & clothing	12	Av. ann. increase in industrial	
Machinery & transport	30	output 1980–93	12.1%

Energy

	'000 TCE		
Total output	28,405	% output exported	67.3
Total consumption	153,689	% consumption imported	110.6
Consumption per head,			
kg coal equivalent	3,483		

Inflation and finance

Consumer price		*av. ann. increase 1989–94*	
inflation 1995	4.5%	Narrow money (M1)	19.7%
Av. ann. inflation 1989–95	6.5%	Broad money	18.6%

Exchange rates

	end 1995		*June 1995*
W per $	768	Effective rates	1990 = 100
W per SDR	1,157	– nominal	..
W per Ecu	1,006	– real	..

Principal exports

	$bn fob		$bn fob
Electronic components	11.8	Ships	4.9
Textiles	7.8		
Clothing	5.7	Total incl. others	**96.0**

Main export destinations

	% of total		% of total
United States	21.4	China	6.5
Japan	14.1	Germany	4.5
Hong Kong	8.3		

Principal imports

	$bn cif		$bn cif
Machinery & transport		Raw materials	9.4
equipment	37.4	Food & live animals	4.8
Mineral fuels & lubricants	15.4		
Chemicals	9.8	Total incl. others	**102.3**

Main origins of imports

	% of total		% of total
Japan	24.8	Germany	5.0
United States	21.1	Saudi Arabia	3.7
China	5.3		

Balance of payments, reserves and debt, $bn

Visible exports fob	93.7	Overall balance	4.6
Visible imports fob	-96.8	Change in reserves	5.4
Trade balance	-3.1	Level of reserves	
Invisibles inflows	21.5	end Dec.	25.8
Invisibles outflows	-23.8	No. months of import cover	2.5
Net transfers	1.6	Foreign debt	54.5
Current account balance	-3.9	– as % of GDP	15.3
– as % of GDP	-1.1	Debt service paid	7.9
Capital balance	10.2	Debt service ratio	6.8

Family life

No. of households	11.4m	Divorces per 1,000 pop.	1.0
Av. no. per household	3.8	Cost of living, Dec. 1995	
Marriages per 1,000 pop.	7.5	New York = 100	118

SPAIN

Area	504,782 sq km	Currency	Peseta (Pta
Capital	Madrid		

People

Population	39.6m	Life expectancy: men	75 yrs
Pop. per sq km	78	women	81 yrs
Av. ann. growth		Adult literacy	98.0%
in pop. 1985–94	0.3%	Fertility rate (per woman)	1.2
Pop. under 15	16.5%		
Pop. over 65	14.9%		*per 1,000 pop*
No. of men per 100 women	96.6	Crude birth rate	9.8
Human Development Index	93	Crude death rate	9.3

The economy

GDP	Pta65,462bn	GDP per head	$13,282
GDP	$525bn	GDP per head in purchasing	
Av. ann. growth in real		power parity (USA=100)	56
GDP 1985–94	2.9%		

Origins of GDP

	% of total		% of total
		Components of GDP	
Agriculture	3.7	Private consumption	63.2
Industry, of which:	32.9	Public consumption	17.0
manufacturing	24.4	Investment	19.8
Services	63.4	Exports	22.3
		Imports	-22.2

Structure of manufacturing

	% of total		% of total
Agric. & food processing	18	Other	48
Textiles & clothing	8	Av. ann. increase in industrial	
Machinery & transport	26	output 1980–88	2.3%

Energy

	'000 TCE		
Total output	41,089	% output exported[a]	34.1
Total consumption	114,627	% consumption imported[a]	90.7
Consumption per head,			
kg coal equivalent	2,901		

Inflation and finance

Consumer price		*av. ann. increase 1989–94*	
inflation 1995	4.7%	Narrow money (M1)	10.2%
Av. ann. inflation 1989–95	5.6%	Broad money	11.0%

Exchange rates

	end 1995		June 1995
			1990 = 100
Pta per $	121.4	Effective rates	
Pta per SDR	180.5	– nominal	81.1
Pta per Ecu	159.0	– real	85.1

Principal exports

	$bn fob		$bn fob
Raw materials & intermediate products	31.0	Capital goods	9.7
		Foodstuffs	9.3
Consumer goods	20.6	Total incl. others	**72.5**

Main export destinations

	% of total		% of total
France	20.1	United Kingdom	8.2
Germany	14.2	United States	4.9
Italy	9.2		

Principal imports

	$bn cif		$bn cif
Raw materials & intermediate products (excl. fuels)	45.6	Energy products	8.8
		Foodstuffs	7.5
Consumer goods	16.6		
Capital goods	14.6	Total incl. others	**93.1**

Main origins of imports

	% of total		% of total
France	17.5	United Kingdom	7.8
Germany	14.6	United States	7.3
Italy	8.9		

Balance of payments, reserves and aid, $bn

Visible exports fob	74.3	Capital balance	7.1
Visible imports fob	-88.9	Overall balance	0.05
Trade balance	-14.6	Change in reserves	0.4
Invisibles inflows	42.9	Level of reserves	
Invisibles outflows	-36.5	end Dec.	47.5
Net transfers	1.7	No. months of import cover	4.6
Current account balance	-6.4	Aid given	1.31
– as % of GDP	-1.2	– as % of GDP	0.28

Family life

No. of households	10.6m	Divorces per 1,000 pop.	0.6
Av. no. per household	3.5	Cost of living, Dec. 1995	
Marriages per 1,000 pop.	5.2	New York = 100	104

Energy trade data are distorted by transitory and oil refining activities.

SWEDEN

Area	449,964 sq km	Currency	Swedish krona (Skr)
Capital	Stockholm		

People

Population	8.7m	Life expectancy: men	76 yrs
Pop. per sq km	20	women	82 yrs
Av. ann. growth		Adult literacy	99.0%
in pop. 1985–94	0.5%	Fertility rate (per woman)	2.1
Pop. under 15	19.0%		
Pop. over 65	17.3%		*per 1,000 pop.*
No. of men per 100 women	98.1	Crude birth rate	13.6
Human Development Index	93	Crude death rate	10.9

The economy

GDP	Skr1,589bn	GDP per head	$23,631
GDP	$206bn	GDP per head in purchasing	
Av. ann. growth in real		power parity (USA=100)	77
GDP 1985–94	0.9%		

Origins of GDP		Components of GDP	
	% of total		*% of total*
Agriculture	3.1	Private consumption	51.8
Industry, of which:	29.7	Public consumption	27.3
manufacturing	23.8	Investment	15.1
Services	67.2	Exports	35.7
		Imports	-29.9

Structure of manufacturing

	% of total		*% of total*
Agric. & food processing	11	Other	54
Textiles & clothing	2	Av. ann. increase in industrial	
Machinery & transport	33	output 1980–93	2.1%

Energy

	'000 TCE		
Total output	32,410	% output exported	44.8
Total consumption	56,649	% consumption imported	71.7
Consumption per head,			
kg coal equivalent	6,516		

Inflation and finance

Consumer price		*av. ann. increase 1989–94*	
inflation 1995	2.5%	Narrow money (M1)	...
Av. ann. inflation 1989–95	5.4%	Broad money	4.3%

Exchange rates

	end 1995		*June 1995*
			1990 = 100
Skr per $	6.66	Effective rates	
Skr per SDR	9.90	– nominal	77.9
Skr per Ecu	8.70	– real	71.2

Principal exports

	$bn fob		$bn fob
Machinery incl.		Transport equipment	9.3
electricals	18.2	Chemicals	5.8
Wood products, pulp &		Iron & steel	3.8
paper	9.7	Total incl. others	**49.9**

Main export destinations

	% of total		% of total
Germany	13.3	Denmark	6.9
United Kingdom	10.2	Netherlands	5.3
Norway	8.1	France	5.1
United States	8.0		

Principal imports

	$bn cif		$bn cif
Machinery incl.		Transport equipment	4.8
electricals	14.8	Clothing, footwear & textiles	2.6
Chemicals	5.9		
Mineral fuels	3.9	Total incl. others	**42.8**

Main origins of imports

	% of total		% of total
Germany	18.4	Finland	6.3
United Kingdom	9.6	Norway	6.1
United States	8.6	France	5.6
Denmark	6.8		

Balance of payments, reserves and aid, $bn

Visible exports fob	60.1	Capital balance	6.1
Visible imports fob	-50.6	Overall balance	2.3
Trade balance	9.6	Change in reserves	4.2
Invisibles inflows	23.8	Level of reserves	
Invisibles outflows	-30.7	end Dec.	25.6
Net transfers	-1.8	No. months of import cover	3.8
Current account balance	0.8	Aid given	1.82
– as % of GDP	0.4	– as % of GDP	0.96

Family life

No. of households	3.8m	Divorces per 1,000 pop.	2.5
Av. no. per household	2.2	Cost of living, Dec. 1995	
Marriages per 1,000 pop.	4.3	New York = 100	119

SWITZERLAND

Area	41,293 sq km	Currency	Swiss franc (SFr)
Capital	Berne		

People

Population	7.1m	Life expectancy: men		75 yrs
Pop. per sq km	174	women		82 yrs
Av. ann. growth		Adult literacy		99.0%
in pop. 1985–94	1.0%	Fertility rate (per woman)		1.7
Pop. under 15	17.7%			
Pop. over 65	14.2%		*per 1,000 pop.*	
No. of men per 100 women	98.2	Crude birth rate		12.3
Human Development Index	93	Crude death rate		9.0

The economy

GDP	SFr513bn	GDP per head	$37,179
GDP	$265bn	GDP per head in purchasing	
Av. ann. growth in real		power parity (USA=100)	95
GDP 1985–94	1.6%		

Origins of GDP[a]		Components of GDP	
	% of total		*% of total*
Agriculture	3.1	Private consumption	58.8
Industry, of which:	34.7	Public consumption	14.3
manufacturing	26.3	Investment	21.9
Services	62.2	Exports	36.2
		Imports	-31.5

Structure of manufacturing

	% of total		*% of total*
Agric. & food processing	...	Other	...
Textiles & clothing	...	Av. ann. increase in industrial	
Machinery & transport	...	output 1980–89[b]	1.8%

Energy

	'000 TCE		
Total output	13,176	% output exported	31.5
Total consumption	33,620	% consumption imported	69.0
Consumption per head,			
kg coal equivalent	4,745		

Inflation and finance

Consumer price		*av. ann. increase 1989–94*	
inflation 1995	1.8%	Narrow money (M1)	0.7%
Av. ann. inflation 1989–95	3.5%	Broad money	4.3%

Exchange rates

	end 1995		*June 1995*
SFr per $	1.15	Effective rates	*1990 = 100*
SFr per SDR	1.71	– nominal	113.4
SFr per Ecu	1.51	– real	117.8

Principal exports

	$bn fob		$bn fob
Machinery	19.1	Metals & metal manufactures	5.7
Chemicals	17.1	Textiles & clothing	3.1
Precision instruments, watches & jewellery	14.6	Total incl. others	**69.9**

Main export destinations

	% of total		% of total
Germany	23.4	Italy	7.5
France	9.2	United Kingdom	6.6
United States	9.1	Japan	3.9

Principal imports

	$bn cif		$bn cif
Machinery	13.9	Textiles & clothing	6.1
Chemicals	9.2	Agric. products	6.1
Precision instruments, watches & jewellery	7.5	Metals & metals manufactures	5.8
Motor vehicles	6.7	Total incl. others	**67.6**

Main origins of imports

	% of total		% of total
Germany	32.8	United Kingdom	6.6
France	11.0	United States	6.2
Italy	9.9	Japan	3.4

Balance of payments, reserves and aid, $bn

Visible exports fob	82.6	Capital balance	-16.5
Visible imports fob	-79.3	Overall balance	1.1
Trade balance	3.3	Change in reserves	1.5
Invisibles inflows	49.8	Level of reserves	
Invisibles outflows	-31.1	end Dec.	66.6
Net transfers	-3.5	No. months of import cover	7.2
Current account balance	18.5	Aid given	0.98
– as % of GDP	7.0	– as % of GDP	0.36

Family life

No. of households	2.5m	Divorces per 1,000 pop.	2.2
Av. no. per household	2.5	Cost of living, Dec. 1995	
Marriages per 1,000 pop.	6.6	New York = 100	156

TAIWAN

Area	36,179 sq km	Currency	Taiwan dollar (T$)
Capital	Taipei		

People

Population	21.1m	Life expectancy: men	...
Pop. per sq km[a]	587	women	...
Av. ann. growth		Adult literacy	...
in pop. 1985–94	1.1%	Fertility rate (per woman)	1.8
Pop. under 15	24.4%		
Pop. over 65	7.4%		*per 1,000 pop.*
No. of men per 100 women	106.2	Crude birth rate	15.2
Human Development Index	...	Crude death rate	5.3

The economy

GDP	T$6,336bn	GDP per head	$11,412
GDP	$241bn	GDP per head in purchasing	
Av. ann. growth in real		power parity (USA=100)	...
GDP 1985–94	6.6%		

Origins of GDP
% of total

Components of GDP
% of total

Agriculture	3.6	Private consumption	58.2
Industry, of which:	37.3	Public consumption	14.8
manufacturing	29.0	Investment	23.8
Services	59.1	Exports	43.8
		Imports	-41.9

Structure of manufacturing

	% of total		*% of total*
Agric. & food processing	...	Other	...
Textiles & clothing	...	Av. ann. increase in industrial	
Machinery & transport	...	output 1980–94	5.9%

Energy

	'000 TCE		
Total output	...	% output exported	3.3
Total consumption	...	% consumption imported	76.7
Consumption per head,			
kg coal equivalent	...		

Inflation and finance

Consumer price		*av. ann. increase 1989–94*	
inflation 1995	3.7%	Narrow money (M1)	8.3%
Av. ann. inflation 1989–95	3.9%	Broad money	14.8%

Exchange rates

	end 1995		*June 1995*
T$ per $	27.29	Effective rates	1990 = 100
T$ per SDR	40.66	– nominal	...
T$ per Ecu	42.37	– real	...

Principal exports

	$bn fob		$bn fob
Machinery & electrical equipment	40.6	Plastic & rubber articles	6.9
		Vehicles, aircraft & ships	5.2
Textiles & clothing	15.0	Toys & sporting goods	2.9
Base metals & manufactures	8.7	Total incl. others	**93.0**

Main export destinations

	% of total		% of total
United States	26.2	Germany	3.5
Hong Kong	22.8	Thailand	2.6
Japan	11.0	Netherlands	2.6
Singapore	3.6	Malaysia	2.4

Principal imports

	$bn cif		$bn cif
Machinery & electrical equipment	32.0	Vehicles, aircraft & ships	7.1
		Crude petroleum	3.2
Metals	11.5	Plastics & plastic products	2.8
Chemicals	10.5	Total incl. others	**85.3**

Main origins of imports

	% of total		% of total
Japan	29.0	Singapore	2.8
United States	21.1	Malaysia	2.7
Germany	5.6	Australia	2.6
South Korea	3.5	Indonesia	2.5

Balance of payments, reserves and debt, $bn

Visible exports fob	92.2	Overall balance	4.7
Visible imports fob	-80.3	Change in reserves	8.9
Trade balance	12.0	Level of reserves	
Invisibles inflows	20.8	end Dec.	92.5
Invisibles outflows	-25.3	No. months of import cover	10.5
Net transfers	-1.4	Foreign debt[b]	10.5
Current account balance	6.2	– as % of GDP	4.5
– as % of GDP	2.5	Debt service	2.3
Capital balance	-0.9	Debt service ratio	2.0

Family life

No. of households	…	Divorces per 1,000 pop.	…
Av. no. per household	…	Cost of living, Dec. 1995	
Marriages per 1,000 pop.	…	New York = 100	113

a 1993.
b Medium and long-term.

THAILAND

Area	513,115 sq km	Currency	Baht (Bt)
Capital	Bangkok		

People

Population	58.7m	Life expectancy: men	65 yrs
Pop. per sq km	115	women	72 yrs
Av. ann. growth		Adult literacy	93.8%
in pop. 1985–94	1.6%	Fertility rate (per woman)	2.1
Pop. under 15	28.3%		
Pop. over 65	5.0%		*per 1,000 pop.*
No. of men per 100 women	100.3	Crude birth rate	19.2
Human Development Index	83	Crude death rate	7.0

The economy

GDP	Bt3,270bn	GDP per head	$2,212
GDP	$130bn	GDP per head in purchasing	
Av. ann. growth in real		power parity (USA=100)	25
GDP 1985–94	9.4%		

Origins of GDP[a]		**Components of GDP**[a]	
	% of total		*% of total*
Agriculture[b]	13.4	Private consumption	55.1
Industry, of which:	37.7	Public consumption	10.1
manufacturing	28.8	Investment	40.1
Services	48.9	Exports	36.4
		Imports	-40.9

Structure of manufacturing

	% of total		*% of total*
Agric. & food processing	16	Other	28
Textiles & clothing	16	Av. ann. increase in industrial	
Machinery & transport	40	output 1980–93	11.0%

Energy

	'000 TCE		
Total output	23,119	% output exported	5.8
Total consumption	55,555	% consumption imported	64.9
Consumption per head,			
kg coal equivalent	965		

Inflation and finance

Consumer price		*av. ann. increase 1989–94*	
inflation 1995	5.8%	Narrow money (M1)	14.6%
Av. ann. inflation 1989–95	5.0%	Broad money	19.9%

Exchange rates

	end 1995		*June 1995*
Bt per $	25.19	Effective rates	*1990 = 100*
Bt per SDR	37.53	– nominal	...
Bt per Ecu	33.00	– real	...

Principal exports[c]

	$bn fob		$bn fob
Textiles & clothing	4.4	Precious stones	1.7
Computers & parts	2.4	Plastic products	1.6
Electrical appliances	2.2	Total incl. others	**37.0**

Main export destinations

	% of total		% of total
United States	21.7	Hong Kong	5.3
Japan	17.2	Germany	4.0
Singapore	12.1		

Principal imports[c]

	$bn cif		$bn cif
Non-electrical machinery	6.9	Chemicals	3.5
Electrical machinery	4.8	Vehicles & parts	3.3
Energy & fuel	3.6	Total incl. others	**46.1**

Main origins of imports

	% of total		% of total
Japan	30.4	Germany	5.4
United States	11.5	Taiwan	5.1
Singapore	6.5		

Balance of payments, reserves and debt, $bn

Visible exports fob	44.5	Overall balance	4.2
Visible imports fob	-48.2	Change in reserves	4.8
Trade balance	-3.7	Level of reserves	
Invisibles inflows	14.1	end Dec.	30.3
Invisibles outflows	-19.9	No. months of import cover	5.3
Net transfers	1.1	Foreign debt	61.0
Current account balance	-8.4	– as % of GDP	43.1
– as % of GDP	-6.5	Debt service paid	9.2
Capital balance	14.1	Debt service ratio	15.6

Family life

No. of households	12.2m	Divorces per 1,000 pop.	0.7
Av. no. per household	4.5	Cost of living, Dec. 1995	
Marriages per 1,000 pop.	8.4	New York = 100	82

a   1992.
b   Includes mining.
c   1993.

TURKEY

Area	779,452 sq km	Currency	Turkish Lira (L)
Capital	Ankara		

People

Population	60.8m	Life expectancy: men	67 yrs
Pop. per sq km	79	women	71 yrs
Av. ann. growth		Adult literacy	81.9%
in pop. 1985–94	2.1%	Fertility rate (per woman)	3.0
Pop. under 15	33.9%		
Pop. over 65	5.0%		*per 1,000 pop*
No. of men per 100 women	104.7	Crude birth rate	24.6
Human Development Index	79	Crude death rate	6.7

The economy

GDP	L4,411,696bn	GDP per head	$2,452
GDP	$149bn	GDP per head in purchasing	
Av. ann. growth in real		power parity (USA=100)	22
GDP 1985–94	4.1%		

Origins of GDP		Components of GDP	
	% of total		*% of total*
Agriculture	15.8	Private consumption	67.1
Industry, of which:	33.8	Public consumption	11.6
manufacturing	27.1	Investment	20.3
Services	50.4	Exports	21.3
		Imports	-20.3

Structure of manufacturing

	% of total		*% of total*
Agric. & food processing	18	Other	49
Textiles & clothing	14	Av. ann. increase in industrial	
Machinery & transport	19	output 1980–93	5.9%

Energy

	'000 TCE		
Total output	26,591	% output exported	10.2
Total consumption	67,529	% consumption imported	71.2
Consumption per head,			
kg coal equivalent	1,133		

Inflation and finance

Consumer price		*av. ann. increase 1989–94*	
inflation 1995	93.6%	Narrow money (M1)	64.8%
Av. ann. inflation 1989–95	74.4%	Broad money	78.9%

Exchange rates

	end 1995		*June 1995*
L per $	59,650	Effective rates	*1990 = 100*
L per SDR	88,669	– nominal	..
L per Ecu	78,142	– real	..

Principal exports

	$bn fob		$bn fob
Clothing	4.6	Synthetic fibres	0.7
Iron & steel	2.4	Leather	0.6
Other textiles & carpets	0.9	Total incl. others	**18.1**

Main export destinations

	% of total		% of total
Germany	21.7	United Kingdom	4.9
United States	8.4	France	4.7
Italy	5.7	Russia	4.5

Principal imports

	$bn cif		$bn cif
Machinery	6.1	Chemicals	1.0
Crude oil	2.4	Plastics	0.8
Iron & steel	2.4	Total incl. others	**23.3**

Main origins of imports

	% of total		% of total
Germany	15.7	France	6.3
United States	10.4	Saudi Arabia	5.3
Italy	8.6	Russia	4.5

Balance of payments, reserves and debt, $bn

Visible exports fob	18.4	Overall balance	0.2
Visible imports fob	-22.6	Change in reserves	0.8
Trade balance	-4.2	Level of reserves	
Invisibles inflows	11.7	end Dec.	8.6
Invisibles outflows	-7.9	No. months of import cover	3.4
Net transfers	3.1	Foreign debt	66.3
Current account balance	2.6	– as % of GDP	51.4
– as % of GDP	1.8	Debt service paid	10.2
Capital balance	-4.2	Debt service ratio	31.2

Family life

No. of households	9.7m	Divorces per 1,000 pop.	0.5
Av. no. per household	5.2	Cost of living, Dec. 1995	
Marriages per 1,000 pop.	8.0	New York = 100	…

UKRAINE

Area	603,700 sq km	Currency	Karbovanets
Capital	Kiev		

People

Population	51.5m	Life expectancy: men		64 yrs
Pop. per sq km	85	women		74 yrs
Av. ann. growth		Adult literacy		95.0%
in pop. 1985–94	0.1%	Fertility rate (per woman)		1.6
No. of men per 100 women	86.8			per 1,000 pop.
		Crude birth rate[a]		11.5
		Crude death rate[a]		13.6

The economy

GDP	$80.9bn	GDP per head	$1,572
Av. ann. growth in real		GDP per head in purchasing	
GDP 1988–94	-11.8%	power parity (USA=100)	21

Origins of NMP[b]		Components of NMP[b]	
	% of total		% of total
Agriculture	30.2	Private consumption	57.4
Industry	42.4	Public consumption	12.6
Construction	10.9	Net investment	30.2
Other	16.5	Net exports	0.2

Inflation and exchange rates

Consumer price			end 1995
inflation 1995	350%	Kabovanets per $	104,133
Av. ann. inflation 1989–95	379%	Kabovanets per Ecu	34,528

Principal exports[c]

	Rb bn		Rb bn
Machinery & metalworking	17.9	Chemicals & products	3.9
Ferrous metallurgy	7.6	Light industry	2.3
Food industry	6.7	Total incl. others	**45.7**

Main export destinations

	% of total		% of total
Russia	43.4	Turkey	6.5
China	7.2	Italy	6.5
Bulgaria	6.6		

Principal imports[c]

	Rb bn		Rb bn
Machinery & metalworking	18.7	Food industry	4.0
Light industry	9.7	Oil & gas	3.9
Chemicals & products	5.7	Total incl. others	**53.8**

Main origins of imports

	% of total		% of total
Russia	63.0	Poland	2.7
Germany	10.5	Italy	2.3

EX-SOVIET REPUBLICS

	Area '000 sq km	Population m	Population[a] per sq km	Capital	Currency
Armenia	29.8	3.77	121	Yerevan	Dram
Azerbaijan	86.6	7.47	87	Baku	Manat
Belarus	207.6	10.16	49	Minsk	Rouble
Estonia	45.2	1.54	34	Tallinn	Kroon
Georgia	69.7	5.45	78	Tbilisi	Lari
Kazakhstan	2,717.3	17.03	6	Alma-Ata	Tenge
Kirgizstan	198.5	4.67	24	Bishkek	Som
Latvia	63.7	2.58	40	Riga	Lats
Lithuania	65.2	3.71	57	Vilnius	Litas
Moldova	33.7	4.42	132	Kishinev	Leu
Tajikistan	143.1	5.93	43	Dushanbe	Rouble
Turkmenistan	488.1	4.01	8	Ashkhabad	Manat
Uzbekistan	447.4	22.35	51	Tashkent	Som

People

	Av. ann. pop. growth 1985–94	Pop. under 15 %	Male life expect.[a] yrs	Birth rate[a]	Death rate[a]	Human Dev. Index
Armenia	1.5	29.7	70	18	6	72
Azerbaijan	1.3	31.8	68	19	6	70
Belarus	0.2	21.6	65	12	12	87
Estonia	nil	20.6	64	11	13	86
Georgia	0.4	23.7	70	15	9	71
Kazakhstan	0.8	29.8	67	19	7	80
Kirgizstan	1.7	37.0	67	26	6	72
Latvia	-0.1	20.6	63	11	13	86
Lithuania	0.4	21.9	65	13	12	77
Moldova	0.5	26.4	64	16	11	76
Tajikistan	2.9	43.1	69	33	6	64
Turkmenistan	2.4	39.5	64	29	7	73
Uzbekistan	2.3	39.9	68	28	6	71

The economy

	GDP $bn	GDP Per head $	GDP PPP USA = 100	Agric. as % of GDP	Exports $m	Imports $m	Foreign debt $m
Armenia	2.5	671	10	48.6	238	419	214
Azerbaijan	3.7	499	11	31.1	637	814	113
Belarus	21.9	2,176	27	24.0	2,626	3,097	1,272
Estonia	4.4	2,823	28	11.1	1,327	1,688	186
Georgia	3.1	563	10	68.0	500	800	1,227
Kazakhstan	18.9	1,110	18	20.8	3,300	4,100	2,704
Kirgizstan	2.8	605	12	32.8	340	436	441
Latvia	5.9	2,292	26	7.8	1,022	1,322	364
Lithuania	5.0	1,347	16	8.1	2,031	2,233	438
Moldova	3.9	872	15	41.7	500	600	492
Tajikistan	2.1	350	7	5.2	512	621	594
Turkmenistan	5.4	1,379	14	11.3	2,425	1,476	418
Uzbekistan	21.1	946	11	28.0	3,218	3,178	1,156

a 1995–2000.
b 1993.
c 1990.

UNITED KINGDOM

Area	242,534 sq km	Currency	Pound (£)
Capital	London		

People

Population	58.1m	Life expectancy: men	74 yrs
Pop. per sq km	239	women	79 yrs
Av. ann. growth		Adult literacy	99.0%
in pop. 1985–94	0.3%	Fertility rate (per woman)	1.8
Pop. under 15	19.5%		
Pop. over 65	15.5%		*per 1,000 pop.*
No. of men per 100 women	95.7	Crude birth rate	12.9
Human Development Index	92	Crude death rate	10.9

The economy

GDP	£698bn	GDP per head	$18,411
GDP	$1,069bn	GDP per head in purchasing	
Av. ann. growth in real		power parity (USA=100)	72
GDP 1985–94	2.2%		

Origins of GDP		Components of GDP	
	% of total		*% of total*
Agriculture	2.0	Private consumption	63.9
Industry, of which:	29.0	Public consumption	21.6
manufacturing	20.9	Investment	15.4
Services	69.0	Exports	23.2
		Imports	-24.1

Structure of manufacturing

	% of total		*% of total*
Agric. & food processing	15	Other	50
Textiles & clothing	5	Av. ann. increase in industrial	
Machinery & transport	30	output 1980–94	1.3%

Energy

	'000 TCE		
Total output	329,701	% output exported	36.9
Total consumption	324,779	% consumption imported	38.2
Consumption per head,			
kg coal equivalent	5,586		

Inflation and finance

Consumer price		*av. ann. increase 1989–94*	
inflation 1995	3.4%	Narrow money (M1)	8.2%
Av. ann. inflation 1989–95	4.9%	Broad money	8.8%

Exchange rates

	end 1995		*June 1995*
£ per $	0.65	Effective rates	*1990 = 100*
£ per SDR	0.96	– nominal	84.2
£ per Ecu	0.83	– real	92.0

Principal exports

	$bn fob		*$bn fob*
Finished manufactured products	111.9	Fuels	13.9
		Basic materials	3.9
Semi-manufactured products	59.3		
Food, beverages & tobacco	15.5	Total incl. others	**206.0**

Main export destinations

	% of total		*% of total*
United States	13.0	Belgium/Luxembourg	5.2
Germany	12.0	Netherlands	5.1
France	9.3	Ireland	3.6

Principal imports

	$bn cif		*$bn cif*
Finished manufactured products	124.4	Fuels	8.8
		Basic materials	8.6
Semi-manufactured products	58.3		
Food, beverages & tobacco	21.4	Total incl. others	**222.2**

Main origins of imports

	% of total		*% of total*
Germany	13.7	Japan	7.4
United States	12.0	Netherlands	6.3
France	9.5	Belgium/Luxembourg	4.5

Balance of payments, reserves and aid, $bn

Visible exports fob	206.1	Capital balance	-25.6
Visible imports fob	-222.3	Overall balance	-19.0
Trade balance	-16.1	Change in reserves	4.1
Invisibles inflows	180.3	Level of reserves	
Invisibles outflows	-158.4	end Dec.	48.1
Net transfers	-8.2	No. months of import cover	1.5
Current account balance	-2.4	Aid given	3.20
– as % of GDP	-0.2	– as % of GDP	0.31

Family life

No. of households	20.0m	Divorces per 1,000 pop.	3.0
Av. no. per household	2.8	Cost of living, Dec. 1995	
Marriages per 1,000 pop.	6.0	New York = 100	109

UNITED STATES

Area	9,372,610 sq km	Currency	US dollar ($)
Capital	Washington DC		

People

Population	260.5m	Life expectancy: men	73 yrs
Pop. per sq km	28	women	80 yrs
Av. ann. growth		Adult literacy	99.0%
in pop. 1985–94	1.0%	Fertility rate (per woman)	2.1
Pop. under 15	22.0%		
Pop. over 65	12.6%		*per 1,000 pop.*
No. of men per 100 women	95.4	Crude birth rate	14.7
Human Development Index	94	Crude death rate	8.7

The economy

GDP	$6,737bn	GDP per head	$25,860
Av. ann. growth in real		GDP per head in purchasing	
GDP 1985–94	2.5%	power parity (USA=100)	100

Origins of GDP

Components of GDP

	% of total		*% of total*
Agriculture	1.9	Private consumption	68.7
Industry, of which:	23.4	Public consumption	17.5
manufacturing	17.9	Investment	15.4
Services	74.9	Exports	10.7
		Imports	-12.1

Structure of manufacturing

	% of total		*% of total*
Agric. & food processing	13	Other	50
Textiles & clothing	5	Av. ann. increase in industrial	
Machinery & transport	30	output 1980–94	3.2%

Energy

	'000 TCE		
Total output	2,236,519	% output exported	5.1
Total consumption	2,789,397	% consumption imported	25.1
Consumption per head,			
kg coal equivalent	10,815		

Inflation and finance

Consumer price		*av. ann. increase 1989–94*	
inflation 1995	2.8%	Narrow money (M1)	7.4%
Av. ann. inflation 1989–95	3.7%	Broad money	3.5%

Exchange rates

	end 1995		*June 1995*
$ per SDR	1.49	Effective rates	*1990 = 100*
$ per Ecu	1.31	– nominal	88.4
		– real	88.1

Principal exports

	$bn fob		*$bn fob*
Capital goods, excl. vehicles	205.4	Vehicles & products	57.6
Industrial supplies	121.6	Food & beverages	42.0
Consumer goods, excl. vehicles	60.0	Total incl. others	**504.5**

Main export destinations

	% of total		*% of total*
Canada	22.9	Germany	3.7
Japan	10.3	South Korea	3.4
Mexico	10.1	Taiwan	3.2
United Kingdom	5.2		

Principal imports

	$bn fob		*$bn fob*
Capital goods, excl. vehicles	184.4	Vehicles & products	118.3
Industrial supplies	164.9	Food & beverages	31.0
Consumer goods, excl. vehicles	146.3	Total incl. others	**668.9**

Main origins of imports

	% of total		*% of total*
Canada	19.1	Germany	4.6
Japan	17.4	Taiwan	3.9
Mexico	7.3	United Kingdom	3.6
China	5.6		

Balance of payments, reserves and aid, $bn

Visible exports fob	504.5	Capital balance	120.2
Visible imports fob	-668.9	Overall balance	-45.0
Trade balance	-164.3	Change in reserves	-1.0
Invisibles inflows	334.3	Level of reserves	
Invisibles outflows	-285.7	end Dec.	163.6
Net transfers	-35.2	No. months of import cover	2.1
Current account balance	-150.9	Aid given	9.93
– as % of GDP	-2.2	– as % of GDP	0.15

Family life

No. of households	95.6m	Divorces per 1,000 pop.	4.6
Av. no. per household	2.6	Cost of living, Dec. 1995	
Marriages per 1,000 pop.	9.0	New York = 100	100

VENEZUELA

Area	912,050 sq km	Currency	Bolivar (Bs)
Capital	Caracas		

People

Population	21.4m	Life expectancy: men	70 yrs
Pop. per sq km	24	women	76 yrs
Av. ann. growth		Adult literacy	89.0%
in pop. 1985–94	2.5%	Fertility rate (per woman)	3.0
Pop. under 15	36.2%		
Pop. over 65	4.1%		*per 1,000 pop.*
No. of men per 100 women	101.5	Crude birth rate	24.9
Human Development Index	86	Crude death rate	4.7

The economy

GDP	Bs8,762bn	GDP per head	$2,761
GDP	$59bn	GDP per head in purchasing	
Av. ann. growth in real		power parity (USA=100)	36
GDP 1985–94	2.8%		

Origins of GDP		**Components of GDP**	
	% of total		*% of total*
Agriculture	7.0	Private consumption	72.7
Industry, of which:	45.1	Public consumption	7.3
manufacturing	16.1	Investment	10.1
Services	47.9	Exports	30.8
		Imports	-20.9

Structure of manufacturing

	% of total		*% of total*
Agric. & food processing	22	Other	64
Textiles & clothing	6	Av. ann. increase in industrial	
Machinery & transport	9	output 1980–93	2.5%

Energy

	'000 TCE		
Total output	238,512	% output exported	67.6
Total consumption	71,083	% consumption imported	1.1
Consumption per head,			
kg coal equivalent	3,399		

Inflation and finance

Consumer price		*av. ann. increase 1989–94*	
inflation 1995	59.6%	Narrow money (M1)	33.7%
Av. ann. inflation 1989–95	48.9%	Broad money	43.9%

Exchange rates

	end 1995		*June 1995*
			1990 = 100
Bs per $	290	Effective rates	
Bs per SDR	431	– nominal	39.4
Bs per Ecu	380	– real	138.5

Principal exports

	$bn fob		$bn fob
Petroleum & products	12.5		
Metals	1.4	Total incl. others	**16.6**

Main export destinations[b]

	% of total		% of total
United States	51.9	Netherlands Antilles	6.3
Colombia	7.1	Suriname	5.3

Principal imports

	$bn fob		$bn fob
Machinery & transport equipment	3.6	Agricultural products	0.8
Chemicals	1.1	Total incl. others	**8.0**

Main origins of imports

	% of total		% of total
United States	46.1	Germany	5.5
Japan	5.6	Colombia	5.0

Balance of payments, reserves and debt, $bn

Visible exports fob	15.9	Overall balance	-1.5
Visible imports fob	-8.2	Change in reserves	-1.2
Trade balance	7.7	Level of reserves	
Invisibles inflows	2.9	end Dec.	12.5
Invisibles outflows	-8.0	No. months of import cover	10.4
Net transfers	-0.2	Foreign debt	36.9
Current account balance	2.5	– as % of GDP	64.0
– as % of GDP	4.2	Debt service paid	3.7
Capital balance	-3.6	Debt service ratio	19.9

Family life

No. households	3.5m	Divorces per 1,000 pop.	1.0
Av. no. per household	5.1	Cost of living, Dec. 1995	
Marriages per 1,000 pop.	5.4	New York = 100	67

a 1991.

ZAIRE

Area	2,345,410 sq km	Currency	Zaire (Z)
Capital	Kinshasa		

People

Population	42.6m	Life expectancy: men	50 yrs
Pop. per sq km	19	women	53 yrs
Av. ann. growth		Adult literacy	74.0%
in pop. 1985–94	3.3%	Fertility rate (per woman)	6.2
Pop. under 15	48.0%		
Pop. over 65	2.9%		*per 1,000 pop.*
No. of men per 100 women	97.7	Crude birth rate	44.8
Human Development Index	38	Crude death rate	13.9

The economy

GDP	Z17,552bn	GDP per head	$345
GDP	$14.7bn	GDP per head in purchasing	
Av. ann. growth in real		power parity (USA=100)	2
GDP 1985–94	-5.0%		

Origins of GDP[a]		Components of GDP[b]	
	% of total		*% of total*
Agriculture	30.2	Private consumption	68.8
Industry, of which:	33.5	Public consumption	21.7
manufacturing	11.2	Investment	6.9
Services	36.3	Exports	21.6
		Imports	-19.0

Structure of manufacturing[c]

	% of total		*% of total*
Agric. & food processing	40	Other	36
Textiles & clothing	16	Av. ann. increase in industrial	
Machinery & transport	8	output 1980–90	2.3%

Energy

	'000 TCE		
Total output	2,660	% output exported	56.6
Total consumption	2,500	% consumption imported	63.6
Consumption per head,			
kg coal equivalent	61		

Inflation and finance

Consumer price		*av. ann. increase 1989–94*	
inflation 1994	23,760%	Narrow money (M1)	1,148%
Av. ann. inflation 1989–94	1,500%	Broad money	1,233%

Exchange rates

	end 1995		*June 1995*
Z per $	10,624	Effective rates	*1990 = 100*
Z per SDR	15,830	– nominal	…
Z per Ecu	13,917	– real	78.4

Principal exports

	$m fob		$m fob
Diamonds	451	Copper & cobalt	184
Coffee	247	Total incl. others	**1,028**

Main export destinations

	% of total		% of total
Belgium/Luxembourg	38	South Africa	9
United States	16	Italy	8

Principal imports

	$m fob		$m fob
Consumer goods	232	Energy products	85
Capital goods	116		
Raw materials	93	Total incl. others	**581**

Main origins of imports

	% of total		% of total
Belgium/Luxembourg	16	Germany	8
South Africa	12	Hong Kong	7

Balance of payments[d], reserves and debt, $bn

Visible exports fob	2.1	Overall balance	-0.8
Visible imports fob	-1.5	Change in reserves	0.1
Trade balance	0.6	Level of reserves	
Invisibles inflows	0.2	end Dec.	0.1
Invisibles outflows	-1.5	No. months of import cover	...
Net transfers	0.1	Foreign debt	12.3
Current account balance	-0.6	– as % of GDP	...
– as % of GDP	-7.9	Debt service paid	0.07
Capital balance	-0.2	Debt service ratio	...

Family life

No. of households	5.7m	Divorces per 1,000 pop.	...
Av. no. per household	5.4	Cost of living, Dec. 1995	
Marriages per 1,000 pop.	...	New York = 100	...

a 1989.
b 1992.
c 1986.
d 1990.

ZIMBABWE

Area	390,759 sq km	Currency	Zimbabwe dollar (Z$)
Capital	Harare		

People

Population	11.0m	Life expectancy: men	50 yrs
Pop. per sq km	29	women	52 yrs
Av. ann. growth		Adult literacy	68.6%
in pop. 1985–94	3.0%	Fertility rate (per woman)	4.5
Pop. under 15	44.1%		
Pop. over 65	2.8%		*per 1,000 pop.*
No. of men per 100 women	98.4	Crude birth rate	36.0
Human Development Index	54	Crude death rate	13.2

The economy

GDP	Z$44.0bn	GDP per head	$493
GDP	$5.4bn	GDP per head in purchasing	
Av. ann. growth in real		power parity (USA=100)	8
GDP 1985–94	2.2%		

Origins of GDP		**Components of GDP**ª	
	% of total		*% of total*
Agriculture	13.6	Private consumption	52.3
Industry, of which:	30.1	Public consumption	23.7
manufacturing	22.9	Investment	23.3
Services	56.3	Exports	29.4
		Imports	-28.7

Structure of manufacturing

	% of total		*% of total*
Agric. & food processing	34	Other	41
Textiles & clothing	14	Av. ann. increase in industrial	
Machinery & transport	11	output 1980–93	2.8%

Energy

	'000 TCE		
Total output	5,474	% output exported	0.8
Total consumption	7,085	% consumption imported	25.1
Consumption per head,			
kg coal equivalent	660		

Inflation and finance

Consumer price			*av. ann. increase 1989–94*
inflation 1994	22.3%	Narrow money (M1)	30.4%
Av. ann. inflation 1989–94	23.9%	Broad money	24.6%

Exchange rates

	end 1995		*June 1995*
Z$ per $	9.31	Effective rates	1990 = 100
Z$ per SDR	13.26	– nominal	...
Z$ per Ecu	12.20	– real	...

Principal exports

	$m fob		$m fob
Tobacco	650	Nickel	81
Gold	227	Total incl. others	**1,970**
Ferro-alloys	115		

Main export destinations[b]

	% of total		% of total
United Kingdom	12.9	Germany	7.1
South Africa	11.8	United States	6.3

Principal imports

	$m fob		$m fob
Machinery & transport equipment	927	Petroleum products & electricity	222
Chemicals	366		
Manufactured products	365	Total incl. others	**2,241**

Main origins of imports

	% of total		% of total
South Africa	32.6	Japan	5.7
United Kingdom	10.3	United States	5.3
Germany	5.9		

Balance of payments[c], reserves and debt, $bn

Visible exports fob	1.6	Overall balance	0.2
Visible imports fob	-1.5	Change in reserves	-0.04
Trade balance	0.1	Level of reserves	
Invisibles inflows	0.4	end Dec.	0.6
Invisibles outflows	-0.9	No. months of import cover	2.8
Net transfers	0.2	Foreign debt	4.4
Current account balance	-0.1	– as % of GDP	85.9
– as % of GDP	-2.0	Debt service paid	0.6
Capital balance	0.3	Debt service ratio	26.9

Family life

No. of households	0.1m	Divorces per 1,000 pop.	...
Av. no. per household	...	Cost of living, Dec. 1995	
Marriages per 1,000 pop.	...	New York = 100	54

a 1990.
b Excluding gold.
c 1993.

Glossary

Balance of payments The record of a country's transactions with the rest of the world. The **current account** of the balance of payments consists of: visible trade (goods); "invisible" trade (services and income); private transfer payments (eg, remittances from those working abroad); official transfers (eg, payments to international organisations, famine relief). Visible imports and exports are normally compiled on rather different definitions to those used in the trade statistics (shown in principal imports and exports) and therefore the statistics do not match. The **capital account** consists of long- and short-term transactions relating to a country's assets and liabilities (eg, loans and borrowings). Adding the current to the capital account gives the **overall balance**. This is compensated by net monetary movements and changes in reserves. In practice methods of statistical recording are neither complete nor accurate and an errors and omissions item, sometimes quite large, will appear. In the country pages of this book this item is included in the overall balance. **Changes in reserves** exclude revaluation effects and are shown without the practice often followed in balance of payments presentations of reversing the sign.

CFA Communauté Financière Africaine. Its members, most of the francophone African nations, share a common currency, the CFA franc, which is maintained at a fixed rate of 1FFr = 100 CFAfr by the French treasury.

Cif/fob Measures of the value of merchandise trade. Imports include the cost of "carriage, insurance and freight" (cif) from the exporting country to the importing. The value of exports des not include these elements and is recorded 'free on board' (fob). Balance of payments statistics are generally adjusted so that both exports and imports are shown fob; the cif elements are included in invisibles.

Commonwealth of Independent States All former Soviet Union Republics, excluding Estonia, Latvia and Lithuania. It was established January 1 1992; Azerbaijan joined in September 1993 and Georgia in December 1993.

Crude birth rate The number of live births in a year per 1,000 population. The crude rate will automatically be relatively high if a large proportion of the population is of childbearing age.

Crude death rate The number of deaths in a year per 1,000 population. Also affected by the population's age structure.

Debt, foreign Financial obligations owed by a country to the rest of the world and repayable in foreign currency. **Debt service paid** is the sum of principal repayments and interest payments actually made. **The debt service ratio** is debt service expressed as a percentage of the country's earnings from exports of goods and services.

EU European Union. Members are: Belgium, Denmark, France, Germany, Greece, Ireland, Italy, Luxembourg, Netherlands, Portugal, Spain and the United Kingdom and, since January 1 1995, Austria, Finland and Sweden. EU data in this book refers only to the first 12 listed member countries.

Ecu European currency unit. An accounting measure used within the EU and composed of a weighted basket of the currencies of 12 EU members.

Effective exchange rate This measures a currency's depreciation (figures below 100) or appreciation (figures over 100) from a base date against a trade weighted basket of the currencies of the country's main trading partners.

Efta European Free Trade Association. An organisation of West European states that are not members of the European Union. Members are: Austria, Finland, Iceland, Liechtenstein, Norway, Sweden and Switzerland.

Fertility rate The average number of children born to a woman who completes her childbearing years.

GDP Gross domestic product. The sum of all output produced by economic activity within a country. GNP (gross national product) includes net income from abroad eg, rent, profits.

Import cover The number of months of imports covered by reserves, ie reserves ÷ ½ annual imports (visibles and invisibles).

Inflation The annual rate at which prices are increasing. The most common measure and the one shown here is the increase in the consumer price index.

Life expectancy The average length of time a baby born today can expect to live.

Literacy is defined by UNESCO as the ability to read and write a simple sentence, but definitions can vary from country to country.

Money supply A measure of the "money" available to buy goods and services. Various definitions exist. The measures shown here are based on definitions used by the IMF and may differ from measures used nationally. Narrow money (M1) consists of cash in circulation and demand deposits (bank deposits that can be withdrawn on demand). "Quasi-money" (time, savings and foreign currency deposits) is added to this to create broad money.

NMP Net material product. The equivalent measure to GDP used in Eastern Europe and certain other economies. It differs from GDP in

excluding certain services and in deducting capital consumption. In general, NMP is between 80-90% of GDP.

OECD Organisation for Economic Co-operation and Development. The "rich countries" club was established in 1961 to promote economic growth and the expansion of world trade. It is based in Paris and now has 26 members.

Opec Organisation of Petroleum Exporting Countries. Set up in 1960 and based in Vienna, Opec is mainly concerned with oil pricing and production issues. Members are; Algeria, Ecuador, Gabon, Indonesia, Iran, Iraq, Kuwait, Libya, Nigeria, Qatar, Saudi Arabia, UAE and Venezuela.

PPP Purchasing power parity. PPP statistics adjust for cost of living differences by replacing normal exchange rates with rates designed to equalise the prices of a standard "basket" of goods and services. These are used to obtain PPP estimates of GDP per head. PPP estimates are normally shown on a scale of 1 to 100, taking the United States, where the average standard of living is highest, as 100.

Real terms Figures adjusted to exclude the effect of inflation.

Reserves The stock of gold and foreign currency held by a country to finance any calls that may be made for the settlement of foreign debt.

SDR Special drawing right. The reserve currency, introduced by the IMF in 1970, was intended to replace gold and national currencies in settling international transactions. The IMF uses SDRs for book-keeping purposes and issues them to member countries. Their value is based on a basket of the five most widely traded currencies: the US dollar, Deutschemark, pound sterling, Japanese yen and French franc.

Sources

Asian Studies Centre, The Heritage Foundation, *US and Asia Statistical Handbook*

BP, *Statistical Review of World Energy*

British Mountaineering Council

Corporate Resources Group, *Quality of Living Report*

The Economist Intelligence Unit, *Cost of Living Survey*

The Economist Intelligence Unit, *Country Forecasts*

The Economist Intelligence Unit, *Country Reports*

ERC Statistics International, *The World Cigarette Market 1995*

Euromonitor, *International Marketing Data and Statistics*

Euromonitor, *European Marketing Data and Statistics*

Europa Publications, *The Europa World Yearbook*

European Bank for Reconstruction and Development, *Transition Report*

FAO, *Production Yearbook*

Financial Times Business Information, *The Banker*

Gold Fields Mineral Services Ltd.

ILO, *Year Book of Labour Statistics*

IMF, *Balance of Payments Statistics Yearbook*

IMF, *Direction of Trade*

IMF, *International Financial Statistics*

IMF, *World Economic Outlook*

International Cocoa Organisation, *Quarterly Bulletin of Cocoa Statistics*

International Civil Aviation Organisation, *Digest of Statistics*

International Coffee Organisation

International Cotton Advisory Committee, *Bulletin*

International Criminal Police Organisation (Interpol), *International Crime Statistics*

International Finance Corporation, *Emerging Stock Markets Factbook*

International Road Federation, *World Road Statistics*

International Rubber Study Group, *Rubber Statistical Bulletin*

International Sugar Organisation, *Sugar Yearbook*

International Tea Committee, *Annual Bulletin of Statistics*

International Telecommunication Union, *World Telecommunication Development Report*

International Wheat Council, *The Grain Market Report*

International Wool Textile Organisation

Lloyd's Register, *Statistical Tables*

Journal de la Marine Marchande et du Transport Multimodal

NTC Publications Ltd in association with Produktschap voor Gedistilleerde Drauken, *World Drink Trends 1995*

OECD, *Economic Outlook*

OECD, *Environmental Data*

ISTA Mielke, *Oil World*

Taiwan Statistical Data Book

The Times, *Atlas of the World*

Time Inc Magazines, *Fortune International*

The World Almanac

UN, *Demographic Yearbook*

UN, *Energy Statistics Yearbook*

UN, *Statistical Chart on World Families*

UN, *World Population Prospects*

UN Development Programme, *Human Development Report*

UNCTAD, *Handbook of International Trade and Development Statistics*

UNESCO, *Statistical Yearbook*

Union International des Chemins de Fer, *Statistiques Internationales des Chemins de Fer*

US Department of Agriculture, *Rice Report*

WHO, *World Health Statistics*

World Bank, *Atlas*

World Bank, *World Debt Tables*

World Bank, *World Development Report*

World Bureau of Metal Statistics, *World Metal Statistics*

World Resources Institute, *World Resources*

World Tourist Organisation, *Yearbook of Tourism Statistics*

World Trade Organisation, *International Trade, Trends and Statistics*

List of countries

Whenever data is available, the world rankings consider 170 countries: all those which had, in 1994, a population of at least 1m or a GDP/GNP of at least $1bn. Here is a list of them.

	Population	GDP		Population	GDP
	'000	$m		'000	$m
Afghanistan	18,879	...	Gabon	1,035	3,669
Albania	3,414	1,229	Gambia, The	1,081	384
Algeria	27,325	46,115	Georgia	5,450	3,071
Angola	10,674	4,400	Germany	81,141	2,075,452
Argentina	34,180	275,657	Ghana	16,944	7,311
Armenia	3,773	2,532	Greece	10,408	80,194
Australia	17,841	320,705	Guadeloupe	420	2,071
Austria	7,915	197,475	Guatemala	10,322	12,237
Azerbaijan	7,472	3,730	Guinea	6,501	3,310
			Guinea-Bissau	1,050	253
Bahamas	272	3,207			
Bahrain	548	4,114	Haiti	7,035	1,542
Bangladesh	117,787	26,636	Honduras	5,493	3,162
Barbados	261	1,704	Hong Kong	5,833	126,286
Belarus	10,163	21,937	Hungary	10,161	39,009
Belgium	10,080	231,051			
Benin	5,246	1,954	Iceland	266	6,545
Bermuda	63	1,881	India	913,600	278,739
Bhutan	1,675	272	Indonesia	189,907	167,632
Bolivia	7,237	5,601	Iran	65,758	58,900
Bosnia &			Iraq	19,951	18,000
Hercegovina	4,383ᵃ	...	Ireland	3,543	48,275
Botswana	1,443	4,037	Israel	5,420	78,113
Brazil	159,143	536,309	Italy	57,154	1,101,258
Brunei	279	3,975			
Bulgaria	8,818	10,255	Jamaica	2,496	3,553
Burkina Faso	10,046	2,982	Japan	124,782	4,321,136
Burundi	6,209	904	Jordan	4,217	5,846
Cambodia	9,968	1,900	Kazakhstan	17,027	18,896
Cameroon	12,871	8,735	Kenya	26,017	6,643
Canada	29,121	569,949	Kirgizstan	4,667	2,825
CAR	3,235	1,191	Kuwait	1,651	31,433
Chad	6,183	1,153			
Chile	14,044	50,051	Laos	4,742	1,496
China	1,190,918	630,202	Latvia	2,583	5,920
Colombia	36,330	58,935	Lebanon	3,930	10,262
Congo	2,516	1,607	Lesotho	1,996	1,398
Costa Rica	3,304	7,856	Liberia	2,941	9,000
Côte d'Ivoire	13,780	7,070	Libya	5,222	22,129
Croatia	4,780	12,093	Lithuania	3,706	4,992
Cuba	10,951	10,000	Luxembourg	401	15,973
Cyprus	734	7,196			
Czech Republic	10,295	33,051	Macao	395	3,456
			Macedonia, FYR	2,093	1,653
Denmark	5,173	145,384	Madagascar	13,101	3,058
Dominican			Malawi	10,843	1,560
Republic	7,684	10,109	Malaysia	19,498	68,674
			Mali	9,524	2,421
Ecuador	11,220	14,703	Malta	364	3,691
Egypt	57,556	40,950	Martinique	375	2,612
El Salvador	5,641	8,365	Mauritania	2,217	1,063
Estonia	1,541	4,351	Mauritius	1,104	3,514
Ethiopia	53,435	6,947	Mexico	91,858	368,679
			Moldova	4,420	3,853
Fiji	771	1,785	Mongolia	2,363	801
Finland	5,083	95,817	Morocco	26,488	30,330
France	57,726	1,355,039	Mozambique	16,614	1,328
			Myanmar	45,555	8,960

	Population	GDP		Population	GDP
	'000	$m		'000	$m
Namibia	1,500	3,045	Spain	39,551	525,334
Nepal	21,360	4,174	Sri Lanka	18,125	11,634
Netherlands	15,391	338,144	Sudan	27,361	1,720
Netherlands			Suriname	418	364
Antilles	197	1,361	Swaziland	906	1,048
New Zealand	3,531	46,578	Sweden	8,735	206,419
Nicaragua	4,275	1,395	Switzerland	7,127	264,974
Niger	8,846	2,040	Syria	14,171	23,939
Nigeria	107,900	29,995			
North Korea	23,472	20,500	Taiwan	21,126	241,100
Norway	4,318	114,328	Tajikistan	5,933	2,075
			Tanzania	28,846	2,449
Oman	2,073	10,779	Thailand	58,718	129,864
			Togo	4,010	1,267
Pakistan	126,284	55,565	Trinidad &		
Panama	2,585	6,905	Tobago	1,292	4,838
Papua New			Tunisia	8,815	15,873
Guinea	4,205	4,857	Turkey	60,771	149,002
Paraguay	4,830	7,606	Turkmenistan	4,010	5,400
Peru	23,331	44,110			
Philippines	66,188	63,311	UAE	1,855	39,910
Poland	38,341	94,613	Uganda	18,592	3,718
Portugal	9,832	92,124	Ukraine	51,465	80,921
Puerto Rico	3,645	26,550	United Kingdom	58,088	1,069,457
			United States	260,529	6,737,367
Qatar	537	7,810	Uruguay	3,167	14,725
			Uzbekistan	22,349	21,142
Réunion	643	6,415			
Romania	22,736	27,921	Venezuela	21,378	59,025
Russia	148,366	392,496	Vietnam	72,500	13,775
Rwanda	7,750	1,493			
			West Bank and		
Saudi Arabia	17,498	126,597	Gaza	2,063	2,932
Senegal	8,102	4,952			
Serbia,			Yemen	13,873	3,884
Montenegro	10,707	15,400	Yugoslavia, Fed.		
Sierra Leone	4,587	698	Rep. see Serbia,		
Singapore	2,819	65,842	Montenegro		
Slovakia	5,333	11,914			
Slovenia	1,995	14,246	Zaire	42,552	14,700
Somalia	9,077	669	Zambia	9,196	3,206
South Africa	41,591	125,225	Zimbabwe	11,002	5,424
South Korea	44,563	366,484			

a 1993.